THEORY OF COLOURS.

CONTENTS.

PART III.

CHEMICAL COLOURS.

Theory of Colours

GOETHE'S

THEORY OF COLOURS;

TRANSLATED FROM THE GERMAN

WITH NOTES BY

CHARLES LOCK EASTLAKE, R.A., F.R.S.

" Cicero varietatem propriè in coloribus nasci, hinc in alienum migrare existimavit.
Certè non alibi natura copiosius aut majore lasciviâ opes suas commendavit. Metalla,
gemmas, marmora, flores, astra, omnia denique quæ progenuit suis etiam coloribus dis-
tinxit; ut venia debeatur si quis in tam numerosâ rerum sylvâ caligaverit."

CELIO CALCAGNINI.

LONDON:
JOHN MURRAY, ALBEMARLE STREET.

1840.

Theory of Colours

JOHANN WOLFGANG VON GOETHE

Translated from the German
with notes by
Charles Lock Eastlake

Introduction by Deane B. Judd

The M.I.T. Press
CAMBRIDGE, MASSACHUSETTS, AND LONDON, ENGLAND

First MIT Press paperback edition, March 1970
Seventh printing, 1985
Reproduced from *Goethe's Theory of Colours,* translated
from the German by Charles Lock Eastlake, published by
John Murray, Albemarle Street, London, 1840

Introduction by Deane B. Judd copyright © 1970 by
The Massachusetts Institute of Technology

ISBN 262 57021 1 (paperback)
Library of Congress catalog card number: 74-84656

Printed in the United States of America

INTRODUCTION.

THE enigma of color has attracted the interest and attention of many of the most gifted intellects of all time. Aristotle, Grimaldi, Newton, Goethe, Hegel, Schopenhauer, Young, Maxwell, Helmholtz, Hering, and Schrödinger all have been intrigued by color and have contributed to our knowledge of it.

Aristotle based his view of color on the observation that sunlight on passage through, or reflection from, an object is always reduced in intensity, or darkened. Since by this operation colors may be produced, he viewed color as a phenomenon arising out of the transition from brightness to darkness, which in a sense it is; or, stated less clearly as it usually is, Aristotle viewed color as a mixture, or blend, or commingling, or superposition, or juxtaposition of black and white. An essential part of this view, widely held up to Newton's time (1642 to 1727), is that all true and pure light, such as light from the sun, has no color, and color must be some sort of constituent or material permeating opaque and transparent objects and media, capable of altering or degrading the pure light incident upon them. Some doubts as to the correctness of Aristotle's view began to arise early in the seventeenth century because of the discovery of what we now name interference colors—colors of thin films, such as soap bubbles—which change markedly with angle of view. These films seem to have every kind of color in them at the same time and to contaminate the incident sunlight in different ways depending on thickness of the film and direction of passage of sunlight through it.

The discovery in 1665 by Newton that light from the sun could be bent to varying degrees by a prism so as to produce a spectrum of colors ranging from red (rays least bent), through orange, yellow, green, and blue, to violet (rays most bent) provided the basis for rejecting Aristotle's view that color comes from objects and permitted substitution for it of the view that color is a property of light. This view has been supported by the great advance in our understanding of the various physical phenomena (interference, scattering, and diffraction as well as refraction and absorption) by which color may appear. This view is, indeed, a view widely held today. It states that wavelength composition of a light beam serves to define its color, and it suggests that physics holds the key to the enigma of color.

We must pause here to make clear that this extreme view that color is a property of light, and of light alone, though it arose among Newton's followers and was based on his discovery, was not shared by Newton himself. He states in a passage, lately much quoted, from his *Opticks:* "And whenever I seem to speak of radiation or rays, coloured or imbued with colour, I should like it always so expressed that it does not sound philosophical or special, but intelligible to the general public; since those ideas are accepted which people, watching experiments of this kind, can themselves comprehend. Indeed, rays, properly expressed, are not coloured. There is nothing else in them but a certain power or disposition which so conditions them that they produce in us the sensation of this or that colour." Newton's view that color is a sensation is also widely held today, but, though Grimaldi, the great Italian pioneer in optics had already expressed a closely similar view in the very year (1665) of Newton's discovery, Newton's followers quickly forgot it.

It must not be supposed, either, that Newton is responsible for the great oversimplification that wavelength of light determines color. Newton's view of light was that it consists of corpuscles or small particles flying through space away from every source of light. The wave theory was not substantiated until many years after Newton's death in 1727 by Thomas Young (1773–1829) who successfully maintained from his experiments on interference that "radiant light consists of undulations of the luminiferous ether." Independently of Young, the French physicist,

Fresnel (1788-1827) disproved Newton's corpuscular theory of light by experiments supporting the view that light is due to wave motion, and that these waves are perpendicular, or transverse, to the direction of propagation of the waves. The wave theory, once established, explained in a simple and brilliant way the colors produced by scattering, diffraction, interference (for example, in thin films), polarization, and refraction. It became easy to ignore Newton's view of color as a sensation, usually, but not always, originating out of radiation, and to say simply that waves of length 400 to 450 nm (billionths of a méter) are violet; 450 to 480, blue; 480 to 560, green; 560 to 590, yellow; 590 to 620, orange; and 620 to 800 nm, red.

To Johann Wolfgang von Goethe (1749–1832), student of the arts, theatrical director, and widely acclaimed author of the master works *Iphigenia at Taurus, Egmont,* and *Faust,* this simple theory of color was the result of mistaking an incidental result for an elemental principle. His study of color phenomena, which extended over many years, had led him to an explanation of color more akin to that of Aristotle than to the new physics that he did not understand. In a period of his life described by one literary critic as "a long interval, marked by nothing of distinguished note" he wrote out a clear and sys-

PART IV.
GENERAL CHARACTERISTICS.

PART V.
RELATION TO OTHER PURSUITS.

PART VI.
EFFECT OF COLOUR WITH REFERENCE TO MORAL ASSOCIATIONS.

OUTLINE

OF A

THEORY OF COLOURS.

" Si vera nostra sunt aut falsa, erunt talia, licet nostra per vitam defen-
dimus. Post fata nostra pueri qui nunc ludunt nostri judices erunt."

THE

TRANSLATOR'S PREFACE.

ENGLISH writers who have spoken of Goethe's
" Doctrine of Colours,"* have generally confined their remarks to those parts of the work
in which he has undertaken to account for the
colours of the prismatic spectrum, and of refraction altogether, on principles different from
the received theory of Newton. The less ques-
tionable merits of the treatise consisting of a
well-arranged mass of observations and experiments, many of which are important and interesting, have thus been in a great measure overlooked. The translator, aware of the opposition
which the theoretical views alluded to have met
with, intended at first to make a selection of

---

* " Farbenlehre"—in the present translation generally rendered
" Theory of Colours."

such of the experiments as seem more directly applicable to the theory and practice of painting. Finding, however, that the alterations this would have involved would have been incompatible with a clear and connected view of the author's statements, he preferred giving the theory itself entire, reflecting, at the same time, that some scientific readers may be curious to hear the author speak for himself even on the points at issue.

In reviewing the history and progress of his opinions and researches, Goethe tells us that he first submitted his views to the public in two short essays entitled "Contributions to Optics." Among the circumstances which he supposes were unfavourable to him on that occasion, he mentions the choice of his title, observing that by a reference to optics he must have appeared to make pretensions to a knowledge of mathematics, a science with which he admits he was very imperfectly acquainted. Another cause to which he attributes the severe treatment he experienced, was his having ventured so openly to question the truth of the established theory : but this last provocation could not be owing to mere inadvertence on his part ; indeed the larger work, in which he alludes to these circumstances, is still more remarkable for the violence of his objections to the Newtonian doctrine.

There can be no doubt, however, that much of the opposition Goethe met with was to be attributed to the manner as well as to the substance of his statements. Had he contented himself with merely detailing his experiments and showing their application to the laws of chromatic harmony, leaving it to others to reconcile them as they could with the pre-established system, or even to doubt in consequence, the truth of some of the Newtonian conclusions, he would have enjoyed the credit he deserved for the accuracy and the utility of his investigations. As it was, the uncompromising expression of his convictions only exposed him to the resentment or silent neglect of a great portion of the scientific world, so that for a time he could not even obtain a fair hearing for the less objectionable or rather highly valuable communications contained in his book. A specimen of his manner of alluding to the Newtonian theory will be seen in the preface.

It was quite natural that this spirit should call forth a somewhat vindictive feeling, and with it not a little uncandid as well as unsparing criticism. "The Doctrine of Colours" met

with this reception in Germany long before it
was noticed in England, where a milder and
fairer treatment could hardly be expected, especially at a time when, owing perhaps to the
limited intercourse with the continent, German
literature was far less popular than it is at present. This last fact, it is true, can be of little
importance in the present instance, for although
the change of opinion with regard to the genius
of an enlightened nation must be acknowledged
to be beneficial, it is to be hoped there is no
fashion in science, and the translator begs to
state once for all, that in advocating the neglected merits of the " Doctrine of Colours," he
is far from undertaking to defend its imputed
errors. Sufficient time has, however, now
elapsed since the publication of this work (in
1810) to allow a calmer and more candid examination of its claims. In this more pleasing task
Germany has again for some time led the way,
and many scientific investigators have followed
up the hints and observations of Goethe with a
due acknowledgment of the acuteness of his
views.*

---

* Sixteen years after the appearance of the Farbenlehre, Dr.
Johannes Müller devoted a portion of his work, " Zur vergleich-
enden Physiologie des Gesichtssinnes des Menschen und der

It may require more magnanimity in English scientific readers to do justice to the merits of one who was so open and, in many respects, it is believed, so mistaken an opponent of Newton; but it must be admitted that the statements of Goethe contain more useful principles in all that relates to harmony of colour than any that have been derived from the established doctrine. It is no derogation of the more important truths of the Newtonian theory to say, that the views it contains seldom appear in a form calculated for direct application to the arts. The principle of contrast, so universally exhibited in nature, so apparent in the action and re-action of the eye itself, is scarcely hinted at. The equal pretensions of seven colours, as

---

Thiere," to the critical examination of Goethe's theory. In his introductory remarks he expresses himself as follows—" For my own part I readily acknowledge that I have been greatly indebted to Goethe's treatise, and can truly say that without having studied it for some years in connexion with the actual phenomena, the present work would hardly have been undertaken. I have no hesitation in confessing more particularly that I have full faith in Goethe's statements, where they are merely descriptive of the phenomena, and where the author does not enter into explanations involving a decision on the great points of controversy." The names of Hegel, Schelling, Seebeck, Steffens, may also be mentioned, and many others might be added, as authorities more or less favourable to the Farbenlehre.

such, and the fanciful analogies which their
assumed proportions could suggest, have rarely
found favour with the votaries of taste,—indeed
they have long been abandoned even by
scientific authorities.*   And here the translator stops : he is quite aware that the defects
which make the Newtonian theory so little
available for æsthetic application, are far from
invalidating its more important conclusions in
the opinion of most scientific men.   In carefully
abstaining therefore from any comparison between the two theories in these latter respects,
he may still be permitted to advocate the clearness and fulness of Goethe's experiments.   The
German philosopher reduces the colours to their

---

* "When Newton attempted to reckon up the rays of light
decomposed by the prism," says Sir John Leslie, "and ventured
to assign the famous number *seven*, he was apparently influenced
by some lurking disposition towards mysticism.   If any unprejudiced person will fairly repeat the experiment, he must soon be
convinced that the various coloured spaces which paint the spectrum slide into each other by indefinite shadings : he may name
four or five principal colours, but the subordinate spaces are evidently so multiplied as to be incapable of enumeration.   The
same illustrious mathematician, we can hardly doubt, was betrayed by a passion for analogy, when he imagined that the primary colours are distributed over the spectrum after the proportions
of the diatonic scale of music, since those intermediate spaces have
really no precise and defined limits."—*Treatises on Various
Subjects of Natural and Chemical Philosophy*, p. 59.

origin and simplest elements ; he sees and constantly bears in mind, and sometimes ably
elucidates, the phenomena of contrast and gradation, two principles which may be said to
make up the artist's world, and to constitute the
chief elements of beauty. These hints occur
mostly in what may be called the scientific part
of the work. On the other hand, in the portion
expressly devoted to the æsthetic application of
the doctrine, the author seems to have made but
an inadequate use of his own principles.

In that part of the chapter on chemical colours which relates to the colours of plants and
animals, the same genius and originality which
are displayed in the Essays on Morphology, and
which have secured to Goethe undisputed rank
among the investigators of nature, are frequently
apparent.

But one of the most interesting features of
Goethe's theory, although it cannot be a recommendation in a scientific point of view, is, that
it contains, undoubtedly with very great improvements, the general doctrine of the ancients
and of the Italians at the revival of letters.
The translator has endeavoured, in some notes,
to point out the connexion between this theory
and the practice of the Italian painters.

The "Doctrine of Colours," as first published in 1810, consists of two volumes in 8vo., and sixteen plates, with descriptions, in 4to. It is divided into three parts, a didactic, a controversial, and an historical part; the present translation is confined to the first of these, with such extracts from the other two as seemed necessary, in fairness to the author, to explain some of his statements. The polemical and historical parts are frequently alluded to in the preface and elsewhere in the present work, but it has not been thought advisable to omit these allusions. No alterations whatever seem to have been made by Goethe in the didactic portion in later editions, but he subsequently wrote an additional chapter on entoptic colours, expressing his wish that it might be inserted in the theory itself at a particular place which he points out. The form of this additional essay is, however, very different from that of the rest of the work, and the translator has therefore merely given some extracts from it in the appendix. The polemical portion has been more than once omitted in later editions.

In the two first parts the author's statements are arranged numerically, in the style of Bacon's Natural History. This, we are told, was for the convenience of reference; but many passages are thus separately numbered which hardly seem to have required it. The same arrangement is, however, strictly followed in the translation to facilitate a comparison with the original where it may be desired; and here the translator observes, that although he has sometimes permitted himself to make slight alterations, in order to avoid unnecessary repetition, or to make the author's meaning clearer, he feels that an apology may rather be expected from him for having omitted so little. He was scrupulous on this point, having once determined to translate the whole treatise, partly, as before stated, from a wish to deal fairly with a controversial writer, and partly because many passages, not directly bearing on the scientific views, are still characteristic of Goethe. The observations which the translator has ventured to add are inserted in the appendix : these observations are chiefly confined to such of the author's opinions and conclusions as have direct reference to the arts ; they seldom interfere with the scientific propositions, even where these have been considered most vulnerable.

PREFACE TO THE FIRST EDITION

OF 1810.

IT may naturally be asked whether, in proposing
to treat of colours, light itself should not first
engage our attention : to this we briefly and
frankly answer that since so much has already
been said on the subject of light, it can hardly
be desirable to multiply repetitions by again
going over the same ground.

Indeed, strictly speaking, it is useless to attempt to express the nature of a thing abstractedly. Effects we can perceive, and a complete
history of those effects would, in fact, sufficiently
define the nature of the thing itself. We should
try in vain to describe a man's character, but let
his acts be collected and an idea of the character
will be presented to us.

The colours are acts of light; its active and
passive modifications : thus considered we may
expect from them some explanation respecting
light itself. Colours and light, it is true, stand
in the most intimate relation to each other, but

we should think of both as belonging to nature as a whole, for it is nature as a whole which manifests itself by their means in an especial manner to the sense of sight.

The completeness of nature displays itself to another sense in a similar way. Let the eye be closed, let the sense of hearing be excited, and from the lightest breath to the wildest din, from the simplest sound to the highest harmony, from the most vehement and impassioned cry to the gentlest word of reason, still it is Nature that speaks and manifests her presence, her power, her pervading life and the vastness of her relations ; so that a blind man to whom the infinite visible is denied, can still comprehend an infinite vitality by means of another organ.

And thus as we descend the scale of being, Nature speaks to other senses—to known, mis-understood, and unknown senses : so speaks she with herself and to us in a thousand modes. To the attentive observer she is nowhere dead nor silent ; she has even a secret agent in inflexible matter, in a metal, the smallest portions of which tell us what is passing in the entire mass. How-ever manifold, complicated, and unintelligible this language may often seem to us, yet its ele-ments remain ever the same. With light poise and counterpoise, Nature oscillates within her prescribed limits, yet thus arise all the varieties and conditions of the phenomena which are presented to us in space and time.

Infinitely various are the means by which we become acquainted with these general movements and tendencies : now as a simple repulsion and attraction, now as an upsparkling and vanishing light, as undulation in the air, as commotion in matter, as oxydation and deoxydation ; but always, uniting or separating, the great purpose is found to be to excite and promote existence in some form or other.

The observers of nature finding, however, that this poise and counterpoise are respectively unequal in effect, have endeavoured to represent such a relation in terms.   They have everywhere remarked and spoken of a greater and lesser principle, an action and resistance, a doing and suffering, an advancing and retiring, a violent and moderating power ; and thus a symbolical language has arisen, which, from its close analogy, may be employed as equivalent to a direct and appropriate terminology.

To apply these designations, this language of Nature to the subject we have undertaken ; to enrich and amplify this language by means of the theory of colours and the variety of their phenomena, and thus facilitate the communication of higher theoretical views, was the principal aim of the present treatise.

The work itself is divided into three parts. The first contains the outline of a theory of colours. In this, the innumerable cases which present themselves to the observer are collected under certain leading phenomena, according to an arrangement which will be explained in the Introduction ; and here it may be remarked, that although we have adhered throughout to experiment, and throughout considered it as our basis, yet the theoretical yiews which led to the arrangement alluded to, could not but be stated. It is sometimes unreasonably required by persons who do not even themselves attend to such a condition, that experimental information should be submitted without any connecting theory to the reader or scholar, who is himself to form his conclusions as he may list. Surely the mere inspection of a subject can profit us but little. Every act of seeing leads to consideration, consideration to reflection, reflection to combination, and thus it may be said that in every attentive look on nature we already theorise. But in order to guard against the possible abuse of this abstract view, in order that the practical deductions we look to should be really useful, we should theorise without forgetting that we are so doing, we should theorise with mental self-possession, and, to use a bold word, with irony.

In the second part* we examine the Newtonian theory; a theory which by its ascendancy and consideration has hitherto impeded a free inquiry into the phenomena of colours. We combat that hypothesis, for although it is no longer found available, it still retains a traditional authority in the world. Its real relations to its subject will require to be plainly pointed out; the old errors must be cleared away, if the theory of colours is not still to remain in the rear of so many other better investigated departments of natural science. Since, however, this second part of our work may appear somewhat dry as regards its matter, and perhaps too vehement and excited in its manner, we may here be permitted to introduce a sort of allegory in a lighter style, as a prelude to that graver portion, and as some excuse for the earnestness alluded to.

We compare the Newtonian theory of colours

---

* The Polemical part.

to an old castle, which was at first constructed
by its architect with youthful precipitation ; it
was, however, gradually enlarged and equipped
by him according to the exigencies of time and
circumstances, and moreover was still further
fortified and secured in consequence of feuds
and hostile demonstrations.

The same system was pursued by his succes-
sors and heirs : their increased wants within,
the harassing vigilance of their opponents without, and various accidents compelled them in
some places to build near, in others in connexion with the fabric, and thus to extend the
original plan.

It became necessary to connect all these incongruous parts and additions by the strangest
galleries, halls and passages.   All damages,
whether inflicted by the hand of the enemy or
the power of time, were quickly made good.   As
occasion required, they deepened the moats,
raised the walls, and took care there should be
no lack of towers, battlements, and embrasures.
This care and these exertions gave rise to a prejudice in favour of the great importance of the
fortress, and still upheld that prejudice, although
the arts of building and fortification were by
this time very much advanced, and people had

learnt to construct much better dwellings and defences in other cases. But the old castle was chiefly held in honour because it had never been taken, because it had repulsed so many assaults, had baffled so many hostile operations, and had always preserved its virgin renown. This renown, this influence lasts even now : it occurs to no one that the old castle is become uninhabitable. Its great duration, its costly construction, are still constantly spoken of. Pilgrims wend their way to it ; hasty sketches of it are shown in all schools, and it is thus recommended to the reverence of susceptible youth. Meanwhile, the building itself is already abandoned; its only inmates are a few invalids, who in simple seriousness imagine that they are prepared for war.

Thus there is no question here respecting a tedious siege or a doubtful war ; so far from it we find this eighth wonder of the world already nodding to its fall as a deserted piece of antiquity, and begin at once, without further ceremony, to dismantle it from gable and roof downwards ; that the sun may at last shine into the old nest of rats and owls, and exhibit to the eye of the wondering traveller that labyrinthine, incongruous style of building, with its scanty,

make-shift contrivances, the result of accident
and emergency, its intentional artifice and
clumsy repairs. Such an inspection will, however, only be possible when wall after wall, arch
after arch, is demolished, the rubbish being at
once cleared away as well as it can be.

To effect this, and to level the site where it is
possible to do so, to arrange the materials thus
acquired, so that they can be hereafter again
employed for a new building, is the arduous
duty we have undertaken in this Second Part.
Should we succeed, by a cheerful application of
all possible ability and dexterity, in razing this
Bastille, and in gaining a free space, it is thus
by no means intended at once to cover the site
again and to encumber it with a new structure;
we propose rather to make use of this area for
the purpose of passing in review a pleasing and
varied series of illustrative figures.

The third part is thus devoted to the historical account of early inquirers and investigators. As we before expressed the opinion that
the history of an individual displays his character, so it may here be well affirmed that the
history of science is science itself. We cannot
clearly be aware of what we possess till we have
the means of knowing what others possessed

before us. We cannot really and honestly re-
joice in the advantages of our own time if we
know not how to appreciate the advantages of
former periods. But it was impossible to write,
or even to prepare the way for a history of the
theory of colours while the Newtonian theory
existed; for no aristocratic presumption has
ever looked down on those who were not of its
order, with such intolerable arrogance as that
betrayed by the Newtonian school in deciding
on all that had been done in earlier times and
all that was done around it. With disgust and
indignation we find Priestley, in his History of
Optics, like many before and after him, dating
the success of all researches into the world of
colours from the epoch of a decomposed ray
of light, or what pretended to be so ; looking
down with a supercilious air on the ancient and
less modern inquirers, who, after all, had proceeded quietly in the right road, and who have
transmitted to us observations and thoughts in
detail which we can neither arrange better nor
conceive more justly.

We have a right to expect from one who proposes to give the history of any science, that he
inform us how the phenomena of which it treats
were gradually known, and what was imagined,

conjectured, assumed, or thought respecting them. To state all this in due connexion is by no means an easy task ; need we say that to write a history at all is always a hazardous affair; with the most honest intention there is always a danger of being dishonest; for in such an undertaking, a writer tacitly announces at the outset that he means to place some things in light, others in shade. The author has, nevertheless, long derived pleasure from the prosecution of his task : but as it is the intention only that presents itself to the mind as a whole, while the execution is generally accomplished portion by portion, he is compelled to admit that instead of a history he furnishes only materials for one. These materials consist in translations, extracts, original and borrowed comments, hints, and notes; a collection, in short, which, if not answering all that is required, has at least the merit of having been made with earnestness and interest. Lastly, such materials,—not altogether untouched it is true, but still not exhausted,— may be more satisfactory to the reflecting reader in the state in which they are, as he can easily combine them according to his own judgment.

This third part, containing the history of the

science, does not, however, thus conclude the
subject : a fourth supplementary portion* is
added. This contains a recapitulation or revi-
sion ; with a view to which, chiefly, the paragraphs are headed numerically. In the execution of a work of this kind some things may be
forgotten, some are of necessity omitted, so as
not to distract the attention, some can only be
arrived at as corollaries, and others may require
to be exemplified and verified : on all these accounts, postscripts, additions and corrections
are indispensable. This part contains, besides,
some detached essays ; for example, that on the
atmospheric colours; for as these are introduced
in the theory itself without any classification,
they are here presented to the mind's eye at
one view. Again, if this essay invites the reader
to consult Nature herself, another is intended to
recommend the artificial aids of science by circumstantially describing the apparatus which
will in future be necessary to assist researches
into the theory of colours.

In conclusion, it only remains to speak of the

---

* This preface must have been written before the work was
finished, for at the conclusion of the historical part there is only
an apology for the non-appearance of the supplement here alluded to.

plates which are added at the end of the work;*
and here we confess we are reminded of that
incompleteness and imperfection which the
present undertaking has, in common with all
others of its class; for as a good play can be in
fact only half transmitted to writing, a great
part of its effect depending on the scene, the
personal qualities of the actor, the powers of
his voice, the peculiarities of his gestures, and
even the spirit and favourable humour of the
spectators; so it is, in a still greater degree,
with a book which treats of the appearances of
nature.   To be enjoyed, to be turned to account,
Nature herself must be present to the reader,
either really, or by the help of a lively imagination.   Indeed, the author should in such cases
communicate his observations orally, exhibiting
the phenomena he describes—as a text, in the
first instance,—partly as they appear to us un-
sought, partly as they may be presented by
contrivance to serve in particular illustration.
Explanation and description could not then fail
to produce a lively impression.

The plates which generally accompany works
like the present are thus a most inadequate sub-

---

* In the present translation the necessary plates accompany
the text.

stitute for all this ; a physical phenomenon exhibiting its effects on all sides is not to be arrested in lines nor denoted by a section. No one ever dreams of explaining chemical experiments with figures ; yet it is customary in physical researches nearly allied to these, because the object is thus found to be in some degree answered. In many cases, however, such diagrams represent mere notions ; they are symbolical resources, hieroglyphic modes of communication, which by degrees assume the place of the phenomena and of Nature herself, and thus rather hinder than promote true knowledge. In the present instance we could not dispense with plates, but we have endeavoured so to construct them that they may be confidently referred to for the explanation of the didactic and polemical portions. Some of these may even be considered as forming part of the apparatus before mentioned.

We now therefore refer the reader to the work itself; first, only repeating a request which many an author has already made in vain, and which the modern German reader, especially, so seldom grants:—

> Si quid novisti rectius istis
> Candidus imperti ; si non, his utere mecum.

INTRODUCTION.

THE desire of knowledge is first stimulated in us when remarkable phenomena attract our attention. In order that this attention be continued, it is necessary that we should feel some interest in exercising it, and thus by degrees we become better acquainted with the object of our curiosity. During this process of observation we remark at first only a vast variety which presses indiscriminately on our view; we are forced to separate, to distinguish, and again to combine; by which means at last a certain order arises which admits of being surveyed with more or less satisfaction.

To accomplish this, only in a certain degree, in any department, requires an unremitting and close application; and we find, for this reason, that men prefer substituting a general theoretical view, or some system of explanation, for the facts themselves, instead of taking the trouble to make themselves first acquainted with cases in detail and then constructing a whole.

The attempt to describe and class the phenomena of colours has been only twice made: first by Theophrastus,* and in modern times by

---

* The treatise to which the author alludes is more generally ascribed to Aristotle.—T.

Boyle. The pretensions of the present essay to the third place will hardly be disputed.

Our historical survey enters into further details. Here we merely observe that in the last century such a classification was not to be thought of, because Newton had based his hypothesis on a phenomenon exhibited in a complicated and secondary state ; and to this the other cases that forced themselves on the attention were contrived to be referred, when they could not be passed over in silence ; just as an astronomer would do, if from whim he were to place the moon in the centre of our system ; he would be compelled to make the earth, sun, and planets revolve round the lesser body, and be forced to disguise and gloss over the error of his first assumption by ingenious calculations and plausible statements.

In our prefatory observations we assumed the reader to be acquainted with what was known respecting light ; here we assume the same with regard to the eye. We observed that all nature manifests itself by means of colours to the sense of sight. We now assert, extraordinary as it may in some degree appear, that the eye sees no form, inasmuch as light, shade, and colour together constitute that which to our vision distinguishes object from object, and the parts of an object from each other. From these three, light, shade, and colour, we construct the visible

world, and thus, at the same time, make painting possible, an art which has the power of
producing on a flat surface a much more perfect
visible world than the actual one can be.

The eye may be said to owe its existence to
light, which calls forth, as it were, a sense that
is akin to itself; the eye, in short, is formed
with reference to light, to be fit for the action
of light; the light it contains corresponding with
the light without.

We are here reminded of a significant adage
in constant use with the ancient Ionian school—
"Like is only known by Like;" and again, of
the words of an old mystic writer, which may
be thus rendered, "If the eye were not sunny,
how could we perceive light? If God's own
strength lived not in us, how could we delight
in Divine things?" This immediate affinity
between light and the eye will be denied by
none; to consider them as identical in substance is less easy to comprehend. It will be
more intelligible to assert that a dormant
light resides in the eye, and that it may be excited by the slightest cause from within or from
without. In darkness we can, by an effort of
imagination, call up the brightest images; in
dreams objects appear to us as in broad day-
light; awake, the slightest external action of
light is perceptible, and if the organ suffers an
actual shock, light and colours spring forth.

Here, however, those who are wont to proceed according to a certain method, may perhaps observe that as yet we have not decidedly explained what colour is. This question, like the definition of light and the eye, we would for the present evade, and would appeal to our inquiry itself, where we have circumstantially shown how colour is produced. We have only therefore to repeat that colour is a law of nature in relation with the sense of sight. We must assume, too, that every one has this sense, that every one knows the operation of nature on it, for to a blind man it would be impossible to speak of colours.

That we may not, however, appear too anxious to shun such an explanation, we would re-state what has been said as follows : colour is an elementary phenomenon in nature adapted to the sense of vision ; a phenomenon which, like all others, exhibits itself by separation and contrast, by commixture and union, by augmentation and neutralization, by communication and dissolution : under these general terms its nature may be best comprehended.

We do not press this mode of stating the subject on any one. Those who, like ourselves, find it convenient, will readily adopt it ; but we have no desire to enter the lists hereafter in its defence. From time immemorial it has been dangerous to treat of colour ; so much so, that

one of our predecessors ventured on a certain
occasion to say, "The ox becomes furious
if a red cloth is shown to him ; but the philosopher, who speaks of colour only in a general
way, begins to rave."

Nevertheless, if we are to proceed to give
some account of our work, to which we have
appealed, we must begin by explaining how
we have classed the different conditions under
which colour is produced. We found three
modes in which it appears; three classes of
colours, or rather three exhibitions of them
all. The distinctions of these classes are easily
expressed.

Thus, in the first instance, we considered colours, as far as they may be said to belong to
the eye itself, and to depend on an action and
re-action of the organ ; next, they attracted our
attention as perceived in, or by means of, colourless mediums ; and lastly, where we could consider them as belonging to particular substances.
We have denominated the first, physiological,
the second, physical, the third, chemical colours.
The first are fleeting and not to be arrested ;
the next are passing, but still for a while enduring; the last may be made permanent for
any length of time.

Having separated these classes and kept them
as distinct as possible, with a view to a clear,
didactic exposition, we have been enabled at

the same time to exhibit them in an unbroken
series, to connect the fleeting with the somewhat
more enduring, and these again with the permanent hues; and thus, after having carefully
attended to a distinct classification in the first
instance, to do away with it again when a larger
view was desirable.

In a fourth division of our work we have
therefore treated generally what was previously
detailed under various particular conditions,
and have thus, in fact, given a sketch for a
future theory of colours. We will here only anticipate our statements so far as to observe, that
light and darkness, brightness and obscurity, or
if a more general expression is preferred, light
and its absence, are necessary to the production
of colour. Next to the light, a colour appears
which we call yellow; another appears next to
the darkness, which we name blue. When
these, in their purest state, are so mixed that
they are exactly equal, they produce a third
colour called green. Each of the two first-named
colours can however of itself produce a new tint
by being condensed or darkened. They thus
acquire a reddish appearance which can be increased to so great a degree that the original
blue or yellow is hardly to be recognised in it:
but the intensest and purest red, especially in
physical cases, is produced when the two extremes of the yellow-red and blue-red are

united. This is the actual state of the appearance and generation of colours. But we can also assume an existing red in addition to the definite existing blue and yellow, and we can produce contrariwise, by mixing, what we directly produced by augmentation or deepening. With these three or six colours, which may be conveniently included in a circle, the elementary doctrine of colours is alone concerned. All other modifications, which may be extended to infinity, have reference more to the application,— have reference to the technical operations of the painter and dyer, and the various purposes of artificial life. To point out another general quality, we may observe that colours throughout are to be considered as half-lights, as half-shadows, on which account if they are so mixed as reciprocally to destroy their specific hues, a shadowy tint, a grey, is produced.

In the fifth division of our inquiry we had proposed to point out the relations in which we should wish our doctrine of colours to stand to other pursuits. Important as this part of our work is, it is perhaps on this very account not so successful as we could wish. Yet when we reflect that strictly speaking these relations cannot be described before they exist, we may console ourselves if we have in some degree failed in endeavouring for the first time to define them. For undoubtedly we should first

wait to see how those whom we have endeavoured to serve, to whom we have intended to
make an agreeable and useful offering, how such
persons, we say, will accept the result of our
utmost exertion : whether they will adopt it,
whether they will make use of it and follow it
up, or whether they will repel, reject, and suffer
it to remain unassisted and neglected.

Meanwhile, we venture to express what we
believe and hope. From the philosopher we
believe we merit thanks for having traced the
phenomena of colours to their first sources, to
the circumstances under which they simply
appear and are, and beyond which no further
explanation respecting them is possible. It will,
besides, be gratifying to him that we have arranged the appearances described in a form that
admits of being easily surveyed, even should he
not altogether approve of the arrangement itself.

The medical practitioner, especially him
whose study it is to watch over the organ of
sight, to preserve it, to assist its defects and
to cure its disorders, we reckon to make especially our friend. In the chapter on the physiological colours, in the Appendix relating to
those that are more strictly pathological, he will
find himself quite in his own province. We are
not without hopes of seeing the physiological
phenomena,—a hitherto neglected, and, we may
add, most important branch of the theory of

colours,—completely investigated through the exertions of those individuals who in our own times are treating this department with success. The investigator of nature should receive us cordially, since we enable him to exhibit the doctrine of colours in the series of other elementary phenomena, and at the same time enable him to make use of a corresponding nomenclature, nay, almost the same words and designations as under the other rubrics. It is true we give him rather more trouble as a teacher, for the chapter of colours is not now to be dismissed as heretofore with a few paragraphs and experiments ; nor will the scholar submit to be so scantily entertained as he has hitherto been, without murmuring. On the other hand, an advantage will afterwards arise out of this : for if the Newtonian doctrine was easily learnt, insurmountable difficulties presented themselvse in its application. Our theory is perhaps more difficult to comprehend, but once known, all is accomplished, for it carries its application along with it.

The chemist who looks upon colours as indications by which he may detect the more secret properties of material things, has hitherto found much inconvenience in the denomination and description of colours ; nay, some have been induced after closer and nicer examination to look upon colour as an uncertain and fallacious criterion in chemical operations. Yet we hope by means of our arrangement and the nomenclature before alluded to, to bring colour again into credit, and to awaken the conviction that a progressive, augmenting, mutable quality, a quality which admits of alteration even to inversion, is not fallacious, but rather calculated to bring to light the most delicate operations of nature.

In looking a little further round us, we are not without fears that we may fail to satisfy another class of scientific men. By an extraordinary combination of circumstances the theory of colours has been drawn into the province and before the tribunal of the mathematician, a tribunal to which it cannot be said to be amenable. This was owing to its affinity with the other laws of vision which the mathematician was legitimately called upon to treat. It was owing, again, to another circumstance: a great mathematician had investigated the theory of colours, and having been mistaken in his observations as an experimentalist, he employed the whole force of his talent to give consistency to this mistake. Were both these circumstances considered, all misunderstanding would presently be removed, and the mathematician would willingly cooperate with us, especially in the physical department of the theory.

To the practical man, to the dyer, on the other hand, our labour must be altogether ac-

ceptable ; for it was precisely those who reflected on the facts resulting from the operations of dyeing who were the least satisfied with
the old theory : they were the first who perceived the insufficiency of the Newtonian doctrine. The conclusions of men are very different
according to the mode in which they approach
a science or branch of knowledge ; from which
side, through which door they enter. The
literally practical man, the manufacturer, whose
attention is constantly and forcibly called to the
facts which occur under his eye, who experiences
benefit or detriment from the application of his
convictions, to whom loss of time and money is
not indifferent, who is desirous of advancing,
who aims at equalling or surpassing what others
have accomplished,—such a person feels the
unsoundness and erroneousness of a theory
much sooner than the man of letters, in whose
eyes words consecrated by authority are at last
equivalent to solid coin; than the mathematician,
whose formula always remains infallible, even
although the foundation on which it is constructed may not square with it. Again, to
carry on the figure before employed, in entering
this theory from the side of painting, from the
side of æsthetic* colouring generally, we shall be

---

* Æsthetic—belonging to taste as mere internal sense, from
αἰσθάνομαι, to feel ; the word was first used by Wolf.—T.

found to have accomplished a most thankworthy office for the artist. In the sixth part we have endeavoured to define the effects of colour as addressed at once to the eye and mind, with a view to making them more available for the purposes of art. Although much in this portion, and indeed throughout, has been suffered to remain as a sketch, it should be remembered that all theory can in strictness only point out leading principles, under the guidance of which, practice may proceed with vigour and be enabled to attain legitimate results.

PART I.

PHYSIOLOGICAL COLOURS.

1.

WE naturally place these colours first, because they belong altogether, or in a great degree, to the *subject* *—to the eye itself. They are the foundation of the whole doctrine, and open to our view the chromatic harmony on which so much difference of opinion has existed. They have been hitherto looked upon as extrinsic and casual, as illusion and infirmity : their appearances have been known from ancient date ; but, as they were too evanescent to be arrested, they were banished into the region of phantoms, and under this idea have been very variously described.

2.

Thus they are called *colores adventicii* by Boyle; *imaginarii* and *phantastici* by Rizetti ; by Buffon, *couleurs accidentelles ;* by Scherfer, *scheinfarben* (apparent colours) ; *ocular illusions* and *deceptions*

---

* The German distinction between *subject* and *object* is so generally understood and adopted, that it is hardly necessary to explain that the subject is the *individual,* in this case the *beholder ;* the object, *all that is without him.*—1.

of sight by many ; by Hamberger, *vitia fugitiva ;* by Darwin, *ocular spectra.*

3.

We have called them physiological because they belong to the eye in a healthy state ; because we consider them as the necessary conditions of vision ; the lively alternating action of which, with reference to external objects and a principle within it, is thus plainly indicated.

4.

To these we subjoin the pathological colours, which, like all deviations from a constant law, afford a more complete insight into the nature of the physiological colours.

EFFECTS OF LIGHT AND DARKNESS ON THE EYE.

5.

The retina, after being acted upon by light or darkness, is found to be in two different states, which are entirely opposed to each other.

6.

If we keep the eyes open in a totally dark place, a certain sense of privation is experienced. The organ is abandoned to itself ; it retires into itself. That stimulating and grateful contact is wanting by means of which it is connected with the external world, and becomes part of a whole.

7.

If we look on a white, strongly illumined surface, the eye is dazzled, and for a time is incapable of distinguishing objects moderately
lighted.

8.

The whole of the retina is acted on in each of
these extreme states, and thus we can only experience one of these effects at a time. In the
one case (6) we found the organ in the utmost
relaxation and susceptibility; in the other (7)
in an overstrained state, and scarcely susceptible
at all.

9.

If we pass suddenly from the one state to the
other, even without supposing these to be the
extremes, but only, perhaps, a change from
bright to dusky, the difference is remarkable,
and we find that the effects last for some time.

10.

In passing from bright daylight to a dusky
place we distinguish nothing at first : by degrees
the eye recovers its susceptibility ; strong eyes
sooner than weak ones ; the former in a minute,
while the latter may require seven or eight
minutes.

11.

The fact that the eye is not susceptible to faint

impressions of light, if we pass from light to comparative darkness, has led to curious mistakes in scientific observations. Thus an observer, whose eyes required some time to recover their tone, was long under the impression that rotten wood did not emit light at noon-day, even in a dark room. The fact was, he did not see the faint light, because he was in the habit of passing from bright sunshine to the dark room, and only subsequently remained so long there that the eye had time to recover itself. The same may have happened to Doctor Wall, who, in the daytime, even in a dark room, could hardly perceive the electric light of amber.

Our not seeing the stars by day, as well as the improved appearance of pictures seen through a double tube, is also to be attributed to the same cause.

12.

If we pass from a totally dark place to one illumined by the sun, we are dazzled. In coming from a lesser degree of darkness to light that is not dazzling, we perceive all objects clearer and better : hence eyes that have been in a state of repose are in all cases better able to perceive moderately distinct appearances.

Prisoners who have been long confined in darkness acquire so great a susceptibility of the retina, that even in the dark (probably a darkness very slightly illumined) they can still distinguish objects.

13.

In the act which we call seeing, the retina is at one and the same time in different and even opposite states. The greatest brightness, short of dazzling, acts near the greatest darkness. In this state we at once perceive all the intermediate gradations of *chiaro-scuro*, and all the varieties of hues.

14.

We will proceed in due order to consider and examine these elements of the visible world, as well as the relation in which the organ itself stands to them, and for this purpose we take the simplest objects.

II.

EFFECTS OF BLACK AND WHITE OBJECTS ON THE EYE.

15.

IN the same manner as the retina generally is affected by brightness and darkness, so it is affected by single bright or dark objects. If light and dark produce different results on the whole retina, so black and white objects seen at the same time produce the same states together which light and dark occasioned in succession.

16.

A dark object appears smaller than a bright one of the same size. Let a white disk be placed on a black ground, and a black disk on a white ground, both being exactly similar in size; let them be seen together at some distance, and we shall pronounce the last to be about a fifth part smaller than the other. If the black circle be made larger by so much, they will appear equal.*

17.

Thus Tycho de Brahe remarked that the moon in conjunction (the darker state) appears about a fifth part smaller than when in opposition (the bright full state). The first crescent appears to belong to a larger disk than the remaining dark portion, which can sometimes be distinguished at the period of the new moon. Black dresses make people appear smaller than light ones. Lights seen behind an edge make an apparent notch in it. A ruler, behind which the flame of a light just appears, seems to us indented. The rising or setting sun appears to make a notch in the horizon.

18.

Black, as the equivalent of darkness, leaves

---

* Plate i. fig. 1.

the organ in a state of repose ; white, as the representative of light, excites it.   We may, perhaps, conclude from the above experiment (16) that the unexcited retina, if left to itself, is drawn together, and occupies a less space than in its active state, produced by the excitement of light.

Hence Kepler says very beautifully : " Certum est vel in retinâ caussâ picturæ, vel in spiritibus caussâ impressionis, exsistere dilatationem lucidorum."—*Paralip. in Vitellionem*, p. 220.   Scherfer expresses a similar conjecture.—Note A.

19.

However this may be, both impressions derived from such objects remain in the organ itself, and last for some time, even when the external cause is removed.   In ordinary experience we scarcely notice this, for objects are seldom presented to us which are very strongly relieved from each other, and we avoid looking at those appearances that dazzle the sight.   In glancing from one object to another ; the succession of images appears to us distinct ; we are not aware that some portion of the impression derived from the object first contemplated passes to that which is next looked at.

20.

If in the morning, on waking, when the eye is very susceptible, we look intently at the bars of a window relieved against the dawning sky, and then shut our eyes or look towards a totally dark place, we shall see a dark cross on a light ground before us for some time.

21.

Every image occupies a certain space on the retina, and of course a greater or less space in proportion as the object is seen near or at a distance. If we shut the eyes immediately after looking at the sun we shall be surprised to find how small the image it leaves appears.

22.

If, on the other hand, we turn the open eye towards the side of a room, and consider the visionary image in relation to other objects, we shall always see it larger in proportion to the distance of the surface on which it is thrown. This is easily explained by the laws of perspective, according to which a small object near covers a great one at a distance.

23.

The duration of these visionary impressions varies with the powers or structure of the eye in different individuals, just as the time necessary for the recovery of the tone of the retina varies in passing from brightness to darkness (10): it can be measured by minutes and seconds, indeed much more exactly than it could formerly have been by causing a lighted linstock to revolve rapidly, so as to appear a circle.—Note B.

24.

But the force with which an impinging light impresses the eye is especially worthy of attention. The image of the sun lasts longest ; other objects, of various degrees of brightness, leave the traces of their appearance on the eye for a proportionate time.

25.

These images disappear by degrees, and diminish at once in distinctness and in size.

26.

They are reduced from the contour inwards, and the impression on some persons has been that in square images the angles become gradually blunted till at last a diminished round image floats before the eye.

27.

Such an image, when its impression is no more observable, can, immediately after, be again revived on the retina by opening and shutting the eye, thus alternately exciting and resting it.

28.

Images may remain on the retina in morbid affections of the eye for fourteen, seventeen minutes, or even longer. This indicates extreme weakness of the organ, its inability to recover itself; while visions of persons or things which are the objects of love or aversion indicate the connexion between sense and thought.

29.

If, while the image of the window-bars before mentioned lasts, we look upon a light grey surface, the cross will then appear light and the panes dark. In the first case (20) the image was like the original picture, so that the visionary impression also could continue unchanged ; but in the present instance our attention is excited by a contrary effect being produced. Various examples have been given by observers of nature.

30.

The scientific men who made observations in the Cordilleras saw a bright appearance round the shadows of their heads on some clouds. This example is a case in point ; for, while they fixed their eyes on the dark shadow, and at the same time moved from the spot, the compensatory light image appeared to float round the real dark one. If we look at a black disk on a light grey surface, we shall presently, by changing the direction of the eyes in the slightest degree, see a bright halo floating round the dark circle.

A similar circumstance happened to myself: for while, as I sat in the open air, I was talking to a man who stood at a little distance from me relieved on a grey sky, it appeared to me, as I slightly altered the direction of my eyes, after having for some time looked fixedly at him, that his head was encircled with a dazzling light.

In the same way probably might be explained the circumstance that persons crossing dewy meadows at sunrise see a brightness round each other's heads ;* the brightness in this case may be also iridescent, as the phenomena of refraction come into the account.

Thus again it has been asserted that the shadows of a balloon thrown on clouds were bordered with bright and somewhat variegated circles.

Beccaria made use of a paper kite in some experiments on electricity. Round this kite appeared a small shining cloud varying in size ; the same brightness was even observed round part of the string. Sometimes it disappeared,

---

* See the Life of Benvenuto Cellini, vol. i. p. 453. Milan edition, 1806. —T.

and if the kite moved faster the light appeared to float to and fro for a few moments on the place before occupied. This appearance, which could not be explained by those who observed it at the time, was the image which the eye retained of the kite relieved as a dark mass on a bright sky ; that image being changed into a light mass on a comparatively dark background.

In optical and especially in chromatic experiments, where the observer has to do with bright lights whether colourless or coloured, great care should be taken that the spectrum which the eye retains in consequence of a previous observation does not mix with the succeeding one, and thus affect the distinctness and purity of the impression.

31.

These appearances have been explained as follows : That portion of the retina on which the dark cross (29) was impressed is to be considered in a state of repose and susceptibility. On this portion therefore the moderately light surface acted in a more lively manner than on the rest of the retina, which had just been impressed with the light through the panes, and which, having thus been excited by a much stronger brightness, could only view the grey surface as a dark.

32.

This mode of explanation appears sufficient for the cases in question, but, in the consideration of phenomena hereafter to be adduced, we are forced to trace the effects to higher sources.

33.

The eye after sleep exhibits its vital elasticity more especially by its tendency to alternate its impressions, which in the simplest form change from dark to light, and from light to dark. The eye cannot for a moment remain in a particular state determined by the object it looks upon. On the contrary, it is forced to a sort of opposition, which, in contrasting extreme with extreme, intermediate degree with intermediate degree, at the same time combines these opposite impressions, and thus ever tends to a whole, whether the impressions are successive, or simultaneous and confined to one image.

34.

Perhaps the peculiarly grateful sensation which we experience in looking at the skilfully treated chiaro-scuro of colourless pictures and similar works of art arises chiefly from the *simultaneous* impression of a whole, which by the organ itself is sought, rather than arrived at, in *succession*, and which, whatever may be the result, can never be arrested.

III.

35.

A MODERATE light is essential to many chromatic experiments. This can be presently obtained by surfaces more or less grey, and thus we have at once to make ourselves acquainted with this simplest kind of middle tint, with regard to which it is hardly necessary to observe, that in many cases a white surface in shadow, or in a low light, may be considered equivalent to a grey.

36.

Since a grey surface is intermediate between brightness and darkness, it admits of our illustrating a phenomenon before described (29) by an easy experiment.

37.

Let a black object be held before a grey surface, and let the spectator, after looking steadfastly at it, keep his eyes unmoved while it is taken away: the space it occupied appears much lighter. Let a white object be held up in the same manner: on taking it away the space it occupied will appear much darker than the rest of the surface. Let the spectator in both cases turn his eyes this way and that on the surface, the visionary images will move in like manner.

38.

A grey object on a black ground appears much brighter than the same object on a white ground. If both comparisons are seen together the spectator can hardly persuade himself that the two greys are identical. We believe this again to be a proof of the great excitability of the retina, and of the silent resistance which every vital principle is forced to exhibit when any definite or immutable state is presented to it. Thus inspiration already presupposes expiration; thus every systole its diastole. It is the universal formula of life which manifests itself in this as in all other cases. When darkness is presented to the eye it demands brightness, and *vice versâ :* it shows its vital energy, its fitness to receive the impression of the object, precisely by spontaneously tending to an opposite state.

IV.

DAZZLING COLOURLESS OBJECTS.

39.

IF we look at a dazzling, altogether colourless object, it makes a strong lasting impression, and its after-vision is accompanied by an appearance of colour.

40.

Let a room be made as dark as possible; let there be a circular opening in the window-shutter about three inches in diameter, which may be closed or not at pleasure. The sun being suffered to shine through this on a white surface, let the spectator from some little distance fix his eyes on the bright circle thus admitted. The hole being then closed, let him look towards the darkest part of the room; a circular image will now be seen to float before him. The middle of this circle will appear bright, colourless, or somewhat yellow, but the border will at the same moment appear red.

After a time this red, increasing towards the centre, covers the whole circle, and at last the bright central point. No sooner, however, is the whole circle red than the edge begins to be blue, and the blue gradually encroaches inwards on the red. When the whole is blue the edge becomes dark and colourless. This darker edge again slowly encroaches on the blue till the whole circle appears colourless. The image then becomes gradually fainter, and at the same time diminishes in size. Here again we see how the retina recovers itself by a succession of vibrations after the powerful external impression it received. (25, 26.)

41.

By several repetitions similar in result, 1 found the comparative duration of these appearances in my own case to be as follows :—

I looked on the bright circle five seconds, and then, having closed the aperture, saw the coloured visionary circle floating before me. After thirteen seconds it was altogether red ; twenty-nine seconds next elapsed till the whole was blue, and forty-eight seconds till it appeared colourless. By shutting and opening the eye I constantly revived the image, so that it did not quite disappear till seven minutes had elapsed.

Future observers may find these periods shorter or longer as their eyes may be stronger or weaker (23), but it would be very remarkable if, notwithstanding such variations, a corresponding proportion as to relative duration should be found to exist.

42.

But this remarkable phenomenon no sooner excites our attention than we observe a new modification of it.

If we receive the impression of the bright circle as before, and then look on a light grey surface in a moderately lighted room, an image again floats before us; but in this instance a dark one : by degrees it is encircled by a green border that gradually spreads inwards over the whole circle, as the red did in the former instance. As soon as this has taken place a dingy yellow appears, and, filling the space as the blue did before, is finally lost in a negative shade.

43.

These two experiments may be combined by placing a black and a white plane surface next each other in a moderately lighted room, and then looking alternately on one and the other as long as the impression of the light circle lasts: the spectator will then perceive at first a red and green image alternately, and afterwards the other changes. After a little practice the two opposite colours may be perceived at once, by causing the floating image to fall on the junction of the two planes. This can be more conveniently done if the planes are at some distance, for the spectrum then appears larger.

44.

I happened to be in a forge towards evening at the moment when a glowing mass of iron was placed on the anvil; I had fixed my eyes steadfastly on it, and, turning round, I looked accidentally into an open coal-shed: a large red image now floated before my eyes, and, as I turned them from the dark opening to the light boards of which the shed was constructed, the image appeared half green, half red, according as it had a lighter or darker ground behind it. I did not at that time take notice of the subsequent changes of this appearance.

45.

The after-vision occasioned by a total dazzling of the retina corresponds with that of a circumscribed bright object. The red colour seen by persons who are dazzled with snow belongs to this class of phenomena, as well as the singularly beautiful green colour which dark objects seem to wear after looking long on white paper in the sun. The details of such experiments may be investigated hereafter by those whose young eyes are capable of enduring such trials further for the sake of science.

46.

With these examples we may also class the black letters which in the evening light appear

red.   Perhaps we might insert under the same
category the story that drops of blood appeared
on the table at which Henry IV. of France had
seated himself with the Duc de Guise to play at
dice.

V.

COLOURED OBJECTS.

47.

WE have hitherto seen the physiological
colours displayed in the after-vision of colourless bright objects, and also in the after-vision
of general colourless brightness ; we shall now
find analogous appearances if a given colour be
presented to the eye: in considering this, all
that has been hitherto detailed must be present
to our recollection.

48.

The impression of coloured objects remains
in the eye like that of colourless ones, but in
this case the energy of the retina, stimulated as
it is to produce the opposite colour, will be more
apparent.

49.

Let a small piece of bright-coloured paper or
silk stuff be held before a moderately lighted
white surface; let the observer look steadfastly

on the small coloured object, and let it be taken
away after a time while his eyes remain unmoved; the spectrum of another colour will then
be visible on the white plane. The coloured
paper may be also left in its place while the eye
is directed to another part of the white plane;
the same spectrum will be visible there too, for
it arises from an image which now belongs to
the eye.

50.

In order at once to see what colour will be
evoked by this contrast, the chromatic circle *
may be referred to. The colours are here arranged in a general way according to the
natural order, and the arrangement will be
found to be directly applicable in the present
case; for the colours diametrically opposed to
each other in this diagram are those which reciprocally evoke each other in the eye. Thus,
yellow demands purple; orange, blue; red,
green; and *vice versâ:* thus again all intermediate gradations reciprocally evoke each other;
the simpler colour demanding the compound,
and *vice versâ.*—Note C.

51.

The cases here under consideration occur
oftener than we are aware in ordinary life; in-

---

* Plate 1, fig. 3.

deed, an attentive observer sees these appearances everywhere, while, on the other hand, the uninstructed, like our predecessors, consider them as temporary visual defects, sometimes even as symptoms of disorders in the eye, thus exciting serious apprehensions. A few remarkable instances may here be inserted.

52.

I had entered an inn towards evening, and, as a well-favoured girl, with a brilliantly fair complexion, black hair, and a scarlet bodice, came into the room, I looked attentively at her as she stood before me at some distance in half shadow. As she presently afterwards turned away, I saw on the white wall, which was now before me, a black face surrounded with a bright light, while the dress of the perfectly distinct figure appeared of a beautiful sea-green.

53.

Among the materials for optical experiments, there are portraits with colours and shadows exactly opposite to the appearance of nature. The spectator, after having looked at one of these for a time, will see the visionary figure tolerably true to nature. This is conformable to the same principles, and consistent with experience, for, in the former instance, a negress with a white head-dress would have given me a white face surrounded with black. In the case of the painted figures, however, which are commonly small, the parts are not distinguishable by every one in the after-image.

54.

A phenomenon which has before excited attention among the observers of nature is to be attributed, I am persuaded, to the same cause.

It has been stated that certain flowers, towards evening in summer, coruscate, become phosphorescent, or emit a momentary light. Some persons have described their observation of this minutely. I had often endeavoured to witness it myself, and had even resorted to artificial contrivances to produce it.

On the 19th of June, 1799, late in the evening, when the twilight was deepening into a clear night, as I was walking up and down the garden with a friend, we very distinctly observed a flame-like appearance near the oriental poppy, the flowers of which are remarkable for their powerful red colour. We approached the place and looked attentively at the flowers, but could perceive nothing further, till at last, by passing and repassing repeatedly, while we looked sideways on them, we succeeded in renewing the appearance as often as we pleased. It proved to be a physiological phenomenon, such as others we have described, and the apparent coruscation was nothing but the spectrum of the flower in the compensatory blue-green colour.

In looking directly at a flower the image is not produced, but it appears immediately as the direction of the eye is altered. Again, by looking sideways on the object, a double image is seen for a moment, for the spectrum then appears near and on the real object.

The twilight accounts for the eye being in a perfect state of repose, and thus very susceptible, and the colour of the poppy is sufficiently powerful in the summer twilight of· the longest days to act with full effect and produce a compensatory image. I have no doubt these appearances might be reduced to experiment, and the same effect produced by pieces of coloured paper. Those who wish to take the most effectual means for observing the appearance in nature—suppose in a garden—should fix the eyes on the bright flowers selected for the purpose, and, immediately after, look on the gravel path. This will be seen studded with spots of the opposite colour. The experiment is practicable on a cloudy day, and even in the brightest sunshine, for the sun-light, by enhancing the brilliancy of the flower, renders it fit to produce the compensatory colour sufficiently distinct to be perceptible even in a bright light. Thus, peonies produce beautiful green, marigolds vivid blue spectra.

55.

As the opposite colour is produced by a constant law in experiments with coloured objects on portions of the retina, so the same effect takes place when the whole retina is impressed with a single colour. We may convince ourselves of this by means of coloured glasses. If we look long through a blue pane of glass, everything will afterwards appear in sunshine to the naked eye, even if the sky is grey and the scene colourless. In like manner, in taking off green spectacles, we see all objects in a red light. Every decided colour does a certain violence to the eye, and forces the organ to opposition.

56.

We have hitherto seen the opposite colours producing each other successively on the retina: it now remains to show by experiment that the same effects can exist simultaneously. If a coloured object impinges on one part of the retina, the remaining portion at the same moment has a tendency to produce the compensatory colour. To pursue a former experiment, if we look on a yellow piece of paper placed on a white surface, the remaining part of the organ has already a tendency to produce a purple hue on the colourless surface: in this case the small portion of yellow is not powerful enough to produce this appearance distinctly, but, if a white paper is placed on a yellow wall, we shall see the white tinged with a purple hue.

57.

Although this experiment may be made with any colours, yet red and green are particularly recommended for it, because these colours seem powerfully to evoke each other. Numerous instances occur in daily experience. If a green paper is seen through striped or flowered muslin, the stripes or flowers will appear reddish. A grey building seen through green pallisades appears in like manner reddish. A modification of this tint in the agitated sea is also a compensatory colour : the light side of the waves appears green in its own colour, and the shadowed side is tinged with the opposite hue. The different direction of the waves with reference to the eye produces the same effect. Objects seen through an opening in a red or green curtain appear to wear the opposite hue. These appearances will present themselves to the attentive observer on all occasions, even to an unpleasant degree.

58.

Having made ourselves acquainted with the simultaneous exhibition of these effects in direct cases, we shall find that we can also observe them by indirect means. If we place a piece of

paper of a bright orange colour on the white
surface, we shall, after looking intently at it,
scarcely perceive the compensatory colour on
the rest of the surface : but when we take the
orange paper away, and when the blue spectrum
appears in its place, immediately as this spectrum becomes fully apparent, the rest of the
surface will be overspread, as if by a flash, with
a reddish-yellow light, thus exhibiting to the
spectator in a lively manner the productive
energy of the organ, in constant conformity with
the same law.

59.

As the compensatory colours easily appear,
where they do not exist in nature, near and
after the original opposite ones, so they are rendered more intense where they happen to mix
with a similar real hue. In a court which was
paved with grey limestone flags, between which
grass had grown, the grass appeared of an extremely beautiful green when the evening clouds
threw a scarcely perceptible reddish light on
the pavement. In an opposite case we find,
in walking through meadows, where we see
scarcely anything but green, the stems of trees
and the roads often gleam with a reddish hue.
This tone is not uncommon in the works of
landscape painters, especially those who practice in water-colours : they probably see it in

nature, and thus, unconsciously imitating it, their colouring is criticised as unnatural.

60.

These phenomena are of the greatest importance, since they direct our attention to the laws of vision, and are a necessary preparation for future observations on colours. They show that the eye especially demands completeness, and seeks to eke out the colorific circle in itself. The purple or violet colour suggested by yellow contains red and blue ; orange, which responds to blue, is composed of yellow and red ; green, uniting blue and yellow, demands red ; and so through all gradations of the most complicated combinations. That we are compelled in this case to assume three leading colours has been already remarked by other observers.

61.

When in this completeness the elements of which it is composed are still appreciable by the eye, the result is justly called harmony. We shall subsequently endeavour to show how the theory of the harmony of colours may be deduced from these phenomena, and how, simply through these qualities, colours may be capable of being applied to æsthetic purposes. This will be shown when we have gone through the whole circle of our observations, returning to the point from which we started.

VI.

COLOURED SHADOWS.

62.

BEFORE, however, we proceed further, we have yet to observe some very remarkable cases of the vivacity with which the suggested colours appear in the neighbourhood of others : we allude to coloured shadows. To arrive at these we first turn our attention to shadows that are colourless or negative.

63.

A shadow cast by the sun, in its full brightness, on a white surface, gives us no impression of colour; it appears black, or, if a contrary light (here assumed to differ only in degree) can act upon it, it is only weaker, half-lighted, grey.

64.

Two conditions are necessary for the existence of coloured shadows : first, that the principal light tinge the white surface with some hue; secondly, that a contrary light illumine to a certain extent the cast shadow.

65.

Let a short, lighted candle be placed at twilight on a sheet of white paper. Between it and the declining daylight let a pencil be placed upright, so that its shadow thrown by the candle may be lighted, but not overcome, by the weak daylight: the shadow will appear of the most beautiful blue.

66.

That this shadow is blue is immediately evident; but we can only persuade ourselves by some attention that the white paper acts as a reddish yellow, by means of which the complemental blue is excited in the eye.—Note D.

67.

In all coloured shadows, therefore, we must presuppose a colour excited or suggested by the hue of the surface on which the shadow is thrown. This may be easily found to be the case by attentive consideration, but we may convince ourselves at once by the following experiment.

68.

Place two candles at night opposite each other on a white surface; hold a thin rod between them upright, so that two shadows be cast by it; take a coloured glass and hold it before one of the lights, so that the white paper appear coloured; at the same moment the shadow cast by the coloured light and slightly illumined by the colourless one will exhibit the complemental hue.

69.

An important consideration suggests itself here, to which we shall frequently have occasion to return. Colour itself is a degree of darkness (σκιερόν); hence Kircher is perfectly right in calling it *lumen opacatum*. As it is allied to shadow, so it combines readily with it; it appears to us readily in and by means of shadow the moment a suggesting cause presents itself. We could not refrain from adverting at once to a fact which we propose to trace and develop hereafter.—Note E.

70.

Select the moment in twilight when the light of the sky is still powerful enough to cast a shadow which cannot be entirely effaced by the light of a candle. The candle may be so placed that a double shadow shall be visible, one from the candle towards the daylight, and another from the daylight towards the candle. If the former is blue the latter will appear orange-yellow: this orange-yellow is in fact, however, only the yellow-red light of the candle diffused over the whole paper, and which *becomes visible in shadow*.

71.

This is best exemplified by the former experiment with two candles and coloured glasses.

The surprising readiness with which shadow assumes a colour will again invite our attention in the further consideration of reflections and elsewhere.

72.

Thus the phenomena of coloured shadows may be traced to their cause without difficulty. Henceforth let any one who sees an instance of the kind observe only with what hue the light surface on which they are thrown is tinged. Nay, the colour of the shadow may be considered as a chromatoscope of the illumined surface, for the spectator may always assume the colour of the light to be the opposite of that of the shadow, and by an attentive examination may ascertain this to be the fact in every instance.

73.

These appearances have been a source of great perplexity to former observers: for, as they were remarked chiefly in the open air, where they commonly appeared blue, they were attributed to a certain inherent blue or blue colouring quality in the air. The inquirer can, however, convince himself, by the experiment with the candle in a room, that no kind of blue light or reflection is necessary to produce the effect in question. The experiment may be made on a cloudy day with white curtains drawn

before the light, and in a room where no trace
of blue exists, and the blue shadow will be only
so much the more beautiful.

74.

De Saussure, in the description of his ascent
of Mont Blanc, says, " A second remark, which
may not be uninteresting, relates to the colour
of the shadows. These, notwithstanding the
most attentive observation, we never found dark
blue, although this had been frequently the case
in the plain. On the contrary, in fifty-nine instances we saw them once yellowish, six times
pale bluish, eighteen times colourless or black,
and thirty-four times pale violet. Some natural
philosophers suppose that these colours arise
from accidental vapours diffused in the air, which
communicate their own hues to the shadows;
not that the colours of the shadows are occasioned by the reflection of any given sky colour
or interposition of any given air colour: the
above observations seem to favour this opinion."
The instances given by De Saussure may be
now explained and classed with analogous examples without difficulty.

At a great elevation the sky was generally
free from vapours, the sun shone in full force on
the snow, so that it appeared perfectly white to
the eye : in this case they saw the shadows
quite colourless. If the air was charged with a

certain degree of vapour, in consequence of which the light snow would assume a yellowish tone, the shadows were violet-coloured, and this effect, it appears, occurred oftenest. They saw also bluish shadows, but this happened less frequently; and that the blue and violet were pale was owing to the surrounding brightness, by which the strength of the shadows was mitigated. Once only they saw the shadow yellowish: in this case, as we have already seen (70), the shadow is cast by a colourless light, and slightly illumined by a coloured one.

75.

In travelling over the Harz in winter, I happened to descend from the Brocken towards evening; the wide slopes extending above and below me, the heath, every insulated tree and projecting rock, and all masses of both, were covered with snow or hoar-frost. The sun was sinking towards the Oder ponds.* During the day, owing to the yellowish hue of the snow, shadows tending to violet had already been observable; these might now be pronounced to be decidedly blue, as the illumined parts exhibited a yellow deepening to orange.

But as the sun at last was about to set, and its rays, greatly mitigated by the thicker va-

---

* Reservoirs in which water is collected from various small streams, to work the mines.—T.

pours, began to diffuse a most beautiful red
colour over the whole scene around me, the
shadow colour changed to a green, in lightness
to be compared to a sea-green, in beauty to the
green of the emerald. The appearance became
more and more vivid : one might have imagined
oneself in a fairy world, for every object had
clothed itself in the two vivid and so beautifully
harmonising colours, till at last, as the sun went
down, the magnificent spectacle was lost in a
grey twilight, and by degrees in a clear moon-
and-starlight night.

76.

One of the most beautiful instances of coloured shadows may be observed during the
full moon. The candle-light and moon-light
may be contrived to be exactly equal in
force ; both shadows may be exhibited with
equal strength and clearness, so that both colours balance each other perfectly. A white
surface being placed opposite the full moon,
and the candle being placed a little on one side
at a due distance, an opaque body is held before the white plane. A double shadow will
then be seen : that cast by the moon and illumined by the candle-light will be a powerful
red-yellow ; and contrariwise, that cast by the
candle and illumined by the moon will appear
of the most beautiful blue. The shadow, composed of the union of the two shadows, where

they cross each other, is black. The yellow shadow (74) cannot perhaps be exhibited in a more striking manner. The immediate vicinity of the blue and the interposing black shadow make the appearance the more agreeable. It will even be found, if the eye dwells long on these colours, that they mutually evoke and enhance each other, the increasing red in the one still producing its contrast, viz. a kind of sea-green.

77.

We are here led to remark that in this, and in all cases, a moment or two may perhaps be necessary to produce the complemental colour. The retina must be first thoroughly impressed with the demanding hue before the responding one can be distinctly observable.

78.

When divers are under water, and the sunlight shines into the diving-bell, everything is seen in a red light (the cause of which will be explained hereafter), while the shadows appear green. The very same phenomenon which I observed on a high mountain (75) is presented to others in the depths of the sea, and thus Nature throughout is in harmony with herself.

79.

Some observations and experiments which equally illustrate what has been stated with regard to coloured objects and coloured shadows may be here added. Let a white paper blind be fastened inside the window on a winter evening; in this blind let there be an opening, through which the snow of some neighbouring roof can be seen. Towards dusk let a candle be brought into the room; the snow seen through the opening will then appear perfectly blue, because the paper is tinged with warm yellow by the candle-light. The snow seen through the aperture is here equivalent to a shadow illumined by a contrary light (76), and may also represent a grey disk on a coloured surface (56).

80.

Another very interesting experiment may conclude these examples. If we take a piece of green glass of some thickness, and hold it so that the window bars be reflected in it, they will appear double owing to the thickness of the glass. The image which is reflected from the under surface of the glass will be green; the image which is reflected from the upper surface, and which should be colourless, will appear red.

The experiment may be very satisfactorily made by pouring water into a vessel, the inner surface of which can act as a mirror; for both reflections may first be seen colourless while the water is pure, and then by tinging it, they will exhibit two opposite hues.

VII.

FAINT LIGHTS.

81.

LIGHT, in its full force, appears purely white, and it gives this impression also in its highest degree of dazzling splendour. Light, which is not so powerful, can also, under various conditions, remain colourless. Several naturalists and mathematicians have endeavoured to measure its degrees—Lambert, Bouguer, Rumfort.

82.

Yet an appearance of colour presently manifests itself in fainter lights, for in their relation to absolute light they resemble the coloured spectra of dazzling objects (39).

83.

A light of any kind becomes weaker, either when its own force, from whatever cause, is diminished, or when the eye is so circumstanced or placed, that it cannot be sufficiently impressed by the action of the light. Those appearances which may be called objective, come under the head of physical colours. We will only advert here to the transition from white to red heat in glowing iron. We may also observe

that the flames of lights at night appear redder
in proportion to their distance from the eye.—
Note F.

84.

Candle-light at night acts as yellow when seen
near; we can perceive this by the effect it produces on other colours. At night a pale yellow
is hardly to be distinguished from white; blue
approaches to green, and rose-colour to orange.

85.

Candle-light at twilight acts powerfully as a
yellow light: this is best proved by the purple
blue shadows which, under these circumstances,
are evoked by the eye.

86.

The retina may be so excited by a strong
light that it cannot perceive fainter lights (11):
if it perceive these they appear coloured : hence
candle-light by day appears reddish, thus resembling, in its relation to fuller light, the spectrum of a dazzling object; nay, if at night we
look long and intently on the flame of a light,
it appears to increase in redness.

87.

There are faint lights which, notwithstanding
their moderate lustre, give an impression of a

white, or, at the most, of a light yellow appearance on the retina ; such as the moon in its full splendour. Rotten wood has even a kind of bluish light. All this will hereafter be the subject of further remarks.

88.

If at night we place a light near a white or greyish wall so that the surface be illumined from this central point to some extent, we find, on observing the spreading light at some distance, that the boundary of the illumined surface appears to be surrounded with a yellow circle, which on the outside tends to red-yellow. We thus observe that when light direct or reflected does not act in its full force, it gives an impression of yellow, of reddish, and lastly even of red. Here we find the transition to halos which we are accustomed to see in some mode or other round luminous points.

VIII.

SUBJECTIVE HALOS.

89.

HALOS may be divided into subjective and objective. The latter will be considered under the physical colours ; the first only belong here. These are distinguished from the objective

halos by the circumstance of their vanishing
when the point of light which produces them on
the retina is covered.

90.

We have before noticed the impression of a
luminous object on the retina, and seen that it
appears larger : but the effect is not at an end
here, it is not confined to the impression of the
image; an expansive action also takes place,
spreading from the centre.

91.

That a nimbus of this kind is produced round
the luminous image in the eye may be best seen
in a dark room, if we look towards a moderately
large opening in the window-shutter. In this
case the bright image is surrounded by a circular misty light. I saw such a halo bounded
by a yellow and yellow-red circle on opening
my eyes at dawn, on an occasion when I passed
several nights in a bed-carriage.

92.

Halos appear most vivid when the eye is susceptible from having been in a state of repose.
A dark background also heightens their appearance. Both causes account for our seeing
them so strong if a light is presented to the eyes

on waking at night. These conditions were combined when Descartes after sleeping, as he sat in a ship, remarked such a vividly-coloured halo round the light.

93.

A light must shine moderately, not dazzle, in order to produce the impression of a halo in the eye ; at all events the halos of dazzling lights cannot be observed. We see a splendour of this kind round the image of the sun reflected from the surface of water.

94.

A halo of this description, attentively observed, is found to be encircled towards its edge with a yellow border: but even here the expansive action, before alluded to, is not at an end, but appears still to extend in varied circles.

95.

Several cases seem to indicate a circular action of the retina, whether owing to the round form of the eye itself and its different parts, or to some other cause.

96.

If the eye is pressed only in a slight degree from the inner corner, darker or lighter circles appear, At night, even without pressure, we can sometimes perceive a succession of such circles emerging from, or spreading over, each other.

97.

We have already seen that a yellow border is apparent round the white space illumined by a light placed near it. This may be a kind of objective halo. (88.)

98.

Subjective halos may be considered as the result of a conflict between the light and a living surface. From the conflict between the exciting principle and the excited, an undulating motion arises, which may be illustrated by a comparison with the circles on water. The stone thrown in drives the water in all directions; the effect attains a maximum, it reacts, and being opposed, continues under the surface. The effect goes on, culminates again, and thus the circles are repeated. If we have ever remarked the concentric rings which appear in a glass of water on trying to produce a tone by rubbing the edge; if we call to mind the intermitting pulsations in the reverberations of bells, we shall approach a conception of what may take place on the retina when the image of a luminous object impinges on it, not to mention that as a living and elastic structure, it has already a circular principle in its organisation.—Note G.

99.

The bright circular space which appears round the shining object is yellow, ending in red : then follows a greenish circle, which is terminated by a red border. This appears to be the usual phenomenon where the luminous body is somewhat considerable in size. These halos become greater the more distant we are from the luminous object.

100.

Halos may, however, appear extremely small and numerous when the impinging image is minute, yet powerful, in its effect. The experiment is best made with a piece of gold-leaf placed on the ground and illumined by the sun. In these cases the halos appear in variegated rays. The iridescent appearance produced in the eye when the sun pierces through the leaves of trees seems also to belong to the same class of phenomena.

PATHOLOGICAL COLOURS.

APPENDIX.

101.

WE are now sufficiently acquainted with the physiological colours to distinguish them from the pathological. We know what appearances belong to the eye in a healthy state, and are necessary to enable the organ to exert its complete vitality and activity.

102.

Morbid phenomena indicate in like manner the existence of organic and physical laws : for if a living being deviates from those rules with reference to which it is constructed, it still seeks to agree with the general vitality of nature in conformity with general laws, and throughout its whole course still proves the constancy of those principles on which the universe has existed, and by which it is held together.

103.

We will here first advert to a very remarkable state in which the vision of many persons is found to be. As it presents a deviation from the ordinary mode of seeing colours, it might be fairly classed under morbid impressions ; but as it is consistent in itself, as it often occurs,

may extend to several members of a family, and
probably does not admit of cure, we may consider it as bordering only on the nosological
cases, and therefore place it first.

104.

I was acquainted with two individuals not
more than twenty years of age, who were thus
affected : both had bluish-grey eyes, an acute
sight for near and distant objects, by day-light
and candle-light, and their mode of seeing
colours was in the main quite similar.

105.

They agreed with the rest of the world in
denominating white, black, and grey in the usual
manner. Both saw white untinged with any
hue. One saw a somewhat brownish appearance in black, and in grey a somewhat reddish
tinge. In general they appeared to have a very
delicate perception of the gradations of light
and dark.

106.

They appeared to see yellow, red-yellow, and
yellow-red,* like others : in the last case they said
they saw the yellow passing as it were over the
red as if glazed : some thickly-ground carmine,
which had dried in a saucer, they called red.

---

* It has been found necessary to follow the author's nomenclature throughout.—T.

107.

But now a striking difference presented itself. If the carmine was passed thinly over the white saucer, they would compare the light colour thus produced to the colour of the sky, and call it blue. If a rose was shown them beside it, they would, in like manner, call it blue ; and in all the trials which were made, it appeared that they could not distinguish light blue from rose-colour. They confounded rose-colour, blue, and violet on all occasions : these colours only appeared to them to be distinguished from each other by delicate shades of lighter, darker, intenser, or fainter appearance.

108.

Again they could not distinguish green from dark orange, nor, more especially, from a red brown.

109.

If any one, accidentally conversing with these individuals, happened to question them about surrounding objects, their answers occasioned the greatest perplexity, and the interrogator began to fancy his own wits were out of order. With some method we may, however, approach to a nearer knowledge of the law of this deviation from the general law.

110.

These persons, as may be gathered from what has been stated, saw fewer colours than other people : hence arose the confusion of different colours. They called the sky rose-colour, and the rose blue, or *vice versâ*. The question now is : did they see both blue or both rose-colour ? did they see green orange, or orange green ?

111.

This singular enigma appears to solve itself, if we assume that they saw no blue, but, instead of it, a light pure red, a rose-colour. We can comprehend what would be the result of this by means of the chromatic diagram.

112.

If we take away blue from the chromatic circle we shall miss violet and green as well. Pure red occupies the place of blue and violet, and in again mixing with yellow the red produces orange where green should be.

113.

Professing to be satisfied with this mode of explanation, we have named this remarkable deviation from ordinary vision " Acyanoblepsia." *
We have prepared some coloured figures for

---

* Non-perception of blue.

its further elucidation, and in explaining these we shall add some further details. Among the examples will be found a landscape, coloured in the mode in which the individuals alluded to appeared to see nature : the sky rose-colour, and all that should be green varying from yellow to brown red, nearly as foliage appears to us in autumn.*—Note **H**.

114.

We now proceed to speak of morbid and other extraordinary affections of the retina, by which the eye may be susceptible of an appearance of light without external light, reserving for a future occasion the consideration of galvanic light.

115.

If the eye receives a blow, sparks seem to spread from it. In some states of body, again, when the blood is heated, and the system much excited, if the eye is pressed first gently, and then more and more strongly, a dazzling and intolerable light may be excited.

116.

If those who have been recently couched experience pain and heat in the eye, they fre-

---

* It has not been thought necessary to copy the plates here referred to.—T.

quently see fiery flashes and sparks : these
symptoms last sometimes for a week or fortnight,
or till the pain and heat diminish.

117.

A person suffering from ear-ache saw sparks
and balls of light in the eye during each attack,
as long as the pain lasted.

118.

Persons suffering from worms often experience
extraordinary appearances in the eye, sometimes
sparks of fire, sometimes spectres of light, sometimes frightful figures, which they cannot by an
effort of the will cease to see : sometimes these
appearances are double.

119.

Hypochondriacs frequently see dark objects,
such as threads, hairs, spiders, flies, wasps.
These appearances also exhibit themselves in
the incipient hard cataract. Many see semi-
transparent small tubes, forms like wings of
insects, bubbles of water of various sizes, which
fall slowly down, if the eye is raised : sometimes these congregate together so as to resemble the spawn of frogs ; sometimes they appear
as complete spheres, sometimes in the form of
lenses.

120.

As light appeared, in the former instances,

without external light, so also these images appear without corresponding external objects. The images are sometimes transient, sometimes they last during the patient's life. Colour, again, frequently accompanies these impressions : for hypochondriacs often see yellow-red stripes in the eye : these are generally more vivid and numerous in the morning, or when fasting.

121.

We have before seen that the impression of any object may remain for a time in the eye : this we have found to be a physiological phenomenon (23) : the excessive duration of such an impression, on the other hand, may be considered as morbid.

122.

The weaker the organ the longer the impression of the image lasts. The retina does not so soon recover itself; and the effect may be considered as a kind of paralysis (28).

123.

This is not to be wondered at in the case of dazzling lights. If any one looks at the sun, he may retain the image in his eyes for several days. Boyle relates an instance of ten years.

124.

The same takes place, in a certain degree, with

regard to objects that are not dazzling. Büsch relates of himself that the image of an engraving, complete in all its parts, was impressed on his eye for seventeen minutes.

125.

A person inclined to fulness of blood retained the image of a bright red calico, with white spots, many minutes in the eye, and saw it float before everything like a veil. It only disappeared by rubbing the eye for some time.

126.

Scherfer observes that the red colour, which is the consequence of a powerful impression of light, may last for some hours.

127.

As we can produce an appearance of light on the retina by pressure on the eyeball, so by a gentle pressure a red colour appears, thus corresponding with the after-image of an impression of light.

128.

Many sick persons, on awaking, see everything in the colour of the morning sky, as if through a red veil : so, if in the evening they doze and wake again, the same appearance presents itself. It remains for some minutes, and

always disappears if the eye is rubbed a little.
Red stars and balls sometimes accompany the
impression. This state may last for a considerable time.

129.

The aëronauts, particularly Zambeccari and
his companions, relate that they saw the moon
blood-red at the highest elevation. As they had
ascended above the vapours of the earth, through
which we see the moon and sun naturally of such
a colour, it may be suspected that this appearance may be classed with the pathological colours. The senses, namely, may be so influenced
by an unusual state, that the whole nervous
system, and particularly the retina, may sink
into a kind of inertness and inexcitability.
Hence it is not impossible that the moon might
act as a very subdued light, and thus produce
the impression of the red colour. The sun even
appeared blood-red to the aëronauts of Ham-
burgh.

If those who are at some elevation in a balloon
scarcely hear each other speak, may not this,
too, be attributed to the inexcitable state of the
nerves as well as to the thinness of the air?

130.

Objects are often seen by sick persons in
variegated colours. Boyle relates an instance

of a lady, who, after a fall by which an eye was bruised, saw all objects, but especially white objects, glittering in colours, even to an intolerable degree.

131.

Physicians give the name of " Chrupsia" to an affection of the sight, occurring in typhoid maladies. In these cases the patients state that they see the boundaries of objects coloured where light and dark meet. A change probably takes place in the humours of the eye, through which their achromatism is affected.

132.

In cases of milky cataract, a very turbid crystalline lens causes the patient to see a red light. In a case of this kind, which was treated by the application of electricity, the red light changed by degrees to yellow, and at last to white, when the patient again began to distinguish objects. These changes of themselves warranted the conclusion that the turbid state of the lens was gradually approaching the transparent state. We shall be enabled easily to trace this effect to its source as soon as we become better acquainted with the physical colours.

133.

If again it may be assumed that a jaundiced

patient sees through an actually yellow-coloured humour, we are at once referred to the department of chemical colours, and it is thus evident that we can only thoroughly investigate the chapter of pathological colours when we have made ourselves acquainted with the whole range of the remaining phenomena. What has been adduced may therefore suffice for the present, till we resume the further consideration of this portion of our subject.

134.

In conclusion we may, however, at once advert to some peculiar states or dispositions of the organ.

There are painters who, instead of rendering the colours of nature, diffuse a general tone, a warm or cold hue, over the picture. In some, again, a predilection for certain colours displays itself; in others a want of feeling for harmony.

135.

Lastly, it is also worthy of remark, that savage nations, uneducated people, and children have a great predilection for vivid colours; that animals are excited to rage by certain colours; that people of refinement avoid vivid colours in their dress and the objects that are about them, and seem inclined to banish them altogether from their presence.—Note I

PART II.

136.

WE give this designation to colours which are produced by certain material mediums : these mediums, however, have no colour themselves, and may be either transparent, semi-transparent yet transmitting light, or altogether opaque. The colours in question are thus produced in the eye through such external given causes, or are merely reflected to the eye when by whatever means they are already produced without us. Although we thus ascribe to them a certain objective character, their distinctive quality still consists in their being transient, and not to be arrested.

137.

They are called by former investigators *colores apparentes, fluxi, fugitivi, phantastici, falsi, variantes.* They are also called *speciosi* and *emphatici*, on account of their striking splendour. They are immediately connected with the physiological colours, and appear to have but little more reality : for, while in the production of the physiological colours the eye itself was chiefly efficient, and we could only perceive the phenomena thus evoked within ourselves, but not without us, we have now to consider the fact that colours are produced in the eye by means of colourless objects ; that we thus too have a colourless surface before us which is acted upon as the retina itself is, and that we can perceive the appearance produced upon it without us. In such a process, however, every observation will convince us that we have to do with colours in a progressive and mutable, but not in a final or complete, state.

138.

Hence, in directing our attention to these physical colours, we find it quite possible to place an objective phenomenon beside a subjective one, and often by means of the union of the two successfully to penetrate farther into the nature of the appearance.

139.

Thus, in the observations by which we become acquainted with the physical colours, the eye is not to be considered as acting alone ; nor is the light ever to be considered in immediate relation with the eye : but we direct our attention especially to the various effects produced by mediums, those mediums being themselves colourless.

140.

Light under these circumstances may be affected by three conditions. First, when it flashes back from the surface of a medium ; in considering which *catoptrical* experiments invite our attention. Secondly, when it passes by the edge of a medium : the phenomena thus produced were formerly called *perioptical ;* we prefer the term *paroptical.* Thirdly, when it passes through either a merely light-transmitting or an actually transparent body ; thus constituting a class of appearances on which *dioptrical* experiments are founded. We have called a fourth class of physical colours *epoptical,* as the phenomena exhibit themselves on the colourless surface of bodies under various conditions, without previous or actual dye (βαφή).—Note K.

141.

In examining these categories with reference to our three leading divisions, according to which we consider the phenomena of colours in a physiological, physical, or chemical view, we find that the catoptrical colours are closely connected with the physiological ; the paroptical are already somewhat more distinct and independent ; the dioptrical exhibit themselves as entirely and strictly physical, and as having a decidedly objective character ; the epoptical, although still only apparent, may be considered as the transition to the chemical colours.

142.

If we were desirous of prosecuting our investigation strictly in the order of nature, we ought to proceed according to the classification which has just been made ; but in didactic treatises it is not of so much consequence to connect as to duly distinguish the various divisions of a subject, in order that at last, when every single class and case has been presented to the mind, the whole may be embraced in one comprehensive view. We therefore turn our attention forthwith to the dioptrical class, in order at once to give the reader the full impression of the physical colours, and to exhibit their characteristics the more strikingly.

IX.

DIOPTRICAL COLOURS.

143.

COLOURS are called dioptrical when a colourless medium is necessary to produce them ; the medium must be such that light and darkness can act through it either on the eye or on opposite surfaces. It is thus required that the medium should be transparent, or at least capable, to a certain degree, of transmitting light.

144.

According to these conditions we divide the dioptrical phenomena into two classes, placing in the first those which are produced by means of imperfectly transparent, yet light-transmitting mediums ; and in the second such as are exhibited when the medium is in the highest degree transparent.

X.

DIOPTRICAL COLOURS OF THE FIRST CLASS.

145.

SPACE, if we assume it to be empty, would have the quality of absolute transparency to our vision. If this space is filled so that the eye cannot perceive that it is so, there exists a more or less material transparent medium, which may be of the nature of air and gas, may be fluid or even solid.

146.

The pure and light-transmitting semi-transparent medium is only an accumulated form of the transparent medium. It may therefore be presented to us in three modes.

147.

The extreme degree of this accumulation is white ; the simplest, brightest, first, opaque occupation of space.

148.

Transparency itself, empirically considered, is already the first degree of the opposite state. The intermediate degrees from this point to opaque white are infinite.

149.

At whatever point short of opacity we arrest the thickening medium, it exhibits simple and remarkable phenomena when placed in relation with light and darkness.

150.

The highest degree of light, such as that of the sun, of phosphorus burning in oxygen, is dazzling and colourless : so the light of the fixed stars is for the most part colourless. This light, however, seen through a medium but very slightly thickened, appears to us yellow. If the density of such a medium be increased, or if its volume become greater, we shall see the light gradually assume a yellow-red hue, which at last deepens to a ruby-colour.—Note L.

151.

If on the other hand darkness is seen through a semi-transparent medium, which is itself illumined by a light striking on it, a blue colour appears : this becomes lighter and paler as the density of the medium is increased, but on the contrary appears darker and deeper the more transparent the medium becomes : in the least degree of dimness short of absolute transparence, always supposing a perfectly colourless medium, this deep blue approaches the most beautiful violet.

152.

If this effect takes place in the eye as here described, and may thus be pronounced to be subjective, it remains further to convince ourselves of this by objective phenomena. For a light thus mitigated and subdued illumines all objects in like manner with a yellow, yellow-red, or red hue ; and, although the effect of darkness through the non-transparent medium does not exhibit itself so powerfully, yet the blue sky displays itself in the camera obscura very distinctly on white paper, as well as every other material colour.

153.

In examining the cases in which this important leading phenomenon appears, we naturally mention the atmospheric colours first: most of these may be here introduced in order.

154.

The sun seen through a certain degree of vapour appears with a yellow disk ; the centre is often dazzlingly yellow when the edges are already red.   The orb seen through a thick yellow mist appears ruby-red (as was the case in 1794, even in the north) ; the same appearance is still more decided, owing to the state of the atmosphere, when the scirocco prevails in southern climates: the clouds generally surrounding the sun in the latter case are of the same colour, which is reflected again on all objects.

The red hues of morning and evening are owing to the same cause.   The sun is announced by a red light, in shining through a greater mass of vapours.   The higher he rises, the yellower and brighter the light becomes.

155.

If the darkness of infinite space is seen through atmospheric vapours illumined by the day-light, the blue colour appears.   On high mountains the sky appears by day intensely blue, owing to the few thin vapours that float before the endless dark space : as soon as we descend in the valleys, the blue becomes lighter; till at last, in certain regions, and in consequence of increasing vapours, it altogether changes to a very pale blue.

156.

The mountains, in like manner, appear to us blue; for, as we see them at so great a distance that we no longer distinguish the local tints, and as no light reflected from their surface acts on our vision, they are equivalent to mere dark objects, which, owing to the interposed vapours, appear blue.

157.

So we find the shadowed parts of nearer objects are blue when the air is charged with thin vapours.

158.

The snow-mountains, on the other hand, at a great distance, still appear white, or approaching to a yellowish hue, because they act on our eyes as brightness seen through atmospheric vapour.

159.

The blue appearance at the lower part of the flame of a candle belongs to the same class of phenomena.   If the flame be held before a white ground, no blue will be seen, but this colour will immediately appear if the flame is opposed to a black ground. This phenomenon may be exhibited most strikingly with a spoonful of lighted spirits of wine. We may thus consider the lower part of the flame as equivalent to the vapour which, although infinitely thin, is still apparent before the dark surface; it is so thin, that one may easily see to read through it: on the other hand, the point of the flame which conceals objects from our sight is to be considered as a self-illuminating body.

160.

Lastly, smoke is also to be considered as a semi-transparent medium, which appears to us yellow or reddish before a light ground, but blue before a dark one.

161.

If we now turn our attention to fluid mediums, we find that water, deprived in a very slight degree of its transparency, produces the same effects.

162.

The infusion of the lignum nephriticum (guilandina Linnæi), which formerly excited so much attention, is only a semi-transparent liquor, which in dark wooden cups must appear blue, but held towards the sun in a transparent glass must exhibit a yellow appearance.

163.

A drop of scented water, of spirit varnish, of several metallic solutions, may be employed to give various degrees of opacity to water for such experiments. Spirit of soap perhaps answers best.

164.

The bottom of the sea appears to divers of a red colour in bright sunshine: in this case the water, owing to its depth, acts as a semi-transparent medium. Under these circumstances, they find the shadows green, which is the complemental colour.

165.

Among solid mediums the opal attracts our attention first: its colours are, at least, partly to be explained by the circumstance that it is, in fact, a semi-transparent medium, through which sometimes light, sometimes dark, substrata are visible.

166.

For these experiments, however, the opal-glass (vitrum astroides, girasole) is the most desirable material. It is prepared in various ways, and its semi-opacity is produced by metallic oxydes. The same effect is produced also by melting pulverised and calcined bones together with the glass, on which account it is also known by the name of *beinglas ;* but, prepared in this mode, it easily becomes too opaque.

167.

This glass may be adapted for experiments in various ways : it may either be made in a very slight degree non-transparent, in which case the light seen through various layers placed one upon the other may be deepened from the lightest yellow to the deepest red, or, if made originally more opaque, it may be employed in thinner or thicker laminæ. The experiments may be successfully made in both ways : in order, however, to see the bright blue colour, the glass should neither be too opaque nor too thick. For, as it is quite natural that darkness must act weakly through the semi-transparent medium, so this medium, if too thick, soon approaches whiteness.

168.

Panes of glass throw a yellow light on objects through those parts where they happen to be semi-opaque, and these same parts appear blue if we look at a dark object through them.

169.

Smoked glass may be also mentioned here, and is, in like manner, to be considered as a semi-opaque medium. It exhibits the sun more or less ruby-coloured ; and, although this appearance may be attributed to the black-brown colour of the soot, we may still convince ourselves that a semi-transparent medium here acts if we hold such a glass moderately smoked, and lit by the sun on the unsmoked side, before a dark object, for we shall then perceive a bluish appearance.

170.

A striking experiment may be made in a dark room with sheets of parchment. If we fasten a piece of parchment before the opening in the window-shutter when the sun shines, it will appear nearly white ; by adding a second, a yellowish colour appears, which still increases as more leaves are added, till at last it changes to red.

171.

A similar effect, owing to the state of the crystalline lens in milky cataract, has been already adverted to (131).

172.

Having now, in tracing these phenomena, arrived at the effect of a degree of opacity scarcely capable of transmitting light, we may here mention a singular appearance which was owing to a momentary state of this kind.

A portrait of a celebrated theologian had been painted some years before the circumstance to which we allude, by an artist who was known to have considerable skill in the management of his materials. The very reverend individual was represented in a rich velvet dress, which was not a little admired, and which attracted the eye of the spectator almost more than the face. The picture, however, from the effect of the smoke of lamps and dust, had lost much of its original vivacity. It was, therefore, placed in the hands of a painter, who was to clean it, and give it a fresh coat of varnish. This person began his operations by carefully washing the picture with a sponge : no sooner, however, had he gone over the surface once or twice, and wiped away the first dirt, than to his amazement the black velvet dress changed suddenly to a light blue plush, which gave the ecclesiastic a very secular, though somewhat old-fashioned, appearance. The painter did not venture to go on with his washing: he could not comprehend how a light blue should be the ground of the deepest black, still less how he could so suddenly have removed a glazing colour capable of converting the one tint to the other.

At all events, he was not a little disconcerted at having spoilt the picture to such an extent. Nothing to characterize the ecclesiastic remained but the richly-curled round wig, which made the exchange of a faded plush for a handsome new velvet dress far from desirable. Meanwhile, the mischief appeared irreparable, and the good artist, having turned the picture to the wall, retired to rest with a mind ill at ease. But what was his joy the next morning, when, on examining the picture, he beheld the black velvet dress again in its full splendour. He could not refrain from again wetting a corner, upon which the blue colour again appeared, and after a time vanished. On hearing of this phenomenon, I went at once to see the miraculous picture. A wet sponge was passed over it in my presence, and the change quickly took place. I saw a somewhat faded, but decidedly light blue plush dress, the folds under the arm being indicated by some brown strokes.

I explained this appearance to myself by the doctrine of the semi-opaque medium. The painter, in order to give additional depth to his black, may have passed some particular varnish over it : on being washed, this varnish imbibed some moisture, and hence became semi-opaque, in consequence of which the black underneath immediately appeared blue. Perhaps those who are practically acquainted with the effect of varnishes may, through accident or contrivance, arrive at some means of exhibiting this singular appearance, as an experiment, to those

who are fond of investigating natural phenomena.   Notwithstanding   many   attempts,   I
could not myself succeed in re-producing it.

173.

Having now traçed the most splendid instances of atmospheric appearances, as well as
other less striking yet sufficiently remarkable
cases, to the leading examples of semi-transparent mediums, we have no doubt that attentive observers of nature will carry such researches further, and accustom themselves to
trace and explain the various appearances
which present themselves in every-day experience on the same principle : we may also hope
that such investigators will provide themselves
with an adequate apparatus in order to place
remarkable facts before the eyes of others who
may be desirous of information.

174.

We venture, once for all, to call the leading
appearance in question, as generally described
in the foregoing pages, a primordial and elementary phenomenon ; and we may here be
permitted at once to state what we understand
by the term.

175.

The circumstances which come under our notice
in ordinary observation are, for the most part, insulated cases, which, with some attention, admit

of being classed under general leading facts. These again range themselves under theoretical rubrics which are more comprehensive, and through which we become better acquainted with certain indispensable conditions of appearances in detail. From henceforth everything is gradually arranged under higher rules and laws, which, however, are not to be made intelligible by words and hypotheses to the understanding merely, but, at the same time, by real phenomena to the senses. We call these primordial phenomena, because nothing appreciable by the senses lies beyond them, on the contrary, they are perfectly fit to be considered as a fixed point to which we first ascended, step by step, and from which we may, in like manner, descend to the commonest case of every-day experience. Such an original phenomenon is that which has lately engaged our attention. We see on the one side light, brightness ; on the other darkness, obscurity : we bring the semi-transparent medium between the two, and from these contrasts and this medium the colours develop themselves, contrasted, in like manner, but soon, through a reciprocal relation, directly tending again to a point of union.*

---

* That is (according to the author's statement 150. 151.) both tend to red ; the yellow deepening to orange as the comparatively dark medium is thickened before brightness ; the blue deepening to violet as the light medium is thinned before darkness.—T.

176.

With this conviction we look upon the mistake that has been committed in the investigation of this subject to be a very serious one, inasmuch as a secondary phenomenon has been thus placed higher in order—the primordial phenomenon has been degraded to an inferior place; nay, the secondary phenomenon has been placed at the head, a compound effect has been treated as simple, a simple appearance as compound: owing to this contradiction, the most capricious complication and perplexity have been introduced into physical inquiries, the effects of which are still apparent.

177.

But when even such a primordial phenomenon is arrived at, the evil still is that we refuse to recognise it as such, that we still aim at something beyond, although it would become us to confess that we are arrived at the limits of experimental knowledge. Let the observer of nature suffer the primordial phenomenon to remain undisturbed in its beauty; let the philosopher admit it into his department, and he will find that important elementary facts are a worthier basis for further operations than insulated cases, opinions, and hypotheses.—Note M.

XI.

DIOPTRICAL COLOURS OF THE SECOND CLASS.—REFRAC-
TION.

178.

DIOPTRICAL colours of both classes are closely connected, as will presently appear on a little examination. Those of the first class appeared through semi-transparent mediums, those of the second class will now appear through transparent mediums. But since every substance, however transparent, may be already considered to partake of the opposite quality (as every accumulation of a medium called transparent proves), so the near affinity of the two classes is sufficiently manifest.

179.

We will, however, first consider transparent mediums abstractedly as such, as entirely free from any degree of opacity, and direct our whole attention to a phenomenon which here presents itself, and which is known by the name of refraction.

180.

In treating of the physiological colours, we have already had occasion to vindicate what were formerly called illusions of sight, as the

active energies of the healthy and duly efficient
eye (2), and we are now again invited to consider similar instances confirming the constancy
of the laws of vision.

181.

Throughout nature, as presented to the senses,
everything depends on the relation which things
bear to each other, but especially on the relation
which man, the most important of these, bears
to the rest.   Hence the world divides itself into
two parts, and the human being as *subject,* stands
opposed to the *object.*   Thus   the practical
man exhausts himself in the accumulation of
facts, the thinker in speculation ; each being
called upon to sustain a conflict which admits
of no peace and no decision.

182.

But still the main point always is, whether
the relations are truly seen.   As our senses, if
healthy, are the surest witnesses of external relations, so we may be convinced that, in all instances where they appear to contradict reality,
they lay the greater and surer stress on true
relations.   Thus a distant object appears to us
smaller ; and precisely by this means we are
aware of distance.   We produced coloured appearances on colourless objects, through colourless mediums, and at the same moment our at-

tention was called to the degree of opacity in the medium.

183.

Thus the different degrees of opacity in so-called transparent mediums, nay, even other physical and chemical properties belonging to them, are known to our vision by means of refraction, and invite us to make further trials in order to penetrate more completely by physical and chemical means into those secrets which are already opened to our view on one side.

184.

Objects seen through mediums more or less transparent do not appear to us in the place which they should occupy according to the laws of perspective. On this fact the dioptrical colours of the second class depend.

185.

Those laws of vision which admit of being expressed in mathematical formulæ are based on the principle that, as light proceeds in straight lines, it must be possible to draw a straight line from the eye to any given object in order that it be seen. If, therefore, a case arises in which the light arrives to us in a bent or broken line, that we see the object by means of a bent or broken line, we are at once informed that the medium between the eye and the object is denser, or that it has assumed this or that foreign nature.

186.

This deviation from the law of right-lined vision is known by the general term of refraction ; and, although we may take it for granted that our readers are sufficiently acquainted with its effects, yet we will here once more briefly exhibit it in its objective and subjective point of view.

187.

Let the sun shine diagonally into an empty cubical vessel, so that the opposite side be illumined, but not the bottom : let water be then poured into this vessel, and the direction of the light will be immediately altered ; for a part of the bottom is shone upon. At the point where the light enters the thicker medium it deviates from its rectilinear direction, and appears broken : hence the phenomenon is called the breaking (*brechung*) or refraction. Thus much of the objective experiment.

188.

We arrive at the subjective fact in the following mode :—Let the eye be substituted for the sun : let the sight be directed in like manner diagonally over one side, so that the opposite inner side be entirely seen, while no part of the bottom is visible.   On pouring in water the eye will perceive a part of the bottom ; and this takes place without our being aware that we do not see in a straight line ; for the bottom appears to us raised, and hence we give the term elevation (*hebung*) to the subjective phenomenon.   Some points, which are particularly remarkable with reference to this, will be adverted to hereafter.

189.

Were we now to express this phenomenon generally, we might here repeat, in conformity with the view lately taken, that the relation of the objects is changed or deranged.

190.

But as it is our intention at present to separate the objective from the subjective appearances, we first express the phenomenon in a subjective form, and say,—a derangement or displacement of the object seen, or to be seen, takes place.

191.

But that which is seen without a limiting outline may be thus affected without our perceiving the change.   On the other hand, if what we look at has a visible termination, we have an evident indication that a displacement occurs. If, therefore, we wish to ascertain the relation or degree of such a displacement, we must chiefly confine ourselves to the alteration of surfaces with visible boundaries ; in other words, to the displacement of circumscribed objects.

192.

The general effect may take place through parallel mediums, for every parallel medium displaces the object by bringing it perpendicularly towards the eye. The apparent change of position is, however, more observable through mediums that are not parallel.

193.

These latter may be perfectly spherical, or may be employed in the form of convex or concave lenses. We shall make use of all these as occasion may require in our experiments. But as they not only displace the object from its position, but alter it in various ways, we shall, in most cases, prefer employing mediums with surfaces, not, indeed, parallel with reference to each other, but still altogether plane, namely, prisms. These have a triangle for their base, and may, it is true, be considered as portions of a lens, but they are particularly available for our experiments, inasmuch as they very perceptibly displace the object from its position, without producing a remarkable distortion.

194.

And now, in order to conduct our observations with as much exactness as possible, and to avoid all confusion and ambiguity, we confine ourselves at first to

SUBJECTIVE EXPERIMENTS,

in which, namely, the object is seen by the observer through a refracting medium. As soon as we have treated these in due series, the objective experiments will follow in similar order.

XII.

REFRACTION WITHOUT THE APPEARANCE OF COLOUR.

195.

REFRACTION can visibly take place without our perceiving an appearance of colour. To whatever extent a colourless or uniformly coloured surface may be altered as to its position by refraction, no colour consequent upon refraction appears within it, provided it has no outline or boundary. We may convince ourselves of this in various ways.

196.

Place a glass cube on any larger surface, and look through the glass perpendicularly or obliquely, the unbroken surface opposite the eye appears altogether raised, but no colour exhibits itself. If we look at a pure grey or blue sky or a uniformly white or coloured wall through a prism, the portion of the surface which the eye thus embraces will be altogether changed as to its position, without our therefore observing the smallest appearance of colour.

XIII.

CONDITIONS OF THE APPEARANCE OF COLOUR.

197.

ALTHOUGH in the foregoing experiments we have found all unbroken surfaces, large or small, colourless, yet at the outlines or boundaries, where the surface is relieved upon a darker or lighter object, we observe a coloured appearance.

198.

Outline, as well as surface, is necessary to constitute a figure or circumscribed object. We therefore express the leading fact thus : circumscribed objects must be displaced by refraction in order to the exhibition of an appearance of colour.

199.

We place before us the simplest object, a light disk on a dark ground (A).* A displacement occurs with regard to this object, if we apparently extend its outline from the centre by magnifying it. This may be done with any convex glass, and in this case we see a blue edge (B).

200.

We can, to appearance, contract the circumference of the same light disk towards the centre by diminishing the object; the edge will then appear yellow (c). This may be done with a concave glass, which, however, should not be ground thin like common eye-glasses, but must have some substance. In order, however, to make this experiment at once with the convex glass, let a smaller black disk be inserted within the light disk on a black ground. If we magnify the black disk on a white ground with a convex glass, the same result takes place as if we diminished the white disk ; for we extend the black outline upon the white, and we thus perceive the yellow edge together with the blue edge (D).

201.

These two appearances, the blue and yellow, exhibit themselves in and upon the white : they

* Plate 2, fig. 1.

both assume a reddish hue, in proportion as they mingle with the black.*

202.

In this short statement we have described the primordial phenomena of all appearance of colour occasioned by refraction. These undoubt-edly may be repeated, varied, and rendered more striking ; may be combined, complicated, confused ; but, after all, may be still restored to their original simplicity.

203.

In examining the process of the experiment just given, we find that in the one case we have, to appearance, extended the white edge upon the dark surface ; in the other we have extended the dark edge upon the white surface, supplanting one by the other, pushing one over the other. We will now endeavour, step by step, to analyse these and similar cases.

204.

If we cause the white disk to move, in appear-ance, entirely from its place, which can be done

---

* The author has omitted the orange and purple in the co-loured diagrams which illustrate these first experiments, from a wish probably to present the elementary contrast, on which he lays a stress, in greater simplicity. The reddish tinge would be apparent, as stated above, where the blue and yellow are in con-tact with the black.—T.

effectually by prisms, it will be coloured according to the direction in which it apparently moves, in conformity with the above laws. If we look at the disk a* through a prism, so that it appear moved to b, the outer edge will appear blue and blue-red, according to the law of the figure B (fig. 1), the other edge being yellow, and yellow-red, according to the law of the figure c (fig. 1). For in the first case the white figure is, as it were, extended over the dark boundary, and in the other case the dark boundary is passed over the white figure. The same happens if the disk is, to appearance, moved from a to c, from a to d, and so throughout the circle.

205.

As it is with the simple effect, so it is with more complicated appearances. If we look through a horizontal prism (a b†) at a white disk placed at some distance behind it at e, the disk will be raised to f, and coloured according to the above law. If we remove this prism, and look through a vertical one (c d) at the same disk, it will appear at h, and coloured according to the same law. If we place the two prisms one upon the other, the disk will appear displaced diagonally, in conformity with a general law of nature, and will be coloured as

* Plate 2, fig. 2.   † Plate 2, fig. 4.

before ; that is, according to its movement in the direction, *e. g. :* *

206.

If we attentively examine these opposite coloured edges, we find that they only appear in the direction of the apparent change of place. A round figure leaves us in some degree uncertain as to this : a quadrangular figure removes all doubt.

207.

The quadrangular figure *a*,† moved in the direction *a b,* or *a d,* exhibits no colour on the sides which are parallel with the direction in which it moves : on the other hand, if moved in the direction *a c,* parallel with its diagonal, all the edges of the figure appear coloured.‡

208.

Thus, a former position (203) is here confirmed ; viz. to produce colour, an object must be so displaced that the light edges be apparently carried over a dark surface, the dark edges over a light surface, the figure over its boundary, the boundary over the figure. But

---

* In this case, according to the author, the refracting medium being increased in mass, the appearance of colour is increased, and the displacement is greater.—**T.**

† Plate 2, fig. 3.

‡ Fig. 2, plate 1, contains a variety of forms, which, when viewed through a prism, are intended to illustrate the statement in this and the following paragraph.

if the rectilinear boundaries of a figure could be indefinitely extended by refraction, so that figure and background might only pursue their course next, but not over each other, no colour would appear, not even if they were prolonged to infinity.

XIV.

CONDITIONS UNDER WHICH THE APPEARANCE OF COLOUR INCREASES.

209.

We have seen in the foregoing experiments that all appearance of colour occasioned by refraction depends on the condition that the boundary or edge be moved in upon the object itself, or the object itself over the ground, that the figure should be, as it were, carried over itself, or over the ground. And we shall now find that, by increased displacement of the object, the appearance of colour exhibits itself in a greater degree. This takes place in subjective experiments, to which, for the present, we confine ourselves, under the following conditions.

210.

First, if, in looking through parallel mediums, the eye is directed more obliquely.

Secondly, if the surfaces of the medium are no longer parallel, but form a more or less acute angle.

Thirdly, owing to the increased proportion of the medium, whether parallel mediums be increased in size, or whether the angle be increased, provided it does not attain a right angle.

Fourthly, owing to the distance of the eye armed with a refracting medium from the object to be displaced.

Fifthly, owing to a chemical property that may be communicated to the glass, and which may be afterwards increased in effect.

211.

The greatest change of place, short of considerable distortion of the object, is produced by means of prisms, and this is the reason why the appearance of colour can be exhibited most powerfully through glasses of this form. Yet we will not, in employing them, suffer ourselves to be dazzled by the splendid appearances they exhibit, but keep the above well-established, simple principles calmly in view.

212.

The colour which is outside, or foremost, in the apparent change of an object by refraction, is always the broader, and we will henceforth call this a *border :* the colour that remains next the outline is the narrower, and this we will call an *edge.*

213.

If we move a dark boundary towards a light surface, the yellow broader border is foremost, and the narrower yellow-red edge follows close to the outline. If we move a light boundary towards a dark surface, the broader violet border is foremost, and the narrower blue edge follows.

214.

If the object is large, its centre remains uncoloured. Its inner surface is then to be considered as unlimited (195): it is displaced, but not otherwise altered: but if the object is so narrow, that under the above conditions the yellow border can reach the blue edge, the space between the outlines will be entirely covered with colour. If we make this experiment with a white stripe on a black ground,* the two extremes will presently meet, and thus produce green. We shall then see the following series of colours :—

Yellow-red.
Yellow.
Green.
Blue.
Blue-red.

215.

If we place a black band, or stripe, on white paper,† the violet border will spread till it meets

---

* Plate 2, fig. 5, *left*.   † Plate 2, fig. 5, *right*.

the yellow-red edge. In this case the intermediate black is effaced (as the intermediate white was in the last experiment), and in its stead a splendid pure red will appear.* The series of colours will now be as follows:—

Blue.

Blue-red.

Red.

Yellow-red.

Yellow.

216.

The yellow and blue, in the first case (214), can by degrees meet so fully, that the two colours blend entirely in green, and the order will then be,

Yellow-red.

Green.

Blue-red.

In the second case (215), under similar circumstances, we see only

Blue.

Red.

Yellow.

This appearance is best exhibited by refracting the bars of a window when they are relieved on a grey sky.†

---

* This pure red, the union of orange and violet, is considered by the author the maximum of the coloured appearance: he has appropriated the term *purpur* to it. See paragraph 703, and *note.*—T.

† The bands or stripes in fig. 4, plate 1, when viewed through a prism, exhibit the colours represented in plate 2, fig. 5.

217.

In all this we are never to forget that this appearance is not to be considered as a complete or final state, but always as a progressive, increasing, and, in many senses, controllable appearance. Thus we find that, by the negation of the above five conditions, it gradually decreases, and at last disappears altogether.

XV.

EXPLANATION OF THE FOREGOING PHENOMENA.

218.

BEFORE we proceed further, it is incumbent on us to explain the first tolerably simple phenomenon, and to show its connexion with the principles first laid down, in order that the observer of nature may be enabled clearly to comprehend the more complicated appearances that follow.

219.

In the first place, it is necessary to remember that we have to do with circumscribed objects. In the act of seeing, generally, it is the circumscribed visible which chiefly invites our observation; and in the present instance, in speaking of the appearance of colour, as occasioned by refraction, the circumscribed visible, the detached object solely occupies our attention.

220.

For our chromatic exhibitions we can, however, divide objects generally into *primary* and *secondary*. The expressions of themselves denote what we understand by them, but our meaning will be rendered still more plain by what follows.

221.

Primary objects may be considered firstly as *original*, as images which are impressed on the eye by things before it, and which assure us of their reality. To these the secondary images may be opposed as *derived* images, which remain in the organ when the object itself is taken away; those apparent after-images, which have been circumstantially treated of in the doctrine of physiological colours.

222.

The primary images, again, may be considered as *direct* images, which, like the original impressions, are conveyed immediately from the object to the eye. In contradistinction to these, the secondary images may be considered as *indirect*, being only conveyed to us, as it were, at second-hand from a reflecting surface. These are the mirrored, or catoptrical, images, which in certain cases can also become double images:

223.

When, namely, the reflecting body is transparent, and has two parallel surfaces, one behind the other: in such a case, an image may be reflected to the eye from both surfaces, and thus arise double images, inasmuch as the upper image does not quite cover the under one: this may take place in various ways.

Let a playing-card be held before a mirror. We shall at first see the distinct image of the card, but the edge of the whole card, as well as that of every spot upon it, will be bounded on one side with a border, which is the beginning of the second reflection. This effect varies in different mirrors, according to the different thickness of the glass, and the accidents of polishing. If a person wearing a white waistcoat, with the remaining part of his dress dark, stands before certain mirrors, the border appears very distinctly, and in like manner the metal buttons on dark cloth exhibit the double reflection very evidently.

224.

The reader who has made himself acquainted with our former descriptions of experiments (80) will the more readily follow the present statement. The window-bars reflected by plates of glass appear double, and by increased thickness of the glass, and a due adaptation of the angle of reflection, the two reflections may be entirely separated from each other. So a vase full of water, with a plane mirror-like bottom, reflects any object twice, the two reflections being more or less separated under the same conditions. In these cases it is to be observed that, where the two reflections cover each other, the perfect vivid image is reflected, but where they are separated they exhibit only weak, transparent, and shadowy images.

225.

If we wish to know which is the under and which the upper image, we have only to take a coloured medium, for then a light object reflected from the under surface is of the colour of the medium, while that reflected from the upper surface presents the complemental colour. With dark objects it is the reverse; hence black and white surfaces may be here also conveniently employed. How easily the double images assume and evoke colours will here again be striking.

226.

Thirdly, the primary images may be considered as *principal* images, while the secondary can be, as it were, annexed to these as *accessory* images. Such an accessory image produces a sort of double form; except that it does not separate itself from the principal object, although it may be said to be always endeavouring to do so. It is

with secondary images of this last description
that we have to do in prismatic appearances.

227.

A surface without a boundary exhibits no
appearance of colour when refracted (195).
Whatever is seen must be circumscribed by an
outline to produce this effect. In other words
a figure, an object, is required; this object
undergoes an apparent change of place by refraction: the change is however not complete,
not clean, not sharp; but incomplete, inasmuch
as an accessory image only is produced.

228.

In examining every appearance of nature,
but especially in examining an important and
striking one, we should not remain in one spot,
we should not confine ourselves to the insulated
fact, nor dwell on it exclusively, but look round
through all nature to see where something similar, something that has affinity to it, appears:
for it is only by combining analogies that we
gradually arrive at a whole which speaks for
itself, and requires no further explanation.

229.

Thus we here call to mind that in certain
cases refraction unquestionably produces double
images, as is the case in Iceland spar: similar

double images are also apparent in cases of refraction through large rock crystals, and in other instances ; phenomena which have not hitherto been sufficiently observed.*

230.

But since in the case under consideration (227) the question relates not to double but to accessory images, we refer to a phenomenon already adverted to, but not yet thoroughly investigated. We allude to an earlier experiment, in which it appeared that a sort of conflict took place in regard to the retina between a light object and its dark ground, and between a dark object and its light ground (16). The light object in this case appeared larger, the dark one smaller.

231.

By a more exact observation of this phenomenon we may remark that the forms are not sharply distinguished from the ground, but that they appear with a kind of grey, in some degree, coloured edge ; in short, with an accessory image. If, then, objects seen only with the naked eye produce such effects, what may not take place when a dense medium is interposed? It is not that alone which presents itself to us

* The date of the publication, 1810, is sometimes to be remembered.—T.

in obvious operation which produces and suffers effects, but likewise all principles that have a mutual relation only of some sort are efficient accordingly, and indeed often in a very high degree.

232.

Thus when refraction produces its effect on an object there appears an accessory image next the object itself: the real form thus refracted seems even to linger behind, as if resisting the change of place ; but the accessory image seems to advance, and extends itself more or less in the mode already shown (212—216).

233.

We also remarked (224) that in double images the fainter appear only half substantial, having a kind of transparent, evanescent character, just as the fainter shades of double shadows must always appear as half-shadows. These latter assume colours easily, and produce them readily (69), the former also (80) ; and the same takes place in the instance of accessory images, which, it is true, do not altogether quit the real object, but still advance or extend from it as half-substantial images, and hence can appear coloured so quickly and so powerfully.

234.

That the prismatic appearance is in fact an

accessory image we may convince ourselves in more than one mode. It corresponds exactly with the form of the object itself. Whether the object be bounded by a straight line or a curve, indented or waving, the form of the accessory image corresponds throughout exactly with the form of the object.*

235.

Again, not only the form but other qualities of the object are communicated to the accessory image. If the object is sharply relieved from its ground, like white on black, the coloured accessory image in like manner appears in its greatest force. It is vivid, distinct, and powerful ; but it is most especially powerful when a luminous object is shown on a dark ground, which may be contrived in various ways.

236.

But if the object is but faintly distinguished from the ground, like grey objects on black or white, or even on each other, the accessory image is also faint, and, when the original difference of tint or force is slight, becomes hardly discernible.

---

* The forms in fig. 2, plate 1, when seen through a prism, are again intended to exemplify this. In the plates to the original work curvilinear figures are added, but the circles, fig. 1, in the same plate, may answer the same end.—T.

237.

The appearances which are observable when coloured objects are relieved on light, dark, or coloured grounds are, moreover, well worthy of attention. In this case a union takes place between the apparent colour of the accessory image and the real colour of the object; a compound colour is the result, which is either assisted and enhanced by the accordance, or neutralised by the opposition of its ingredients.

238.

But the common and general characteristic both of the double and accessory image is semi-transparence. The tendency of a transparent medium to become only half transparent, or merely light-transmitting, has been before adverted to (147, 148). Let the reader assume that he sees within or through such a medium a visionary image, and he will at once pronounce this latter to be a semi-transparent image.

239.

Thus the colours produced by refraction may be fitly explained by the doctrine of the semi-transparent mediums. For where dark passes over light, as the border of the semi-transparent accessory image advances, yellow appears; and, on the other hand, where a light outline passes over the dark background, blue appears (150, 151).

240.

The advancing foremost colour is always the broader. Thus the yellow spreads over the light with a broad border, but the yellow-red appears as a narrower stripe and is next the dark, according to the doctrine of augmentation, as an effect of shade.*

241.

On the opposite side the condensed blue is next the edge, while the advancing border, spreading as a thinner veil over the black, produces the violet colour, precisely on the principles before explained in treating of semi-transparent mediums, principles which will hereafter be found equally efficient in many other cases.

242.

Since an analysis like the present requires to be confirmed by ocular demonstration, we beg every reader to make himself acquainted with the experiments hitherto adduced, not in a superficial manner, but fairly and thoroughly. We have not placed arbitrary signs before him instead of the appearances themselves; no modes of expression are here proposed for his

---

* The author has before observed that colour is a degree of darkness, and he here means that increase of darkness, produced by transparent mediums, is, to a certain extent, increase of colour.—T.

adoption which may be repeated for ever without the exercise of thought and without leading any one to think ; but we invite him to examine intelligible appearances, which must be present to the eye and mind, in order to enable him clearly to trace these appearances to their origin, and to explain them to himself and to others.

XVI.

DECREASE OF THE APPEARANCE OF COLOUR.

243.

We need only take the five conditions (210) under which the appearance of colour increases in the contrary order, to produce the contrary or decreasing state; it may be as well, however, briefly to describe and review the corresponding modifications which are presented to the eye.

244.

At the highest point of complete junction of the opposite edges, the colours appear as follows (216) :—

Yellow-red.	Blue.
Green.	Red.
Blue-red.	Yellow.

245.

Where the junction is less complete, the appearance is as follows (214, 215) :—

Yellow-red.	Blue.
Yellow.	Blue-red.
Green.	Red.
Blue.	Yellow-red.
Blue-red.	Yellow.

Here, therefore, the surface still appears completely coloured, but neither series is to be considered as an elementary series, always developing itself in the same manner and in the same degrees; on the contrary, they can and should be resolved into their elements; and, in doing this, we become better acquainted with their nature and character.

216.

These elements then are (199, 200, 201)—

Yellow-red.	Blue.
Yellow.	Blue-red.
White.	Black.
Blue.	Yellow-red.
Blue-red.	Yellow.

Here the surface itself, the original object, which has been hitherto completely covered, and as it were lost, again appears in the centre of the colours, asserts its right, and enables us

fully to recognise the secondary nature of the
accessory images which exhibit themselves as
" edges " and " borders."—Note N.

247.

We can make these edges and borders as narrow as we please ; nay, we can still have refraction in reserve after having done away with all
appearance of colour at the boundary of the
object.

Having now sufficiently investigated the exhibition of colour in this phenomenon, we repeat
that we cannot admit it to be an elementary
phenomenon.   On the contrary, we have traced
it to an antecedent and a simpler one ; we have
derived it, in connexion with the theory of secondary images, from the primordial phenomenon of light and darkness, as affected or acted
upon by semi-transparent mediums.   Thus prepared, we proceed to describe the appearances
which refraction produces on grey and coloured
objects,. and this will complete the section of
subjective phenomena.

XVII.

248.

Hitherto we have confined our attention to black and white objects relieved on respectively opposite grounds, as seen through the prism, because the coloured edges and borders are most clearly displayed in such cases. We now repeat these experiments with grey objects, and again find similar results.

249.

As we called black the equivalent of darkness, and white the representative of light (18), so we now venture to say that grey represents half-shadow, which partakes more or less of light and darkness, and thus stands between the two. We invite the reader to call to mind the following facts as bearing on our present view.

250.

Grey objects appear lighter on a black than on a white ground (33); they appear as a light on a black ground, and larger; as a dark on the white ground, and smaller. (16.)

251.

The darker the grey the more it appears as a faint light on black, as a strong dark on white, and *vice versâ;* hence the accessory images of dark-grey on black are faint, on white strong: so the accessory images of light-grey on white are faint, on black strong.

252.

Grey on black, seen through the prism, will exhibit the same appearances as white on black; the edges are coloured according to the same law, only the borders appear fainter. If we relieve grey on white, we have the same edges and borders which would be produced if we saw black on white through the prism.—Note O.

253.

Various shades of grey placed next each other in gradation will exhibit at their edges, either blue and violet only, or red and yellow only, according as the darker grey is placed over or under.

254.

A series of such shades of grey placed horizontally next each other will be coloured conformably to the same law according as the whole series is relieved, on a black or white ground above or below.

255.

The observer may see the phenomena exhibited by the prism at one glance, by enlarging the plate intended to illustrate this section.*

256.

It is of great importance duly to examine and consider another experiment in which a grey object is placed partly on a black and partly on a white surface, so that the line of division passes vertically through the object.

257.

The colours will appear on this grey object in conformity with the usual law, but according to the opposite relation of the light to the dark, and will be contrasted in a line. For as the grey is as a light to the black, so it exhibits the red and yellow above the blue and violet below: again, as the grey is as a dark to the white, the blue and violet appear above the red and yellow below. This experiment will be found of great importance with reference to the next chapter.

---

* It has been thought unnecessary to give all the examples in the plate alluded to, but the leading instance referred to in the next paragraph will be found in plate 3, fig. 1. The grey square when seen through a prism will exhibit the effects described in par. 257.—T.

XVIII.

258.

An unlimited coloured surface exhibits no prismatic colour in addition to its own hue, thus not at all differing from a black, white, or grey surface. To produce the appearance of colour, light and dark boundaries must act on it either accidentally or by contrivance. Hence experiments and observations on coloured surfaces, as seen through the prism, can only be made when such surfaces are separated by an outline from another differently tinted surface, in short when *circumscribed objects* are coloured,

259.

All colours, whatever they may be, correspond so far with grey, that they appear darker than white and lighter than black. This shade-like quality of colour (σχιερόν) has been already alluded to (69), and will become more and more evident. If then we begin by placing coloured objects on black and white surfaces, and examine them through the prism, we shall again have all that we have seen exhibited with grey surfaces.

260.

If we displace a coloured object by refraction, there appears, as in the case of colourless objects and according to the same laws, an accessory image. This accessory image retains, as far as colour is concerned, its usual nature, and acts on one side as a blue and blue-red, on the opposite side as a yellow and yellow-red. Hence the apparent colour of the edge and border will be either homogeneous with the real colour of the object, or not so. In the first case the apparent image identifies itself with the real one, and appears to increase it, while, in the second case, the real image may be vitiated, rendered indistinct, and reduced in size by the apparent image. We proceed to review the cases in which these effects are most strikingly exhibited.

261.

If we take a coloured drawing enlarged from the plate, which illustrates this experiment,* and examine the red and blue squares placed next each other on a black ground, through the prism as usual, we shall find that as both colours are lighter than the ground, similarly coloured edges and borders will appear above and below,

---

* Plate ʻ3, fig. 1. The author always recommends making the experiments on an increased scale, in order to see the prismatic effects distinctly.

at the outlines of both, only they will not appear
equally distinct to the eye.

262.

Red is proportionally much lighter on black
than blue is. The colours of the edges will
therefore appear stronger on the red than on
the blue, which here acts as a dark-grey, but
little different from black. (251.)

263.

The extreme red edge will identify itself with
the vermilion colour of the square, which will
thus appear a little elongated in this direction ;
while the yellow border immediately underneath
it only gives the red surface a more brilliant
appearance, and is not distinguished without
attentive observation.

264.

On the other hand the red edge and yellow
border are heterogeneous with the blue square ;
a dull red appears at the edge, and a dull green
mingles with the figure, and thus the blue
square seems, at a hasty glance, to be comparatively diminished on this side.

265.

At the lower outline of the two squares a blue
edge and a violet border will appear, and will

produce the contrary effect; for the blue edge, which is heterogeneous with the warm red surface, will vitiate it and produce a neutral colour, so that the red on this side appears comparatively reduced and driven upwards, and the violet border on the black is scarcely perceptible.

266.

On the other hand, the blue apparent edge will identify itself with the blue square, and not only not reduce, but extend it. The blue edge and even the violet border next it have the apparent effect of increasing the surface, and elongating it in that direction.

267.

The effect of homogeneous and heterogeneous edges, as I have now minutely described it, is so powerful and singular that the two squares at the first glance seem pushed out of their relative horizontal position and moved in opposite directions, the red upwards, the blue downwards. But no one who is accustomed to observe experiments in a certain succession, and respectively to connect and trace them, will suffer himself to be deceived by such an unreal effect.

268.

A just impression with regard to this important phenomenon will, however, much depend on some nice and even troublesome conditions, which are necessary to produce the illusion in question. Paper should be tinged with vermilion or the best minium for the red square, and with deep indigo for the blue square. The blue and red prismatic edges will then unite imperceptibly with the real surfaces where they are respectively homogeneous; where they are not, they vitiate the colours of the squares without producing a very distinct middle tint. The real red should not incline too much to yellow, otherwise the apparent deep red edge above will be too distinct; at the same time it should be somewhat yellow, otherwise the transition to the yellow border will be too observable. The blue must not be light, otherwise the red edge will be visible, and the yellow border will produce a too decided green, while the violet border underneath would not give us the impression of being part of an elongated light blue square.

269.

All this will be treated more circumstantially hereafter, when we speak of the apparatus intended to facilitate the experiments connected with this part of our subject.* Every inquirer

---

* Neither the description of the apparatus nor the recapitulation of the whole theory, so often alluded to by the author, were ever given.—T.

should prepare the figures himself, in order fairly to exhibit this specimen of ocular deception, and at the same time to convince himself that the coloured edges, even in this case, cannot escape accurate examination.

270.

Meanwhile various other combinations, as exhibited in the plate, are fully calculated to remove all doubt on this point in the mind of every attentive observer.

271.

If, for instance, we look at a white square, next the blue one, on a black ground, the prismatic hues of the opposite edges of the white, which here occupies the place of the red in the former experiment, will exhibit themselves in their utmost force. The red edge extends itself above the level of the blue almost in a greater degree than was the case with the red square itself in the former experiment. The lower blue edge, again, is visible in its full force next the white, while, on the other hand, it cannot be distinguished next the blue square. The violet border underneath is also much more apparent on the white than on the blue.

272.

If the observer now compares these double

squares, carefully prepared and arranged one above the other, the red with the white, the two blue squares together, the blue with the red, the blue with the white, he will clearly perceive the relations of these surfaces to their coloured edges and borders.

273.

The edges and their relations to the coloured surfaces appear still more striking if we look at the coloured squares and a black square on a white ground; for in this case the illusion before mentioned ceases altogether, and the effect of the edges is as visible as in any case that has come under our observation. Let the blue and red squares be first examined through the prism. In both the blue edge now appears above; this edge, homogeneous with the blue surface, unites with it, and appears to extend it upwards, only the blue edge, owing to its lightness, is somewhat too distinct in its upper portion; the violet border underneath it is also sufficiently evident on the blue. The apparent blue edge is, on the other hand, heterogeneous with the red square; it is neutralised by contrast, and is scarcely visible; meanwhile the violet border, uniting with the real red, produces a hue resembling that of the peach-blossom.

274.

If thus, owing to the above causes, the upper

outlines of these squares do not appear level
with each other, the correspondence of the
under outlines is the more observable ; for since
both colours, the red and the blue, are darks
compared with the white (as in the former case
they were light compared with the black), the
red edge with its yellow border appears very
distinctly under both. It exhibits itself under
the warm red surface in its full force, and
under the dark blue nearly as it appears under
the black : as may be seen if we compare the
edges and borders of the figures placed one
above the other on the white ground.

275.

In order to present these experiments with
the greatest variety and perspicuity, squares
of various colours are so arranged* that
the boundary of the black and white passes
through them vertically. According to the
laws now known to us, especially in their application to coloured objects, we shall find the
squares as usual doubly coloured at each edge ;
each square will appear to be split in two, and
to be elongated upwards or downwards. We
may here call to mind the experiment with the
grey figure seen in like manner on the line of
division between black and white (257).†

---

* Plate iii. fig. 1.

† The grey square is introduced in the same plate, fig. 1, above
the coloured squares.

276.

A phenomenon was before exhibited, even to illusion, in the instance of a red and blue square on a black ground; in the present experiment the elongation upwards and downwards of two differently coloured figures is apparent in the two halves of one and the same figure of one and the same colour. Thus we are still referred to the coloured edges and borders, and to the effects of their homogeneous and heterogeneous relations with respect to the real colours of the objects.

277.

I leave it to observers themselves to compare the various gradations of coloured squares, placed half on black half on white, only inviting their attention to the apparent alteration which takes place in contrary directions; for red and yellow appear elongated upwards if on a black ground, downwards if on a white; blue, downwards if on a black ground, upwards if on a white. All which, however, is quite in accordance with the diffusely detailed examples above given.

278.

Let the observer now turn the figures so that the before-mentioned squares placed on the line of division between black and white may be in a horizontal series; the black above, the white underneath. On looking at these squares through the prism, he will observe that the red square gains by the addition of two red edges ; on more accurate examination he will observe the yellow border on the red figure, and the lower yellow border upon the white will be perfectly apparent.

279.

The upper red edge on the blue square is on the other hand hardly visible; the yellow border next it produces a dull green by mingling with the figure; the lower red edge and the yellow border are displayed in lively colours.

280.

After observing that the red figure in these cases appears to gain by an addition on both sides, while the dark blue, on one side at least, loses something; we shall see the contrary effect produced by turning the same figures upside down, so that the white ground be above, the black below.

281.

For as the homogeneous edges and borders now appear above and below the blue square, this appears elongated, and a portion of the surface itself seems even more brilliantly coloured: it is only by attentive observation that we can distinguish the edges and borders from the colour of the figure itself.

282.

The yellow and red squares, on the other hand, are comparatively reduced by the heterogeneous edges in this position of the figures, and their colours are, to a certain extent, vitiated. The blue edge in both is almost invisible. The violet border appears as a beautiful peach-blossom hue on the red, as a very pale colour of the same kind on the yellow; both the lower edges are green; dull on the red, vivid on the yellow; the violet border is but faintly perceptible under the red, but is more apparent under the yellow.

283.

Every inquirer should make it a point to be thoroughly acquainted with all the appearances here adduced, and not consider it irksome to follow out a single phenomenon through so many modifying circumstances. These experiments, it is true, may be multiplied to infinity by differently coloured figures, upon and between differently coloured grounds. Under all such circumstances, however, it will be evident to every attentive observer that coloured squares only appear relatively altered, or elongated, or reduced by the prism, because an addition of homogeneous or heterogeneous edges produces an illusion. The inquirer will now be enabled to do away with this illusion if he has the patience to go through the experiments one after the other, always comparing the effects together, and satisfying himself of their correspondence.

Experiments with coloured objects might have been contrived in various ways : why·they have been exhibited precisely in the above mode, and with so much minuteness, will be seen hereafter. The phenomena, although formerly not unknown, were much misunderstood ; and it was necessary to investigate them thoroughly to render some portions of our intended historical view clearer.

284.

In conclusion, we will mention a contrivance by means of which our scientific readers may be enabled to see these appearances distinctly at one view, and even in their greatest splendour. Cut in a piece of pasteboard five perfectly similar square openings of about an inch, next each other, exactly in a horizontal line : behind these openings place five coloured glasses in the natural order, orange, yellow, green, blue, violet. Let the series thus adjusted be fastened in an opening of the camera obscura, so that the bright sky may be seen through the squares, or that the sun may shine on them ; they will thus appear very powerfully coloured. Let the spectator now examine them through the prism, and observe the appearances, already

familiar by the foregoing experiments, with
coloured objects, namely, the partly assisting,
partly neutralising effects of the edges and borders, and the consequent apparent elongation or
reduction of the coloured squares with reference
to the horizontal line. The results witnessed by
the observer in this case, entirely correspond
with those in the cases before analysed ; we do
not, therefore, go through them again in detail,
especially as we shall find frequent occasions
hereafter to return to the subject.—Note P.

XIX.

ACHROMATISM AND HYPERCHROMATISM.

285.

FORMERLY when much that is regular and constant in nature was considered as mere aber-
ration and accident, the colours arising from refraction were but little attended to, and were
looked upon as an appearance attributable to
particular local circumstances.

286.

But after it had been assumed that this appearance of colour accompanies refraction at all
times, it was natural that it should be considered
as intimately and exclusively connected with
that phenomenon ; the belief obtaining that the

measure of the coloured appearance was in proportion to the measure of the refraction, and that they must advance *pari passu* with each other.

287.

If, again, philosophers ascribed the phenomenon of a stronger or weaker refraction, not indeed wholly, but in some degree, to the different density of the medium, (as purer atmospheric air, air charged with vapours, water, glass, according to their increasing density, increase the so-called refraction, or displacement of the object;) so they could hardly doubt that the appearance of colour must increase in the same proportion ; and hence took it for granted, in combining different mediums which were to counteract refraction, that as long as refraction existed, the appearance of colour must take place, and that as soon as the colour disappeared, the refraction also must cease.

288.

Afterwards it was, however, discovered that this relation which was assumed to correspond, was, in fact, dissimilar ; that two mediums can refract an object with equal power, and yet produce very dissimilar coloured borders.

289.

It was found that, in addition to the physical principle to which refraction was ascribed, a chemical one was also to be taken into the account. We propose to pursue this subject hereafter, in the chemical division of our inquiry, and we shall have to describe the particulars of this important discovery in our history of the doctrine of colours. What follows may suffice for the present.

290.

In mediums of similar or nearly similar refracting power, we find the remarkable circumstance that a greater and lesser appearance of colour can be produced by a chemical treatment ; the greater effect is owing, namely, to acids, the lesser to alkalis. If metallic oxydes are introduced into a common mass of glass, the coloured appearance through such glasses becomes greatly increased without any perceptible change of refracting power. That the lesser effect, again, is produced by alkalis, may be easily supposed.

291.

Those kinds of glass which were first employed after the discovery, are called flint and crown glass ; the first produces the stronger, the second the fainter appearance of colour.

292.

We shall make use of both these denominations as technical terms in our present statement,

and assume that the refractive power of both is
the same, but that flint-glass produces the
coloured appearance more strongly by one-third
than the crown-glass. The diagram (Plate 3,
fig. 2,) may serve in illustration.

293.

A black surface is here divided into compartments for more convenient demonstration :
let the spectator imagine five white squares between the parallel lines a, b, and c, d. The
square No. 1, is presented to the naked eye unmoved from its place.

294.

But let the square No. 2, seen through a
crown-glass prism g, be supposed to be displaced by refraction three compartments, exhibiting the coloured borders to a certain extent ;
again, let the square No. 3, seen through a flint
glass prism h, in like manner be moved downwards three compartments, when it will exhibit
the coloured borders by about a third wider
than No. 2.

295.

Again, let us suppose that the square No. 4,
has, like No. 2, been moved downwards three
compartments by a prism of crown-glass, and
that then by an oppositely placed prism h, of

flint-glass, it has been again raised to its former situation, where it now stands.

296.

Here, it is true, the refraction is done away with by the opposition of the two ; but as the prism h, in displacing the square by refraction through three compartments, produces coloured borders wider by a third than those produced by the prism g, so, notwithstanding the refraction is neutralised, there must be an excess of coloured border remaining. (The position of this colour, as usual, depends on the direction of the apparent motion (204) communicated to the square by the prism h, and, consequently, it is the reverse of the appearance in the two squares 2 and 3, which have been moved in an opposite direction.) This excess of colour we have called Hyperchromatism, and from this the achromatic state may be immediately arrived at.

297.

For assuming that it was the square No. 5 which was removed three compartments from its first supposed place, like No. 2, by a prism of crown-glass g, it would only be necessary to reduce the angle of a prism of flint-glass h, and to connect it, reversed, to the prism g, in order to raise the square No. 5 two degrees or compartments ; by which means the Hyperchromatism of the first case would cease, the figure would not quite return to its first position, and yet be already colourless. The prolonged lines of the united prisms, under No. 5, show that a single complete prism remains : again, we have only to suppose the lines curved, and an object-glass presents itself. Such is the principle of the achromatic telescopes.

298.

For these experiments, a small prism composed of three different prisms, as prepared in England, is extremely well adapted. It is to be hoped our own opticians will in future enable every friend of science to provide himself with this necessary instrument.

XX.

ADVANTAGES OF SUBJECTIVE EXPERIMENTS.—TRANSITION TO THE OBJECTIVE.

299.

WE have presented the appearances of colour as exhibited by refraction, first, by means of subjective experiments ; and we have so far arrived at a definite result, that we have been enabled to deduce the phenomena in question from the doctrine of semi-transparent mediums and double images.

300.

In statements which have reference to nature, everything depends on ocular inspection, and these experiments are the more satisfactory as they may be easily and conveniently made. Every amateur can procure his apparatus without much trouble or cost, and if he is a tolerable adept in pasteboard contrivances, he may even prepare a great part of his machinery himself. A few plain surfaces, on which black, white, grey, and coloured objects may be exhibited alternately on a light and dark ground, are all that is necessary. The spectator fixes them before him, examines the appearances at the edge of the figures conveniently, and as long as he pleases ; he retires to a greater distance, again approaches, and accurately observes the progressive states of the phenomena.

301.

Besides this, the appearances may be observed with sufficient exactness through small prisms, which need not be of the purest glass. The other desirable requisites in these glass instruments will, however, be pointed out in the section which treats of the apparatus.*

---

* This description of the apparatus was never given.

302.

A great advantage in these experiments, again, is, that they can be made at any hour of the day in any room, whatever aspect it may have. We have no need to wait for sunshine, which in general is not very propitious to northern observers.

OBJECTIVE EXPERIMENTS.

303.

THE objective experiments, on the contrary, necessarily require the sun-light which, even when it is to be had, may not always have the most desirable relation with the apparatus placed opposite to it. Sometimes the sun is too high, sometimes too low, and withal only a short time in the meridian of the best situated room. It changes its direction during the observation, the observer is forced to alter his own position and that of his apparatus, in consequence of which the experiments in many cases become uncertain. If the sun shines through the prism it exhibits all inequalities, lines, and bubbles in the glass, and thus the appearance is rendered confused, dim, and discoloured.

304.

Yet both kinds of experiments must be investigated with equal accuracy. They appear to be opposed to each other, and yet are always parallel. What one order of experiments exhibits the other exhibits likewise, and yet each has its peculiar capabilities, by means of which certain effects of nature are made known to us in more than one way.

305.

In the next place there are important phenomena which may be exhibited by the union of subjective and objective experiments. The latter experiments again have this advantage, that we can in most cases represent them by diagrams, and present to view the component relations of the phenomena. In proceeding, therefore, to describe the objective experiments, we shall so arrange them that they may always correspond with the analogous subjective examples; for this reason, too, we annex to the number of each paragraph the number of the former corresponding one. But we set out by observing generally that the reader must consult the plates, that the scientific investigator must be familiar with the apparatus in order that the twin-phenomena in one mode or the other may be placed before them.

XXI.

REFRACTION WITHOUT THE APPEARANCE OF COLOUR.

306 (195, 196).

THAT refraction may exhibit its effects without producing an appearance of colour, is not to be demonstrated so perfectly in objective as in subjective experiments. We have, it is true, unlimited spaces which we can look at through the prism, and thus convince ourselves that no colour appears where there is no boundary; but we have no unlimited source of light which we can cause to act through the prism. Our light comes to us from circumscribed bodies; and the sun, which chiefly produces our prismatic appearances, is itself only a small, circumscribed, luminous object.

307.

We may, however, consider every larger opening through which the sun shines, every larger medium through which the sun-light is transmitted and made to deviate from its course, as so far unlimited that we can confine our attention to the centre of the surface without considering its boundaries.

308 (197).

If we place a large water-prism in the sun, a

large bright space is refracted upwards by it on the plane intended to receive the image, and the middle of this illumined space will be colourless. The same effect may be produced if we make the experiment with glass prisms having angles of few degrees : the appearance may be produced even through glass prisms, whose refracting angle is sixty degrees, provided we place the recipient surface near enough.

XXII.

CONDITIONS OF THE APPEARANCE OF COLOUR.

309 (198).

ALTHOUGH, then, the illumined space before mentioned appears indeed refracted and moved from its place, but not coloured, yet on the horizontal edges of this space we observe a coloured appearance. That here again the colour is solely owing to the displacement of a circumscribed object may require to be more fully proved.

The luminous body which here acts is circumscribed : the sun, while it shines and diffuses light, is still an insulated object. However small the opening in the lid of a camera obscura be made, still the whole image of the sun will penetrate it. The light which streams from all parts of the sun's disk, will cross itself in the smallest opening, and form the angle which corresponds with the sun's apparent diameter. On the outside we have a cone narrowing to the orifice; within, this apex spreads again, producing on an opposite surface a round image, which still increases in size in proportion to the distance of the recipient surface from the apex. This image, together with all other objects of the external landscape, appears reversed on the white surface in question in a dark room.

310.

How little therefore we have here to do with single sun-rays, bundles or fasces of rays, cylinders of rays, pencils, or whatever else of the kind may be imagined, is strikingly evident. For the convenience of certain diagrams the sun-light may be assumed to arrive in parallel lines, but it is known that this is only a fiction; a fiction quite allowable where the difference between the assumption and the true appearance is unimportant; but we should take care not to suffer such a postulate to be equivalent to a fact, and proceed to further operations on such a fictitious basis.

311.

Let the aperture in the window-shutter be now enlarged at pleasure, let it be made round or square, nay, let the whole shutter be opened, and let the sun shine into the room through the whole window; the space which the sun illumines will always be larger according to the angle which its diameter makes; and thus even the whole space illumined by the sun through the largest window is only the image of the sun *plus* the size of the opening. We shall hereafter have occasion to return to this.

312 (199).

If we transmit the image of the sun through convex glasses we contract it towards the focus. In this case, according to the laws before explained, a yellow border and a yellow-red edge must appear when the spectrum is thrown on white paper. But as this experiment is dazzling and inconvenient, it may be made more agreeably with the image of the full moon. On contracting this orb by means of a convex glass, the coloured edge appears in the greatest splendor; for the moon transmits a mitigated light in the first instance, and can thus the more readily produce colour which to a certain extent accompanies the subduing of light: at the same time the eye of the observer is only gently and agreeably excited.

313 (200).

If we transmit a luminous image through concave glasses, it is dilated. Here the image appears edged with blue.

314.

The two opposite appearances may be produced by a convex glass, simultaneously or in succession ; simultaneously by fastening an opaque disk in the centre of the convex glass, and then transmitting the sun's image. In this case the luminous image and the black disk within it are both contracted, and, consequently, the opposite colours must appear. Again, we can present this contrast in succession by first contracting the luminous image towards the focus, and then suffering it to expand again beyond the focus, when it will immediately exhibit a blue edge.

315 (201).

Here too what was observed in the subjective experiments is again to be remarked, namely, that blue and yellow appear in and upon the white, and that both assume a reddish appearance in proportion as they mingle with the black.

316 (202, 203).

These elementary phenomena occur in all subsequent objective experiments, as they constituted the groundwork of the subjective ones.

The process too which takes place is the same; a light boundary is carried over a dark surface, a dark surface is carried over a light boundary. The edges must advance, and as it were push over each other in these experiments as in the former ones.

317 (204).

If we admit the sun's image through a larger or smaller opening into the dark room, if we transmit it through a prism so placed that its refracting angle, as usual, is underneath; the luminous image, instead of proceeding in a straight line to the floor, is refracted upwards on a vertical surface placed to receive it. This is the moment to take notice of the opposite modes in which the subjective and objective refractions of the object appear.

318.

If we *look* through a prism, held with its refracting angle underneath, at an object above us, the object is moved downwards; whereas a luminous image refracted through the same prism is moved upwards. This, which we here merely mention as a matter of fact for the sake of brevity, is easily explained by the laws of refraction and elevation.

319.

The luminous object being moved from its place in this manner, the coloured borders appear in the order, and according to the laws before explained. The violet border is always foremost, and thus in objective cases proceeds upwards, in subjective cases downwards.

320 (205).

The observer may convince himself in like manner of the mode in which the appearance of colour takes place in the diagonal direction when the displacement is effected by means of two prisms, as has been plainly enough shown in the subjective example ; for this experiment, however, prisms should be procured of few degrees, say about fifteen.

321 (206, 207).

That the colouring of the image takes place here too, according to the direction in which it moves, will be apparent if we make a *square* opening of moderate size in a shutter, and cause the luminous image to pass through a water-prism ; the spectrum being moved first in the horizontal and vertical directions, then diagonally, the coloured edges will change their position accordingly.

322 (208).

Whence it is again evident that to produce colour the boundaries must be carried over each other, not merely move side by side.

XXIII.

CONDITIONS OF THE INCREASE OF COLOUR.

323 (209).

HERE too an increased displacement of the object produces a greater appearance of colour.

324 (210).

This increased displacement occurs,

1. By a more oblique direction of the impinging luminous object through mediums with parallel surfaces.

2. By changing the parallel form for one more or less acute angled.

3. By increased proportion of the medium, whether parallel or acute angled; partly because the object is by this means more powerfully displaced, partly because an effect depending on the mere mass co-operates.

4. By the distance of the recipient surface from the refracting medium so that the coloured

spectrum emerging from the prism may be said to have a longer way to travel.

5. When a chemical property produces its effects under all these circumstances: this we have already entered into more fully under the head of achromatism and hyperchromatism.

325 (211).

The objective experiments have this advantage that the progressive states of the phenomenon may be arrested and clearly represented by diagrams, which is not the case with the subjective experiments.

326.

We can observe the luminous image after it has emerged from the prism, step by step, and mark its increasing colour by receiving it on a plane at different distances, thus exhibiting before our eyes various sections of this cone, with an elliptical base: again, the phenomenon may at once be rendered beautifully visible throughout its whole course in the following manner:—Let a cloud of fine white dust be excited along the line in which the image passes through the dark space ; the cloud is best produced by fine, perfectly dry, hair-powder. The more or less coloured appearance will now be painted on the white atoms, and presented in its whole length and breadth to the eye of the spectator.

327.

By this means we have prepared some diagrams, which will be found among the plates. In these the appearance is exhibited from its first origin, and by these the spectator can clearly comprehend why the luminous image is so much more powerfully coloured through prisms than through parallel mediums.

328 (212).

At the two opposite outlines of the image an opposite appearance presents itself, beginning from an acute angle ;* the appearance spreads as it proceeds further in space, according to this angle. On one side, in the direction in which the luminous image is moved, a violet border advances on the dark, a narrower blue edge remains next the outline of the image. On the opposite side a yellow border advances into the light of the image itself, and a yellow-red edge remains at the outline.

329 (213).

Here, therefore, the movement of the dark against the light, of the light against the dark, may be clearly observed.

---

* Plate iv. fig. 1.

330 (214).

The centre of a large object remains long un-coloured, especially with mediums of less density and smaller angles; but at last the opposite borders and edges touch each other, upon which a green appears in the centre of the luminous image.

331 (215).

Objective experiments have been usually made with the sun's image: an objective experiment with a dark object has hitherto scarcely been thought of. We have, however, prepared a convenient contrivance for this also. Let the large water-prism before alluded to be placed in the sun, and let a round pasteboard disk be fastened either inside or outside. The coloured appearance will again take place at the outline, beginning according to the usual law; the edges will appear, they will spread in the same proportion, and when they meet, red will appear in the centre.* An intercepting square may be added near the round disk, and placed in any direction *ad libitum*, and the spectator can again convince himself of what has been before so often described.

332 (216).

If we take away these dark objects from the

---

* Plate iv. fig. 2.

prism, in which case, however, the glass is to be carefully cleaned, and hold a rod or a large pencil before the centre of the horizontal prism, we shall then accomplish the complete immixture of the violet border and the yellow-red edge, and see only the three colours, the external blue, and yellow, and the central red.

333.

If again we cut a long horizontal opening in the middle of a piece of pasteboard, fastened on the prism, and then cause the sun-light to pass through it, we shall accomplish the complete union of the yellow border with the blue edge upon the light, and only see yellow-red, green and violet.　The details of this are further entered into in the description of the plates.

334 (217).

The prismatic appearance is thus by no means complete and final when the luminous image emerges from the prism.　It is then only that we perceive its elements in contrast; for as it increases these contrasting elements unite, and are at last intimately joined.　The section of this phenomenon arrested on a plane surface is different at every degree of distance from the prism; so that the notion of an immutable series of colours, or of a pervading similar proportion between them, cannot be a question for a moment.

XXIV.

EXPLANATION OF THE FOREGOING PHENOMENA.

335 (218).

As we have already entered into this analysis circumstantially while treating of the subjective experiments, as all that was of force there is equally valid here, it will require no long details in addition to show that the phenomena, which are entirely parallel in the two cases, may also be traced precisely to the same sources.

336 (219).

That in objective experiments also we have to do with circumscribed images, has been already demonstrated at large. The sun may shine through the smallest opening, yet the image of the whole disk penetrates beyond. The largest prism may be placed in the open sun-light, yet it is still the sun's image that is bounded by the edges of the refracting surfaces, and produces the accessory images of this boundary. We may fasten pasteboard, with many openings cut in it, before the water-prism, yet we still merely see multiplied images which, after having been moved from their place by refraction, exhibit coloured edges and borders, and in these mere accessory images.

337 (235).

In subjective experiments we have seen that objects strongly relieved from each other produce a very lively appearance of colour, and this will be the case in objective experiments in a much more vivid and splendid degree. The sun's image is the most powerful brightness we know; hence its accessory image will be energetic in proportion, and notwithstanding its really secondary dimmed and darkened character, must be still very brilliant. The colours thrown by the sun-light through the prism on any object, carry a powerful light with them, for they have the highest and most intense source of light, as it were, for their ground.

338.

That we are warranted in calling even these accessory images semi-transparent, thus deducing the appearances from the doctrine of the semi-transparent mediums, will be clear to every one who has followed us thus far, but particularly to those who have supplied themselves with the necessary apparatus, so as to be enabled at all times to witness the precision and vivacity with which semi-transparent mediums act.

XXV.

DECREASE OF THE APPEARANCE OF COLOUR.

339 (243).

IF we could afford to be concise in the description of the decreasing coloured appearance in subjective cases, we may here be permitted to proceed with still greater brevity while we refer to the former distinct statement. One circumstance, only on account of its great importance, may be here recommended to the reader's especial attention as a leading point of our whole thesis.

340 (244, 247).

The decline of the prismatic appearance must be preceded by its separation, by its resolution into its elements. At a due distance from the prism, the image of the sun being entirely coloured, the blue and yellow at length mix completely, and we see only yellow-red, green, and blue-red. If we bring the recipient surface nearer to the refracting medium, yellow and blue appear again, and we see the five colours with their gradations. At a still shorter distance the yellow and blue separate from each other entirely, the green vanishes, and the image itself appears, colourless, between the coloured edges and borders. The nearer we bring the recipient surface to the prism, the narrower the edges and borders become, till at last, when in contact with the prism, they are reduced to nothing.

XXVI.

GREY OBJECTS.

341 (218).

WE have exhibited grey objects as very important to our inquiry in the subjective experiments. They show, by the faintness of the accessory images, that these same images are in all cases derived from the principal object. If we wish here, too, to carry on the objective experiments parallel with the others, we may conveniently do this by placing a more or less dull ground glass before the opening through which the sun's image enters. By this means a subdued image would be produced, which on being refracted would exhibit much duller colours on the recipient plane than those immediately derived from the sun's disk ; and thus, even from the intense sun-image, only a faint accessory image would appear, proportioned to the mitigation of the light by the glass. This experiment, it is true, will only again and again confirm what is already sufficiently familiar to us.

XXVII.

COLOURED OBJECTS.

342 (260).

THERE are various modes of producing coloured images in objective experiments. In the first place, we can fix coloured glass before the opening, by which means a coloured image is at once produced; secondly, we can fill the water-prism with coloured fluids; thirdly, we can cause the colours, already produced in their full vivacity by the prism, to pass through proportionate small openings in a tin plate, and thus prepare small circumscribed colours for a second operation. This last mode is the most difficult; for owing to the continual progress of the sun, the image cannot be arrested in any direction at will. The second method has also its inconveniences, since not all coloured liquids can be prepared perfectly bright and clear. On these accounts the first is to be preferred, and deserves the more to be adopted because natural philosophers have hitherto chosen to consider the colours produced from the sun-light through the prism, those produced through liquids and glasses, and those which are already fixed on paper or cloth, as exhibiting effects equally to be depended on, and equally available in demonstration.

343.

As it is thus merely necessary that the image

should be coloured, so the large water-prism before alluded to affords us the best means of effecting this. A pasteboard screen may be contrived to slide before the large surfaces of the prism, through which, in the first instance, the light passes uncoloured. In this screen openings of various forms may be cut, in order to produce different images, and consequently different accessory images. This being done, we need only fix coloured glasses before the openings, in order to observe what effect refraction produces on coloured images in an objective sense.

344.

A series of glasses may be prepared in a mode similar to that before described (284); these should be accurately contrived to slide in the grooves of the large water-prism. Let the sun then shine through them, and the coloured images refracted upwards will appear bordered and edged, and will vary accordingly: for these borders and edges will be exhibited quite distinctly on some images, and on others will be mixed with the specific colour of the glass, which they will either enhance or neutralize. Every observer will be enabled to convince himself here again that we have only to do with the same simple phenomenon so circumstantially described subjectively and objectively.

XXVIII.

ACHROMATISM AND HYPERCHROMATISM.

345 (285, 290).

It is possible to make the hyperchromatic and achromatic experiments objectively as well as subjectively.   After what has been already stated, a short description of the method will suffice, especially as we take it for granted that the compound prism before mentioned is in the hands of the observer.

346.

Let the sun's image pass through an acute-angled prism of few degrees, prepared from crown-glass, so that the spectrum be refracted upwards on an opposite surface ; the edges will appear coloured, according to the constant law, namely, the violet and blue above and outside, the yellow and yellow-red below and within the image.   As the refracting angle of this prism is undermost, let another proportionate prism of flint-glass be placed against it, with its refracting angle uppermost.   The sun's image will by this means be again moved to its place, where, owing to the excess of the colouring power of the prism of flint-glass, it will still appear a little coloured, and, in consequence of the direction in which it has been moved, the blue and violet will now appear underneath and outside, the yellow and yellow-red above and inside.

347.

If the whole image be now moved a little upwards by a proportionate prism of crown-glass, the hyperchromatism will disappear, the sun's image will be moved from its place, and yet will appear colourless.

348.

With an achromatic object-glass composed of three glasses, this experiment may be made step by step, if we do not mind taking out the glasses from their setting. The two convex glasses of crown-glass in contracting the sun's image towards the focus, the concave glass of flint-glass in dilating the image beyond it, exhibit at the edges the usual colours. A convex glass united with a concave one exhibits the colours according to the law of the latter. If all three glasses are placed together, whether we contract the sun's image towards the focus, or suffer it to dilate beyond the focus, coloured edges never appear, and the achromatic effect intended by the optician is, in this case, again attained.

349.

But as the crown-glass has always a greenish tint, and as a tendency to this hue may be more decided in large and strong object-glasses, and under certain circumstances produce the compensatory red, (which, however, in repeated experiments with several instruments of this kind did not occur to us,) philosophers have resorted to the most extraordinary modes of explaining such a result; and having been compelled, in support of their system, theoretically to prove the impossibility of achromatic telescopes, have felt a kind of satisfaction in having some apparent ground for denying so great an improvement. Of this, however, we can only treat circumstantially in our historical account of these discoveries.

XXIX.

COMBINATION OF SUBJECTIVE AND OBJECTIVE EXPERIMENTS.

350.

HAVING shown above (318) that refraction, considered objectively and subjectively, must act in opposite directions, it will follow that if we combine the experiments, the effects will reciprocally destroy each other.

351.

Let the sun's image be thrown upwards on a

vertical plane, through a horizontally-placed prism. If the prism is long enough to admit of the spectator also looking through it, he will see the image elevated by the objective refraction again depressed, and in the same place in which it appeared without refraction.

352.

Here a remarkable case presents itself, but at the same time a natural result of a general law. For since, as often before stated, the objective sun's image thrown on the vertical plane is not an ultimate or unchangeable state of the phenomenon, so in the above operation the image is not only depressed when seen through the prism, but its edges and borders are entirely robbed of their hues, and the spectrum is reduced to a colourless circular form.

353.

By employing two perfectly similar prisms placed next each other, for this experiment, we can transmit the sun's image through one, and look through the other.

354.

If the spectator advances nearer with the prism through which he looks, the image is again elevated, and by degrees becomes coloured according to the law of the first prism. If he again retires till he has brought the image to the neutralized point, and then retires still farther away, the image, which had become round and colourless, moves still more downwards and becomes coloured in the opposite sense, so that if we look through the prism and upon the refracted spectrum at the same time, we see the same image coloured according to subjective and objective laws.

355.

The modes in which this experiment may be varied are obvious. If the refracting angle of the prism, through which the sun's image was objectively elevated, is greater than that of the prism through which the observer looks, he must retire to a much greater distance, in order to depress the coloured image so low on the vertical plane that it shall appear colourless, and *vice versâ*.

356.

It will be easily seen that we may exhibit achromatic and hyperchromatic effects in a similar manner, and we leave it to the amateur to follow out such researches more fully. Other complicated experiments in which prisms and lenses are employed together, others again, in which objective and subjective experiments are variously intermixed, we reserve for a future occasion, when it will be our object to trace such effects to the simple phenomena with which we are now sufficiently familiar.

XXX.

TRANSITION.

357.

In looking back on the description and analysis of dioptrical colours, we do not repent either that we have treated them so circumstantially, or that we have taken them into consideration before the other physical colours, out of the order we ourselves laid down. Yet, before we quit this branch of our inquiry, it may be as well to state the reasons that have weighed with us.

358.

If some apology is necessary for having treated the theory of the dioptrical colours, particularly those of the second class, so diffusely, we should observe, that the exposition of any branch of knowledge is to be considered partly with reference to the intrinsic importance of the subject, and partly with reference to the particular necessities of the time in which the inquiry is undertaken. In our own case we were forced to keep both these considerations constantly in view. In the first place we had to state a mass of experiments with our consequent convictions ; next, it was our especial aim to exhibit certain phenomena (known, it is true, but misunderstood, and above all, exhibited in false connection,) in that natural and progressive development which is strictly and truly conformable to observation ; in order that hereafter, in our polemical or historical investigations, we might be enabled to bring a complete preparatory analysis to bear on, and elucidate, our general view. The details we have entered into were on this account unavoidable ; they may be considered as a reluctant consequence of the occasion. Hereafter, when philosophers will look upon a simple principle as simple, a combined effect as combined ; when they will acknowledge the first elementary, and the second complicated states, for what they are ; then, indeed, all this statement may be abridged to a narrower form ; a labour which, should we ourselves not be able to accomplish it, we bequeath to the active interest of contemporaries and posterity.

359.

With respect to the order of the chapters, it should be remembered that natural phenomena,

which are even allied to each other, are not connected in any particular sequence or constant
series ; their efficient causes act in a narrow
circle, so that it is in some sort indifferent what
phenomenon is first or last considered ; the main
point is, that all should be as far as possible
present to us, in order that we may embrace
them at last from one point of view, partly according to their nature, partly according to
generally received methods.

360.

Yet, in the present particular instance, it may
be asserted that the dioptrical colours are justly
placed at the head of the physical colours ; not
only on account of their striking splendour and
their importance in other respects, but because,
in tracing these to their source, much was necessarily entered into which will assist our subsequent enquiries.

361.

For, hitherto, light has been considered as a
kind of abstract principle, existing and acting
independently ; to a certain extent self-modified,
and on the slightest cause, producing colours
out of itself. To divert the votaries of physical
science from this mode of viewing the subject ;
to make them attentive to the fact, that in prismatic and other appearances we have not to do

with light as an uncircumscribed and modifying principle, but as circumscribed and modified ; that we have to do with a luminous image ;
with images or circumscribed objects generally,
whether light or dark : this was the purpose we
had in view, and such is the problem to be solved.

362.

All that takes place in dioptrical cases,—
especially those of the second class which are
connected with the phenomena of refraction,—is
now sufficiently familiar to us, and will serve
as an introduction to what follows.

363.

Catoptrical appearances remind us of the
physiological phenomena, but as we ascribe a
more objective character to the former, we
thought ourselves justified in classing them
with the physical examples. It is of importance, however, to remember that here again it
is not light, in an abstract sense, but a luminous
image that we have to consider.

364.

In proceeding onwards to the paroptrical
class, the reader, if duly acquainted with the
foregoing facts, will be pleased to find himself
once more in the region of circumscribed forms.
The shadows of bodies, especially, as secondary

images, so exactly accompanying the object, will serve greatly to elucidate analogous appearances.

365.

We will not, however, anticipate these statements, but proceed as heretofore in what we consider the regular course.

XXXI.

366.

CATOPTRICAL colours are such as appear in consequence of a mirror-like reflection. We assume, in the first place, that the light itself, as well as the surface from which it is reflected, is perfectly colourless. In this sense the appearances in question come under the head of physical colours. They arise in consequence of reflection, as we found the dioptrical colours of the second class appear by means of refraction. Without further general definitions, we turn our attention at once to particular cases, and to the conditions which are essential to the exhibition of these phenomena.

367.

If we unroll a coil of bright steel-wire, and after suffering it to spring confusedly together again, place it at a window in the light, we shall see the prominent parts of the circles and convolutions illumined, but neither resplendent nor iridescent. But if the sun shines on the wire, this light will be condensed into a point, and we perceive a small resplendent image of the sun, which, when seen near, exhibits no colour. On retiring a little, however, and fixing the eyes on this refulgent appearance, we discern several small mirrored suns, coloured in the most varied manner; and although the impression is that green and red predominate, yet, on a more accurate inspection, we find that the other colours are also present.

368.

If we take an eye-glass, and examine the appearance through it, we find the colours have vanished, as well as the radiating splendour in which they were seen, and we perceive only the small luminous points, the repeated images of the sun. We thus find that the impression is subjective in its nature, and that the appearance is allied to those which we have adverted to under the name of radiating halos (100).

369.

We can, however, exhibit this phenomenon objectively. Let a piece of white paper be fastened beneath a small aperture in the lid of a camera-obscura, and when the sun shines through this aperture, let the confusedly-rolled steel-wire be held in the light, so that it be opposite to the paper. The sun-light will impinge on and in the circles of the wire, and will not, as in the concentrating lens of the eye, display itself in a point; but, as the paper can receive the reflection of the light in every part of its surface will be seen in hair-like lines, which are also iridescent.

370.

This experiment is purely catoptrical; for as we cannot imagine that the light penetrates the surface of the steel, and thus undergoes a change, we are soon convinced that we have here a mere reflection which, in its subjective character, is connected with the theory of faintly acting lights, and the after-image of dazzling lights, and as far as it can be considered objective, announces even in the minutest appearances, a real effect, independent of the action and reaction of the eye.

371.

We have seen that to produce these effects

not merely light but a powerful light is necessary; that this powerful light again is not an abstract and general quality, but a circumscribed light, a luminous image. We can convince ourselves still further of this by analogous cases.

372.

A polished surface of silver placed in the sun reflects a dazzling light, but in this case no colour is seen. If, however, we slightly scratch the surface, an iridescent appearance, in which green and red are conspicuous, will be exhibited at a certain angle. In chased and carved metals the effect is striking: yet it may be remarked throughout that, in order to its appearance, some form, some alternation of light and dark must co-operate with the reflection; thus a window-bar, the stem of a tree, an accidentally or purposely interposed object produces a perceptible effect. This appearance, too, may be exhibited objectively in the camera-obscura.

373.

If we cause a polished plated surface to be so acted on by aqua fortis that the copper within is touched, and the surface itself thus rendered rough, and if the sun's image be then reflected from it, the splendour will be reverberated from every minutest prominence, and the surface will appear iridescent. So, if we hold a sheet of black unglazed paper in the sun, and look at it attentively, it will be seen to glisten in its minutest points with the most vivid colours.

374.

All these examples are referable to the same conditions. In the first case the luminous image is reflected from a thin line ; in the second probably from sharp edges; in the third from very small points. In all a very powerful and circumscribed light is requisite. For all these appearances of colour again it is necessary that the eye should be at a due distance from the reflecting points.

375.

If these observations are made with the microscope, the appearance will be greatly increased in force and splendour, for we then see the smallest portion of the surfaces, lit by the sun, glittering in these colours of reflection, which, allied to the hues of refraction, now attain their highest degree of brilliancy. In such cases we may observe a vermiform iridescence on the surface of organic bodies, the further description of which will be given hereafter.

376.

Lastly, the colours which are chiefly exhi-

bited in reflection are red and green, whence
we may infer that the linear appearance especially consists of a thin line of red, bounded by
blue on one side and yellow on the other. If
these triple lines approach very near together,
the intermediate space must appear green; a
phenomenon which will often occur to us as we
proceed.

377.

We frequently meet with these colours in
nature. The colours of the spider's web might
be considered exactly of the same class with
those reflected from the steel wire, except that
the non-translucent quality of the former is not
so certain as in the case of steel ; on which account some have been inclined to class the
colours of the spider's web with the phenomena
of refraction.

378.

In mother-of-pearl we perceive infinitely fine
organic fibres and lamellæ in juxta-position,
from which, as from the scratched silver before
alluded to, varied colours, but especially red and
green, may arise.

379.

The changing colours of the plumage of birds
may also be mentioned here, although in all or-

ganic instances a chemical principle and an
adaptation of the colour to the structure may be
assumed ; considerations to which we shall return in treating of chemical colours.

380.

That the appearances of objective halos also
approximate catoptrical phenomena will be
readily admitted, while we again do not deny
that refraction as well may here come into
the account. For the present we restrict ourselves to one or two observations ; hereafter we
may be enabled to make a fuller application of
general principles to particular examples.

381.

We first call to mind the yellow and red
circles produced on a white or grey wall by a
light placed near it (88). Light when reflected
appears subdued, and a subdued light excites
the impression of yellow, and subsequently of
red.

382.

Let the wall be illumined by a candle placed
quite close to it. The farther the light is diffused the fainter it becomes ; but it is still the
effect of the flame, the continuation of its
action, the dilated effect of its image. We
might, therefore, very fairly call these circles

reiterated images, because they constitute the successive boundaries of the action of the light, and yet at the same time only present an extended image of the flame.

383.

If the sky is white and luminous round the sun owing to the atmosphere being filled with light vapours; if mists or clouds pass before the moon, the reflection of the disk mirrors itself in them ; the halos we then perceive are single or double, smaller or greater, sometimes very large, often colourless, sometimes coloured.

384.

I witnessed a very beautiful halo round the moon the 15th of November, 1799, when the barometer stood high ; the sky was cloudy and vapoury. The halo was completely coloured, and the circles were concentric round the light as in subjective halos. That this halo was objective I was presently convinced by covering the moon's disk, when the same circles were nevertheless perfectly visible.

385.

The different extent of the halos appears to have a relation with the proximity or distance of the vapour from the eye of the observer.

386.

As window-panes lightly breathed upon increase the brilliancy of subjective halos, and in some degree give them an objective character, so, perhaps, with a simple contrivance in winter, during a quickly freezing temperature, a more exact definition of this might be arrived at.

387.

How much reason we have in considering these circles to insist on the *image* and its effects, is apparent in the phenomenon of the so-called double suns. Similar double images always occur in certain points of halos and circles, and only present in a circumscribed form what takes place in a more general way in the whole circle. All this will be more conveniently treated in connexion with the appearance of the rainbow.—Note Q.

388.

In conclusion it is only necessary to point out the affinity between the catoptrical and paroptical colours.

We call those paroptical colours which appear when the light passes by the edge of an opaque colourless body. How nearly these are allied to the dioptrical colours of the second class will be easily seen by those who are convinced with us that the colours of refraction take place only at the edges of objects. The affinity again between the catoptrical and paroptical colours will be evident in the following chapter.

XXXII.

PAROPTICAL COLOURS.

389.

THE paroptical colours have been hitherto called peri-optical, because a peculiar effect of light was supposed to take place as it were round the object, and was ascribed to a certain flexibility of the light to and from the object.

390.

These colours again may be divided into subjective and objective, because they appear partly without us, as it were, painted on surfaces, and partly within us, immediately on the retina. In this chapter we shall find it more to our purpose to take the objective cases first, since the subjective are so closely connected with other appearances already known to us, that it is hardly possible to separate them.

391.

The paroptical colours then are so called be-

cause the light must pass by an outline or edge
to produce them. They do not, however, always
appear in this case ; to produce the effect very
particular conditions are necessary besides.

392.

It is also to be observed that in this instance
again light does not act as an abstract diffusion
(361), the sun shines towards an edge. The
volume of light poured from the sun-image
passes by the edge of a substance, and occasions
shadows. Within these shadows we shall presently find colours appear.

393.

But, above all, we should make the experiments and observations that bear upon our present inquiry in the fullest light. We, therefore, place the observer in the open air before
we conduct him to the limits of a dark room.

394.

A person walking in sun-shine in a garden, or
on any level path, may observe that his shadow
only appears sharply defined next the foot on
which he rests ; farther from this point, especially round the head, it melts away into the
bright ground. For as the sun-light proceeds
not only from the middle of the sun, but also
acts cross-wise from the two extremes of every

diameter, an objective parallax takes place which produces a half-shadow on both sides of the object.

395.

If the person walking raises and spreads his hand, he distinctly sees in the shadow of each finger the diverging separation of the two half-shadows outwards, and the diminution of the principal shadow inwards, both being effects of the cross action of the light.

396.

This experiment may be repeated and varied before a smooth wall, with rods of different thicknesses, and again with balls; we shall always find that the farther the object is removed from the surface of the wall, the more the weak double shadow spreads, and the more the forcible main shadow diminishes, till at last the main shadow appears quite effaced, and even the double shadows become so faint, that they almost disappear; at a still greater distance they are, in fact, imperceptible.

397.

That this is caused by the cross-action of the light we may easily convince ourselves; for the shadow of a pointed object plainly exhibits two points. We must thus never lose sight of the fact that in this case the whole sun-image acts, produces shadows, changes them to double shadows, and finally obliterates them.

398.

Instead of solid bodies let us now take openings cut of various given sizes next each other, and let the sun shine through them on a plane surface at some little distance ; we shall find that the bright image produced by the sun on the surface, is larger than the opening ; this is because one edge of the sun shines towards the opposite edge of the opening, while the other edge of the disk is excluded on that side. Hence the bright image is more weakly lighted towards the edges.

399.

If we take square openings of any size we please, we shall find that the bright image on a surface nine feet from the opening, is on every side about an inch larger than the opening ; thus nearly corresponding with the angle of the apparent diameter of the sun.

400.

That the brightness should gradually diminish towards the edges of the image is quite natural, for at last only a minimum of the light can act cross-wise from the sun's circumference through the edge of the aperture.

401.

Thus we here again see how much reason we have in actual observation to guard against the assumption of parallel rays, bundles and fasces of rays, and the like hypothetical notions.

402.

We might rather consider the splendour of the sun, or of any light, as an infinite specular multiplication of the circumscribed luminous image, whence it may be explained that all square openings through which the sun shines, at certain distances, according as the apertures are greater or smaller, must give a round image of light.

403.

The above experiments may be repeated through openings of various shapes, and sizes, and the same effect will always take place at proportionate distances. In all these cases, however, we may still observe that in a full light and while the sun merely shines past an edge, no colour is apparent.

404.

We therefore proceed to experiments with a subdued light, which is essential to the appearance of colour. Let a small opening be made in the window-shutter of a dark room; let the crossing sun-light which enters, be received on a surface of white paper, and we shall find that the smaller the opening is, the dimmer the light image will be. This is quite obvious, because the paper does not receive light from the whole sun, but partially from single points of its disk.

405.

If we look attentively at this dim image of the sun, we find it still dimmer towards the outlines where a yellow border is perceptible. The colour is still more apparent if a vapour or a transparent cloud passes before the sun, thus subduing and dimming its brightness. The halo on the wall, the effect of the decreasing brightness of a light placed near it, is here forced on our recollection. (88.)

406.

If we examine the image more accurately, we perceive that this yellow border is not the only appearance of colour; we can see, besides, a bluish circle, if not even a halo-like repetition of the coloured border. If the room is quite dark, we discern that the sky next the sun also has its effect : we see the blue sky, nay, even the whole landscape, on the paper, and are thus again convinced that as far as regards the sun, we have here only to do with a luminous image.

407.

If we take a somewhat larger square opening, so large that the image of the sun shining through it does not immediately become round, we may distinctly observe the half-shadows of every edge or side, the junction of these in the corners, and their colours ; just as in the above-mentioned appearance with the round opening.

408.

We have now subdued a parallactic light by causing it to shine through small apertures, but we have not taken from it its parallactic character; so that it can produce double shadows of bodies, although with diminished power. These double shadows which we have hitherto been describing, follow each other in light and dark, coloured and colourless circles, and produce repeated, nay, almost innumerable halos. These effects have been often represented in drawings and engravings. By placing needles, hairs, and other small bodies, in the subdued light, the numerous halo-like double shadows may be increased ; thus observed, they have been ascribed to an alternating flexile action of the light, and the same assumption has been employed to explain the obliteration of the central shadow, and the appearance of a light in the place of the dark.

409.

For ourselves, we maintain that these again
are parallactic double shadows, which appear
edged with coloured borders and halos.

410.

After having seen and investigated the foregoing phenomena, we can proceed to the experiments with knife-blades,* exhibiting effects
which may be referred to the contact and parallactic mutual intersection of the half-shadows
and halos already familiar to us.

411.

Lastly, the observer may follow out the experiments with hairs, needles, and wires, in the
half-light produced as before described by the
sun, as well as in that derived from the blue
sky, and indicated on the white paper. He will
thus make himself still better acquainted with
the true nature of this phenomenon.

412.

But since in these experiments everything
depends on our being persuaded of the parallactic action of the light, we can make this
more evident by means of two sources of light,
the two shadows from which intersect each
other, and may be altogether separated. By
day this may be contrived with two small

---

* See Newton's Optics, book iii.

openings in a window-shutter; by night, with two candles. There are even accidental effects in interiors, on opening and closing shutters, by means of which we can better observe these appearances than with the most careful apparatus. But still, all and each of these may be reduced to experiment by preparing a box which the observer can look into from above, and gradually diminishing the openings after having caused a double light to shine in. In this case, as might be expected, the coloured shadow, considered under the physiological colours, appears very easily.

413.

It is necessary to remember, generally, what has been before stated with regard to the nature of double shadows, half-lights, and the like. Experiments also should especially be made with different shades of grey placed next each other, where every stripe will appear light by a darker, and dark by a lighter stripe next it. If at night, with three or more lights, we produce shadows which cross each other successively, we can observe this phenomenon very distinctly, and we shall be convinced that the physiological case before more fully treated, here comes into the account (38).

414.

To what extent the appearances that accompany the paroptical colours, may be derived from the doctrine of subdued lights, from half-shadows, and from the physiological disposition of the retina, or whether we shall be forced to take refuge in certain intrinsic qualities of light, as has hitherto been done, time may teach. Suffice it here to have pointed out the conditions under which the paroptical colours appear, and we may hope that our allusion to their connexion with the facts before adduced by us will not remain unnoticed by the observers of nature.

415.

The affinity of the paroptical colours with the dioptrical of the second class will also be readily seen and followed up by every reflecting investigator. Here, as in those instances, we have to do with edges or boundaries; here, as in those instances, with a light, which appears at the outline. How natural, therefore, it is to conclude that the paroptical effects may be heightened, strengthened, and enriched by the dioptrical. Since, however, the luminous image actually shines through the medium, we can here only have to do with objective cases of refraction : it is these which are strictly allied to the paroptical cases. The subjective cases of refraction, where we see objects through the medium, are quite distinct from the paroptical.

We have already recommended them on account of their clearness and simplicity.

416.

The connexion between the paroptical colours and the catoptrical may be already inferred from what has been said : for as the catoptrical colours only appear on scratches, points, steel-wire, and delicate threads, so it is nearly the same case as if the light shone past an edge. The light must always be reflected from an edge in order to produce colour. Here again, as before pointed out, the partial action of the luminous image and the subduing of the light are both to be taken into the account.

417.

We add but few observations on the subjective paroptical colours, because these may be classed partly with the physiological colours, partly with the dioptrical of the second order. The greater part hardly seem to belong here, but, when attentively considered, they still diffuse a satisfactory light over the whole doctrine, and establish its connexion.

418.

If we hold a ruler before the eyes so that the flame of a light just appears above it, we see t he ruler as it were indented and notched at the

place where the light appears. This seems deducible from the expansive power of light acting
on the retina (18).

419.

The same phenomenon on a large scale is exhibited at sun-rise ; for when the orb appears
distinctly, but not too powerfully, so that we can
still look at it, it always makes a sharp indent-
ation in the horizon.

420.

If, when the sky is grey, we approach a window, so that the dark cross of the window-bars
be relieved on the sky ; if after fixing the eyes
on the horizontal bar we bend the head a little
forward ; on half closing the eyes as we look up,
we shall presently perceive a bright yellow-red
border under the bar, and a bright light-blue
one above it. The duller and more monotonous
the grey of the sky, the more dusky the room,
and, consequently, the more previously unexcited the eye, the livelier the appearance will
be ; but it may be seen by an attentive observer
even in bright daylight.

421.

If we move the head backwards while half
closing the eyes, so that the horizontal bar be
seen below, the phenomenon will appear re-

versed. The upper edge will appear yellow, the under edge blue.

422.

Such observations are best made in a dark room. If white paper is spread before the opening where the solar microscope is commonly fastened, the lower edge of the circle will appear blue, the upper yellow, even while the eyes are quite open, or only by half-closing them so far that a halo no longer appears round the white. If the head is moved backwards the colours are reversed.

423.

These phenomena seem to prove that the humours of the eye are in fact only really achromatic in the centre where vision takes place, but that towards the circumference, and in unusual motions of the eyes, as in looking horizontally when the head is bent backwards or forwards, a chromatic tendency remains, especially when distinctly relieved objects are thus looked at. Hence such phenomena may be considered as allied to the dioptrical colours of the second class.

424.

Similar colours appear if we look on black and white objects, through a pin-hole in a card.

Instead of a white object we may take the minute light aperture in the tin plate of a camera obscura, as prepared for paroptical experiments.

425.

If we look through a tube, the farther end of which is contracted or variously indented, the same colours appear.

426.

The following phenomena appear to me to be more nearly allied to the paroptical appearances. If we hold up a needle near the eye, the point appears double. A particularly remarkable effect again is produced if we look towards a grey sky through the blades of knives prepared for paroptical experiments. We seem to look through a gauze; a multitude of threads appear to the eye; these are in fact only the reiterated images of the sharp edges, each of which is successively modified by the next, or perhaps modified in a parallactic sense by the oppositely acting one, the whole mass being thus changed to a thread-like appearance.

427.

Lastly, it is to be remarked that if we look through the blades towards a minute light in the window-shutter, coloured stripes and halos appear on the retina as on the paper.

428.

The present chapter may be here terminated, the less reluctantly, as a friend has undertaken to investigate this subject by further experiments. In our recapitulation, in the description of the plates and apparatus, we hope hereafter to give an account of his observations.*

XXXIII.

EPOPTICAL COLOURS.

429.

WE have hitherto had to do with colours which appear with vivacity, but which immediately vanish again when certain conditions cease. We have now to become acquainted with others, which it is true are still to be considered as transient, but which, under certain circumstances, become so fixed that, even after the conditions which first occasioned their appearance cease, they still remain, and thus con-

---

* The observations here alluded to never appeared.

stitute the link between the physical and the chemical colours.

430.

They appear from various causes on the surface of a colourless body, originally, without communication, die or immersion (βαφή) ; and we now proceed to trace them, from their faintest indication to their most permanent state, through the different conditions of their appearance, which for easier survey we here at once summarily state.

431.

First condition.—The contact of two smooth surfaces of hard transparent bodies.

First case: if masses or plates of glass, or if lenses are pressed against each other.

Second case : if a crack takes place in a solid mass of glass, chrystal, or ice.

Third case : if lamellæ of transparent stones become separated.

Second condition.—If a surface of glass or a polished stone is breathed upon.

Third condition.—The combination of the two last ; first, breathing on the glass, then placing another plate of glass upon it, thus exciting the colours by pressure ; then removing the upper glass, upon which the colours begin to fade and vanish with the breath.

Fourth condition.—Bubbles of various liquids, soap, chocolate, beer, wine, fine glass bubbles.

Fifth condition.—Very fine pellicles and lamellæ, produced by the decomposition of minerals and metals. The pellicles of lime, the surface of stagnant water, especially if impregnated with iron, and again pellicles of oil on water, especially of varnish on aqua fortis.

Sixth condition.—If metals are heated; the operation of imparting tints to steel and other metals.

Seventh condition.—If the surface of glass is beginning to decompose.

432.

First condition, first case. If two convex glasses, or a convex and plane glass, or, best of all, a convex and concave glass come in contact, concentric coloured circles appear. The phenomenon exhibits itself immediately on the slightest pressure, and may then be gradually carried through various successive states. We will describe the complete appearance at once, as we shall then be better enabled to follow the different states through which it passes.

433.

The centre is colourless; where the glasses are, so to speak, united in one by the strongest pressure, a dark grey point appears with a silver

white space round it : then follow, in decreasing
distances, various insulated rings, all consisting
of three colours, which are in immediate contact with each other. Each of these rings, of
which perhaps three or four might be counted,
is yellow on the inner side, blue on the outer,
and red in the centre. Between two rings there
appears a silver white interval. The rings
which are farthest from the centre are always
nearer together : they are composed of red and
green without a perceptible white space between them.

434.

We will now observe the appearances in their
gradual formation, beginning from the slightest
pressure.

435.

On the slightest pressure the centre itself appears of a green colour. Then follow as far as
the concentric circles extend, red and green
rings. They are wide, accordingly, and no trace
of a silver white space is to be seen between
them. The green is produced by the blue of an
imperfectly developed circle, mixing with the
yellow of the first circle. All the remaining
circles are, in this slight contact, broad ; their
yellow and blue edges mix together, thus producing a beautiful green. The red, however, of

each circle, remains pure and untouched ; hence the whole series is composed of these two colours.

436.

A somewhat stronger pressure separates the first circle by a slight interval from the imperfectly developed one : it is thus detached, and may be said to appear in a complete state. The centre is now a blue point ; for the yellow of the first circle is now separated from this central point by a silver white space. From the centre of the blue a red appears, which is thus, in all cases, bounded on the outside by its blue edge. The second and third rings from the centre are quite detached. Where deviations from this order present themselves, the observer will be enabled to account for them, from what has been or remains to be stated.

437.

On a stronger pressure the centre becomes yellow ; this yellow is surrounded by a red and blue edge : at last, the yellow also retires from the centre ; the innermost circle is formed and is bounded with yellow. The whole centre itself now appears silver white, till at last, on the strongest pressure, the dark point appears, and the phenomenon, as described at first, is complete.

438.

The relative size of the concentric circles and their intervals depends on the form of the glasses which are pressed together.

439.

We remarked above, that the coloured centre is, in fact, an undeveloped circle. It is, however, often found, on the slightest pressure, that several undeveloped circles exist there, as it were, in the germ; these can be successively developed before the eye of the observer.

440.

The regularity of these rings is owing to the form of the convex glasses, and the diameter of the coloured appearance depends on the greater or lesser section of a circle on which a lens is polished. We easily conclude from this, that by pressing plane glasses together, irregular appearances only will be produced; the colours, in fact, undulate like watered silks, and spread from the point of pressure in all directions. Yet, the phenomenon as thus exhibited is much more splendid than in the former instance, and cannot fail to strike every spectator. If we make the experiment in this mode, we shall distinctly see, as in the other case, that, on a slight pressure, the green and red waves appear; on a stronger, stripes of blue, red, and yellow, become detached. At first, the outer sides of these stripes touch ; on increased pressure they are separated by a silver white space.

441.

Before we proceed to a further description of this phenomenon, we may point out the most convenient mode of exhibiting it. Place a large convex glass on a table near the window ; upon this glass lay a plate of well-polished mirror-glass, about the size of a playing-card, and the mere weight of the plate will press sufficiently to produce one or other of the phenomena above described. So, also, by the different weight of plates of glass, by other accidental circumstances, for instance, by slipping the plate on the side of the convex glass where the pressure cannot be so strong as in the centre, all the gradations above described can be produced in succession.

442.

In order to observe the phenomenon it is necessary to look obliquely on the surface where it appears. But, above all, it is to be remarked that by stooping still more, and looking at the appearance under a more acute angle, the circles not only grow larger but other circles are developed from the centre, of which no trace is to be discovered when we look perpendicularly, even through the strongest magnifiers.

443.

In order to exhibit the phenomenon in its greatest beauty, the utmost attention should be paid to the cleanness of the glasses. If the experiment is made with plate-glass adapted for mirrors, the glass should be handled with gloves. The inner surfaces, which must come in contact with the utmost nicety, may be most conveniently cleaned before the experiment, and the outer surfaces should be kept clean while the pressure is increased.

444.

From what has been said it will be seen that an exact contact of two smooth surfaces is necessary. Polished glasses are best adapted for the purpose. Plates of glass exhibit the most brilliant colours when they fit closely together, and for this reason the phenomenon will increase in beauty if exhibited under an air-pump, by exhausting the air.

445.

The appearance of the coloured rings may be produced in the greatest perfection by placing a convex and concave glass together which have been ground on similar segments of circles. I have never seen the effect more brilliant than with the object-glass of an achromatic telescope,

Fig. 1.

PLATE I

Fig. 2.

Fig. 3.

Red

Purple

Orange

Blue

Yellow

Green

Fig. 4.

PLATE II

Fig. 1.

Fig. 2.

Fig. 3.

Fig. 4.

Fig. 5.

PLATE III

Fig. 1.

Fig. 2.

PLATE IV

Fig. 1.

Fig. 2.

in which the crown-glass and flint-glass were necessarily in the closest contact.

446.

A remarkable appearance takes place when dissimilar surfaces are pressed together; for example, a polished crystal and a plate of glass. The appearance does not at all exhibit itself in large flowing waves, as in the combination of glass with glass, but it is small and angular, and, as it were, disjointed: thus it appears that the surface of the polished crystal, which consists of infinitely small sections of lamellæ, does not come so uninterruptedly in contact with the glass as another glass-plate would.

447.

The appearance of colour vanishes on the strongest pressure, which so intimately unites the two surfaces that they appear to make but one substance. It is this which occasions the dark centre, because the pressed lens no longer reflects any light from this point, for the very same point, when seen against the light, is perfectly clear and transparent. On relaxing the pressure, the colours, in like manner, gradually diminish, and disappear entirely when the surfaces are separated.

448.

These same appearances occur in two similar cases. If entirely transparent masses become partially separated, the surfaces of their parts being still sufficiently in contact, we see the same circles and waves more or less. They may be produced in great beauty by plunging a hot mass of glass in water; the different fissures and cracks enabling us to observe the colours in various forms. Nature often exhibits the same phenomena in split rock crystals.

449.

This appearance, again, frequently displays itself in the mineral world in those kinds of stone which by nature have a tendency to exfoliate. These original lamellæ are, it is true, so intimately united, that stones of this kind appear altogether transparent and colourless, yet, the internal layers become separated, from various accidental causes, without altogether destroying the contact : thus the appearance, which is now familiar to us by the foregoing description, often occurs in nature, particularly in calcareous spars; the specularis, adularia, and other minerals of similar structure. Hence it shows an ignorance of the proximate causes of an appearance so often accidentally produced, to consider it so important in mineralogy, and to attach especial value to the specimens exhibiting it.

450.

We have yet to speak of the very remarkable inversion of this appearance, as related by men of science. If, namely, instead of looking at the colours by a reflected light, we examine them by a transmitted light, the opposite colours are said to appear, and in a mode corresponding with that which we have before described as physiological ; the colours evoking each other. Instead of blue, we should thus see red-yellow ; instead of red, green, &c., and *vice versâ*. We reserve experiments in detail, the rather as we have ourselves still some doubts on this point.

451.

If we were now called upon to give some general explanation of these epoptical colours, as they appear under the first condition, and to show their connexion with the previously detailed physical phenomena, we might proceed to do so as follows :—

452.

The glasses employed for the experiments are to be regarded as the utmost possible practical approach to transparence. By the intimate contact, however, occasioned by the pressure applied to them, their surfaces, we are persuaded, immediately become in a very slight degree dimmed. Within this semi-transparence

the colours immediately appear, and every circle
comprehends the whole scale; for when the two
opposites, yellow and blue, are united by their
red extremities, pure red appears: the green,
on the other hand, as in prismatic experiments,
when yellow and blue touch.

453.

We have already repeatedly found that where
colour exists at all, the whole scale is soon
called into existence; a similar principle may be
said to lurk in the nature of every physical
phenomenon; it already follows, from the idea
of polar opposition, from which an elementary
unity or completeness results.

454.

The fact that a colour exhibited by transmitted light is different from that displayed by
reflected light, reminds us of those dioptrical
colours of the first class which we found were
produced precisely in the same way through
semi-opacity. That here, too, a diminution of
transparency exists there can scarcely be a
doubt; for the adhesion of the perfectly smooth
plates of glass (an adhesion so strong that they
remain hanging to each other) produces a degree of union which deprives each of the two
surfaces, in some degree, of its smoothness and
transparence. The fullest proof may, however,

be found in the fact that in the centre, where
the lens is most strongly pressed on the other
glass, and where a perfect union is accomplished, a complete transparence takes place,
in which we no longer perceive any colour. All
this may be hereafter confirmed in a recapitulation of the whole.

455.

Second condition.—If after breathing on a
plate of glass, the breath is merely wiped away
with the finger, and if we then again immediately breathe on the glass, we see very vivid
colours gliding through each other; these, as
the moisture evaporates, change their place,
and at last vanish altogether. If this operation
is repeated, the colours are more vivid and
beautiful, and remain longer than they did the
first time.

456.

Quickly as this appearance passes, and confused as it appears to be, I have yet remarked
the following effects :—At first all the principal
colours appear with their combinations ; on
breathing more strongly, the appearance may
be perceived in some order. In this succession
it may be remarked, that when the breath in
evaporating becomes contracted from all sides

towards the centre, the blue colour vanishes
last.

457.

The phenomenon appears most readily between
the minute lines, which the action of passing
the fingers leaves on the clear surface; a somewhat rough state of the surface of the glass is
otherwise requisite. On some glass the appearance may be produced by merely breathing; in
other cases the wiping with the fingers is necessary : I have even met with polished mirror-
glasses, one side of which immediately showed
the colours vividly; the other not. To judge
from some remaining pieces, the former was originally the front of the glass, the latter the side
which was covered with quicksilver.

458.

These experiments may be best made in cold
weather, because the glass may be more quickly
and distinctly breathed upon, and the breath
evaporates more suddenly. In severe frost the
phenomenon may be observed on a large scale
while travelling in a carriage; the glasses being
well cleaned, and all closed. The breath of the
persons within is very gently diffused over the
glass, and immediately produces the most vivid
play of colours. How far they may present a
regular succession I have not been able to re-

mark ; but they appear particularly vivid when they have a dark object as a background. This alternation of colours does not, however, last long; for as soon as the breath gathers in drops, or freezes to points of ice, the appearance is at once at an end.

459.

Third condition.—The two foregoing experiments of the pressure and breathing may be united ; namely, by breathing on a plate of glass, and immediately after pressing the other upon it. The colours then appear as in the case of two glasses unbreathed upon, with this difference, that the moisture occasions here and there an interruption of the undulations. On pushing one glass away from the other the moisture appears iridescent as it evaporates.

460.

It might, however, be asserted that this combined experiment exhibits no more than each single experiment; for it appears the colours excited by pressure disappear in proportion as the glasses are less in contact, and the moisture then evaporates with its own colours.

461.

Fourth condition.—Iridescent appearances are observable in almost all bubbles ; soap-bubbles are the most commonly known, and the effect in question is thus exhibited in the easiest mode ; but it may be observed in wine, beer, in pure spirit, and again, especially, in the froth of chocolate.

462.

As in the above cases we required an infinitely narrow space between two surfaces which are in contact, so we can consider the pellicle of the soap-bubble as an infinitely thin lamina between two elastic bodies ; for the appearance in fact takes place between the air within, which distends the bubble, and the atmospheric air.

463.

The bubble when first produced is colourless ; then coloured stripes, like those in marble paper, begin to appear : these at length spread over the whole surface, or rather are driven round it as it is distended.

464.

In a single bubble, suffered to hang from the straw or tube, the appearance of colour is difficult to observe, for the quick rotation prevents any accurate observation, and all the colours seem to mix together ; yet we can perceive that the colours begin at the orifice of the tube. The solution itself may, however, be blown into carefully, so that only one bubble shall appear. This remains white (colourless) if not much agitated; but if the solution is not too watery, circles appear round the perpendicular axis of the bubble; these being near each other, are commonly composed alternately of green and red. Lastly, several bubbles may be produced together by the same means; in this case the colours appear on the sides where two bubbles have pressed each other flat.

465.

The bubbles of chocolate-froth may perhaps be even more conveniently observed than those of soap; though smaller, they remain longer. In these, owing to the heat, an impulse, a movement, is produced and sustained, which appears necessary to the development and succession of the appearances.

466.

If the bubble is small, or shut in between others, coloured lines chase each other over the surface, resembling marbled paper; all the colours of the scale are seen to pass through each other; the pure, the augmented, the combined, all distinctly clear and beautiful. In small bubbles the appearance lasts for a considerable time.

467.

If the bubble is larger, or if it becomes by degrees detached, owing to the bursting of others near, we perceive that this impulsion and attraction of the colours has, as it were, an end in view; for on the highest point of the bubble we see a small circle appear, which is yellow in the centre; the other remaining coloured lines move constantly round this with a vermicular action.

468.

In a short time the circle enlarges and sinks downwards on all sides; in the centre the yellow remains; below and on the outside it becomes red, and soon blue; below this again appears a new circle of the same series of colours: if they approximate sufficiently, a green is produced by the union of the border-colours.

469.

When I could count three such leading circles, the centre was colourless, and this space became by degrees larger as the circles sank lower, till at last the bubble burst.

470.

Fifth condition.—Very delicate pellicles may be formed in various ways: on these films we discover a very lively play of colours, either in the usual order, or more confusedly passing through each other. The water in which lime has been slaked soon skims over with a coloured pellicle: the same happens on the surface of stagnant water, especially if impregnated with iron. The lamellæ of the fine tartar which adheres to bottles, especially in red French wine, exhibit the most brilliant colours, on being exposed to the light, if carefully detached. Drops of oil on water, brandy, and other fluids, produce also similar circles and brilliant effects: but the most beautiful experiment that can be made is the following:—Let aqua fortis, not too strong, be poured into a flat saucer, and then with a brush drop on it some of the varnish used by engravers to cover certain portions during the process of biting their plates. After quick commotion there presently appears a film which spreads itself out in circles, and immediately produces the most vivid appearances of colour.

471.

Sixth condition.—When metals are heated, colours rapidly succeeding each other appear on the surface: these colours can, however, be arrested at will.

472.

If a piece of polished steel is heated, it will, at a certain degree of warmth, be overspread with yellow. If taken suddenly away from the fire, this yellow remains.

473.

As the steel becomes hotter, the yellow appears darker, intenser, and presently passes into red. This is difficult to arrest, for it hastens very quickly to bright blue.

474.

This beautiful blue is to be arrested if the steel is suddenly taken out of the heat and buried in ashes. The blue steel works are produced in this way. If, again, the steel is held longer over the fire, it soon becomes a light blue, and so it remains.

475.

These colours pass like a breath over the plate of steel; each seems to fly before the other, but, in reality, each successive hue is constantly developed from the preceding one.

476.

If we hold a penknife in the flame of a light, a coloured stripe will appear across the blade. The portion of the stripe which was nearest to the flame is light blue; this melts into blue-red; the red is in the centre; then follow yellow-red and yellow.

477.

This phenomenon is deducible from the preceding ones ; for the portion of the blade next the handle is less heated than the end which is in the flame, and thus all the colours which in other cases exhibited themselves in succession, must here appear at once, and may thus be permanently preserved.

478.

Robert Boyle gives this succession of colours as follows :—" A florido flavo ad flavum saturum et rubescentem (quem artifices sanguineum vocant) inde ad languidum, postea ad saturiorem cyaneum." This would be quite correct if the words "languidus" and "saturior" were to change places. How far the observation is correct, that the different colours have a relation to the degree of temper which the metal afterwards acquires, we leave to others to decide. The colours are here only indications of the different degrees of heat.—Note R.

479.

When lead is calcined, the surface is first greyish. This greyish powder, with greater heat, becomes yellow, and then orange. Silver, too, exhibits colours when heated ; the fracture of silver in the process of refining belongs to the same class of examples. When metallic glasses melt, colours in like manner appear on the surface.

480.

Seventh condition.—When the surface of glass becomes decomposed. The accidental opacity (blindwerden) of glass has been already noticed : the term (blindwerden) is employed to denote that the surface of the glass is so affected as to appear dim to us.

481.

White glass becomes "blind" soonest; cast, and afterwards polished glass is also liable to be so affected ; the bluish less, the green least.

482.

Of the two sides of a plate of glass one is called the mirror side; it is that which in the oven lies uppermost, on which one may observe roundish elevations : it is smoother than the other, which is undermost in the oven, and on which scratches may be sometimes observed. On this account the mirror side is placed facing the interior of rooms, because it is less affected by the moisture adhering to it from within, than the other would be, and the glass is thus less liable to become " blind."

483.

This half-opacity or dimness of the glass assumes by degrees an appearance of colour which may become very vivid, and in which perhaps a certain succession, or otherwise regular order, might be discovered

484.

Having thus traced the physical colours from their simplest effects to the present instances, where these fleeting appearances are found to be fixed in bodies, we are, in fact, arrived at the point where the chemical colours begin; nay, we have in some sort already passed those limits; a circumstance which may excite a favourable prejudice for the consistency of our statement. By way of conclusion to this part of our inquiry, we subjoin a general observation, which may not be without its bearing on the common connecting principle of the phenomena that have been adduced.

485.

The colouring of steel and the appearances analogous to it, might perhaps be easily deduced from the doctrine of the semi-opaque mediums. Polished steel reflects light powerfully: we may consider the colour produced by the heat as a slight degree of dimness: hence a bright yellow must immediately appear; this, as the dimness increases, must still appear deeper, more condensed, and redder, and at last pure and ruby-red. The colour has now reached the extreme point of depth, and if we suppose the same de-

gree of semi-opacity still to continue, the dimness would now spread itself over a dark ground,
first producing a violet, then a dark-blue, and at
last a light-blue, and thus complete the series of
the appearances.

We will not assert that this mode of explanation will suffice in all cases; our object is rather
to point out the road by which the all-compre-
hensive formula, the very key of the enigma,
may be at last discovered.—Note S.

PART III.

CHEMICAL COLOURS.

486.

WE give this denomination to colours which we can produce, and more or less fix, in certain bodies; which we can render more intense, which we can again take away and communicate to other bodies, and to which, therefore, we ascribe a certain permanency : duration is their prevailing characteristic.

487.

In this view the chemical colours were formerly distinguished with various epithets; they were called *colores proprii, corporei, materiales, veri, permanentes, fixi.*

488.

In the preceding chapter we observed how the fluctuating and transient nature of the physical colours becomes gradually fixed, thus forming the natural transition to our present subject.

489.

Colour becomes fixed in bodies more or less permanently ; superficially, or thoroughly.

490.

All bodies are susceptible of colour ; it can

either be excited, rendered intense, and gradually fixed in them, or at least communicated to them.

XXXIV.

CHEMICAL CONTRAST.

491.

In the examination of coloured appearances we had occasion everywhere to take notice of a principle of contrast: so again, in approaching the precincts of chemistry, we find a chemical contrast of a remarkable nature. We speak here, with reference to our present purpose, only of that which is comprehended under the general names of acid and alkali.

492.

We characterised the chromatic contrast, in conformity with all other physical contrasts as a *more* and *less ;* ascribing the *plus* to the yellow side, the *minus* to the blue ; and we now find that these two divisions correspond with the chemical contrasts. The yellow and yellow-red affect the acids, the blue and blue-red the alkalis ; thus the phenomena of chemical colours, although still necessarily mixed up with other considerations, admit of being traced with sufficient simplicity.

493.

The principal phenomena in chemical colours are produced by the oxydation of metals, and it will be seen how important this consideration is at the outset. Other facts which come into the account, and which are worthy of attention, will be examined under separate heads ; in doing this we, however, expressly state that we only propose to offer some preparatory suggestions to the chemist in a very general way, without entering into the nicer chemical problems and questions, or presuming to decide on them. Our object is only to give a sketch of the mode in which, according to our conviction, the chemical theory of colours may be connected with general physics.

XXXV.

WHITE.

494.

In treating of the dioptrical colours of the first class (155) we have already in some degree anticipated this subject. Transparent substances may be said to be in the highest class of inorganic matter. With these, colourless semitransparence is closely connected, and white may be considered the last opaque degree of this.

495.

Pure water crystallised to snow appears white, for the transparence of the separate parts makes no transparent whole. Various crystallised salts, when deprived to a certain extent of moisture, appear as a white powder. The accidentally opaque state of a pure transparent substance might be called white; thus pounded glass appears as a white powder. The cessation of a combining power, and the exhibition of the atomic quality of the substance might at the same time be taken into the account.

496.

The known undecomposed earths are, in their pure state, all white. They pass to a state of transparence by natural crystallization. Silex becomes rock-crystal; argile, mica; magnesia, talc; calcareous earth and barytes appear transparent in various spars.—Note **T**.

497.

As in the colouring of mineral bodies the

metallic oxydes will often invite our attention, we observe, in conclusion, that metals, when slightly oxydated, at first appear white, as lead is converted to white lead by vegetable acid.

XXXVI.

BLACK.

498.

BLACK is not exhibited in so elementary a state as white. We meet with it in the vegetable kingdom in semi-combustion ; and charcoal, a substance especially worthy of attention on other accounts, exhibits a black colour. Again, if woods—for example, boards, owing to the action of light, air, and moisture, are deprived in part of their combustibility, there appears first the grey then the black colour. So again, we can convert even portions of animal substance to charcoal by semi-combustion.

499.

In the same manner we often find that a sub-oxydation takes place in metals when the black colour is to be produced. Various metals, particularly iron, become black by slight oxyda-

tion, by vinegar, by mild acid fermentations ;
for example, a decoction of rice, &c.

500.

Again, it may be inferred that a de-oxydation
may produce black. This occurs in the preparation of ink, which becomes yellow by the
solution of iron in strong sulphuric acid, but
when partly de-oxydised by the infusion of gall-
nuts, appears black.

XXXVII.

FIRST EXCITATION OF COLOUR.

501.

In the division of physical colours, where semi-
transparent mediums were considered, we saw
colours antecedently to white and black. In
the present case we assume a white and black
already produced and fixed ; and the question
is, how colour can be excited in them ?

502.

Here, too, we can say, white that becomes
darkened or dimmed inclines to yellow ; black,
as it becomes lighter, inclines to blue.—Note U.

503.

Yellow appears on the active (plus) side, immediately in the light, the bright, the white. All white surfaces easily assume a yellow tinge ; paper, linen, wool, silk, wax : transparent fluids again, which have a tendency to combustion, easily become yellow ; in other words they easily pass into a very slight state of semi-transparence.

504.

So again the excitement on the passive side, the tendency to obscure, dark, black, is immediately accompanied with blue, or rather with a reddish-blue. Iron dissolved in sulphuric acid, and much diluted with water, if held to the light in a glass, exhibits a beautiful violet colour as soon as a few drops only of the infusion of gall-nuts are added. This colour presents the peculiar hues of the dark topaz, the *orphninon* of a burnt-red, as the ancients expressed it.

505.

Whether any colour can be excited in the pure earths by the chemical operations of nature and art, without the admixture of metallic oxydes, is an important question, generally, indeed, answered in the negative. It is perhaps connected with the question—to what extent changes may be produced in the earths through oxydation ?

506.

Undoubtedly the negation of the above question is confirmed by the circumstance that wherever mineral colours are found, some trace of metal, especially of iron, shows itself; we are thus naturally led to consider how easily iron becomes oxydised, how easily the oxyde of iron assumes different colours, how infinitely divisible it is, and how quickly it communicates its colour. It were to be wished, notwithstanding, that new experiments could be made in regard to the above point, so as either to confirm or remove any doubt.

507.

However this may be, the susceptibility of the earths with regard to colours already existing is very great; aluminous earth is thus particularly distinguished.

508.

In proceeding to consider the metals, which in the inorganic world have the almost exclusive prerogative of appearing coloured, we find that, in their pure, independent, natural state, they are already distinguished from the pure earths by a tendency to some one colour or other.

509.

While silver approximates most to pure white, —nay, really represents pure white, heightened by metallic splendor,—steel, tin, lead, and so forth, incline towards pale blue-grey; gold, on the other hand, deepens to pure yellow, copper approaches a red hue, which, under certain circumstances, increases almost to bright red, but which again returns to a yellow golden colour when combined with zinc.

510.

But if metals in their pure state have so specific a determination towards this or that exhibition of colour, they are, through the effect of oxydation, in some degree reduced to a common character; for the elementary colours now come forth in their purity, and although this or that metal appears to have a particular tendency to this or that colour, we find some that can go through the whole circle of hues, others, that are capable of exhibiting more than one colour; tin, however, is distinguished by its comparative inaptitude to become coloured. We propose to give a table hereafter, showing how far the different metals can be more or less made to exhibit the different colours.

511.

When the clean, smooth surface of a pure metal, on being heated, becomes overspread with a mantling colour, which passes through a series of appearances as the heat increases, this, we are persuaded, indicates the aptitude of the metal to pass through the whole range of colours. We find this phenomenon most beautifully exhibited in polished steel; but silver, copper, brass, lead, and tin, easily present similar appearances. A superficial oxydation is probably here taking place, as may be inferred from the effects of the operation when continued, especially in the more easily oxydizable metals.

512.

The same conclusion may be drawn from the fact that iron is more easily oxydizable by acid liquids when it is red hot, for in this case the two effects concur with each other. We observe, again, that steel, accordingly as it is hardened in different stages of its colorification, may exhibit a difference of elasticity: this is quite natural, for the various appearances of colour indicate various degrees of heat.*

513.

If we look beyond this superficial mantling,

---

* See par. 478.

this pellicle of colour, we observe that as metals are oxydized throughout their masses, white or black appears with the first degree of heat, as may be seen in white lead, iron, and quicksilver.

514.

If we examine further, and look for the actual exhibition of colour, we find it most frequently on the *plus* side. The mantling, so often mentioned, of smooth metallic surfaces begins with yellow. Iron passes presently into yellow ochre, lead from white lead to massicot, quicksilver from æthiops to yellow turbith. The solutions of gold and platinum in acids are yellow.

515.

The exhibitions on the *minus* side are less frequent. Copper slightly oxydized appears blue. In the preparation of Prussian-blue, alkalis are employed.

516.

Generally, however, these appearances of colour are of so mutable a nature that chemists look upon them as deceptive tests, at least in the nicer gradations. For ourselves, as we can only treat of these matters in a general way, we merely observe that the appearances of colour in metals may be classed according to their origin, manifold appearance, and cessation, as various results of oxydation, hyper-oxydation, ab-oxydation, and de-oxydation.*

XXXVIII.

AUGMENTATION OF COLOUR.†

517.

THE augmentation of colour exhibits itself as a condensation, a fulness, a darkening of the hue. We have before seen, in treating of colourless mediums, that by increasing the degree of opacity in the medium, we can deepen a bright object from the lightest yellow to the intensest ruby-red. Blue, on the other hand, increases to the most beautiful violet, if we rarefy and diminish a semi-opaque medium, itself lighted, but through which we see darkness (150, 151).

518.

If the colour is positive, a similar colour appears in the intenser state. Thus if we fill a white porcelain cup with a pure yellow liquor, the fluid will appear to become gradually redder

---

* As these terms are afterwards referred to (par. 525), it was necessary to preserve them.

† Steigerung, literally *gradual ascent*. See the note to par. 523.

towards the bottom, and at last appears orange. If we pour a pure blue solution into another cup, the upper portion will exhibit a sky-blue, that towards the bottom, a beautiful violet. If the cup is placed in the sun, the shadowed side, even of the upper portion, is already violet. If we throw a shadow with the hand, or any other substance, over the illumined portion, the shadow in like manner appears reddish.

519.

This is one of the most important appearances connected with the doctrine of colours, for we here manifestly find that a difference of quantity produces a corresponding qualified impression on our senses. In speaking of the last class of epoptical colours (452, 485), we stated our conjecture that the colouring of steel might perhaps be traced to the doctrine of the semi-transparent mediums, and we would here again recall this to the reader's recollection.

520.

All chemical augmentation of colour, again, is the immediate consequence of continued excitation. The augmentation advances constantly and unremittingly, and it is to be observed that the increase of intenseness is most common on the *plus* side. Yellow iron ochre increases, as well by fire as by other operations, to a very strong red: massicot is increased to red lead, turbith to vermilion, which last attains a very high degree of the yellow-red. An intimate saturation of the metal by the acid, and its separation to infinity, take place together with the above effects.

521.

The augmentation on the *minus* side is less frequent; but we observe that the more pure and condensed the Prussian-blue or cobalt glass is prepared, the more readily it assumes a reddish hue and inclines to the violet.

522.

The French have a happy expression for the less perceptible tendency of yellow and blue towards red: they say the colour has "un œil de rouge," which we might perhaps express by a reddish glance (einen röthlichen blick).

XXXIX.

CULMINATION.*

523.

THIS is the consequence of still progressing augmentation. Red, in which neither yellow nor

---

* *Culmination*, the original word. It might have been ren-

blue is to be detected, here constitutes the acme.

524.

If we wish to select a striking example of a culmination on the *plus* side, we again find it in the coloured steel, which attains the bright red acme, and can be arrested at this point.

525.

Were we here to employ the terminology before proposed, we should say that the first oxydation produces yellow, the hyper-oxydation yellow-red ; that here a kind of maximum exists, and that then an ab-oxydation, and lastly a de-oxydation takes place.

526.

High degrees of oxydation produce a bright red. Gold in solution, precipitated by a solution of tin, appears bright red : oxyde of arsenic, in combination with sulphur, produces a ruby colour.

527.

How far, however, a kind of sub-oxydation may co-operate in some culminations, is matter for inquiry ; for an influence of alkalis on the

---

dered *maximum of colour*, but as the author supposes an *ascent* through yellow and blue to red, his meaning is better expressed by his own term.

yellow-red also appears to produce the culmination; the colour reaching the acme by being forced towards the *minus* side.

528.

The Dutch prepare a colour known by the name of vermilion, from the best Hungarian cinnabar, which exhibits the brightest yellow-red. This vermilion is still only a cinnabar, which, however, approximates the pure red, and it may be conjectured that alkalis are used to bring it nearer to the culminating point.

529.

Vegetable juices, treated in this way, offer very striking examples of the above effects. The colouring-matter of turmeric, annotto, dyer's saffron,* and other vegetables, being extracted with spirits of wine, exhibits tints of yellow, yellow-red, and hyacinth-red; these, by the admixture of alkalis, pass to the culminating point, and even beyond it to blue-red.

530.

No instance of a culmination on the *minus* side has come to my knowledge in the mineral and vegetable kingdoms. In the animal kingdom the juice of the murex is remarkable; of its augmentation and culmination on the *minus* side, we shall hereafter have occasion to speak.

---

* Curcuma, Bixa Orellana, Carthamus Tinctorius.

XL.

FLUCTUATION.

531.

THE mutability of colour is so great, that even those pigments, which may have been considered to be defined and arrested, still admit of slight variations on one side or the other. This mutability is most remarkable near the culminating point, and is effected in a very striking manner by the alternate employment of acids and alkalis.

532.

To express this appearance in dyeing, the French make use of the word " virer," to turn from one side to the other; they thus very adroitly convey an idea which others attempt to express by terms indicating the component hues.

533.

The effect produced with litmus is one of the most known and striking of this kind. This colouring substance is rendered red-blue by means of alkalis. The red-blue is very readily changed to red-yellow by means of acids, and again returns to its first state by again employing alkalis. The question whether a culminating point is to be discovered and arrested by

nice experiments, is left to those who are practised in these operations. Dyeing, especially
scarlet-dyeing, might afford a variety of examples of this fluctuation.

XLI.

PASSAGE THROUGH THE WHOLE SCALE.

534.

THE first excitation and gradual increase of
colour take place more on the *plus* than on the
minus side. So, also, in passing through the
whole scale, colour exhibits itself most on the
plus side.

535.

A passage of this kind, regular and evident to
the senses, from yellow through red to blue, is
apparent in the colouring of steel.

536.

The metals may be arrested at various points
of the colorific circle by various degrees and
kinds of oxydation.

537.

As they also appear green, a question arises
whether chemists know any instance in the

mineral kingdom of a constant transition from yellow, through green, to blue, and *vice versâ.* Oxyde of iron, melted with glass, produces first a green, and with a more powerful heat, a blue colour.

538.

We may here observe of green generally, that it appears, especially in an atomic sense, and certainly in a pure state, when we mix blue and yellow : but, again, an impure and dirty yellow soon gives us the impression of green ; yellow and black already produce green ; this, however, is owing to the affinity between black and blue. An imperfect yellow, such as that of sulphur, gives us the impression of a greenish hue : thus, again, an imperfect blue appears green. The green of wine bottles arises, it appears, from an imperfect union of the oxyde of iron with the glass. If we produce a more complete union by greater heat, a beautiful blue-glass is the result.

539.

From all this it appears that a certain chasm exists in nature between yellow and blue, the opposite characters of which, it is true, may be done away atomically by due immixture, and, thus combined, to green ; but the true reconciliation between yellow and blue, it seems, only takes place by means of red.

540.

The process, however, which appears unattainable in inorganic substances, we shall find to be possible when we turn our attention to organic productions ; for in these, the passage through the whole circle from yellow, through green and blue, to red, really takes place.

XLII.

INVERSION.

541.

AGAIN, an immediate inversion or change to the totally opposite hue, is a very remarkable appearance which sometimes occurs ; at present, we are merely enabled to adduce what follows.

542.

The mineral chameleon, a name which has been given to an oxyde of manganese, may be considered, in its perfectly dry state, as a green powder. If we strew it in water, the green colour displays itself very beautifully in the first moment of solution, but it changes presently to the bright red opposite to green, without any apparent intermediate state.

543.

The same occurs with the sympathetic ink, which may be considered a reddish liquid, but which, when dried by warmth, appears as a green colour on paper.

544.

In fact, this phenomenon appears to be owing to the conflict between a dry and moist state, as has been already observed, if we are not mistaken, by the chemists. We may look to the improvements of time to point out what may further be deduced from these phenomena, and to show what other facts they may be connected with.

XLIII.

FIXATION.

545.

MUTABLE as we have hitherto found colour to be, even as a substance, yet under certain circumstances it may at last be fixed.

546.

There are bodies capable of being entirely converted into colouring matter : here it may be said that the colour fixes itself in its own substance, stops at a certain point, and is there defined. Such colouring substances are found throughout nature ; the vegetable world affords a great quantity of examples, among which some are particularly distinguished, and may be considered as the representatives of the rest; such as, on the active side, madder, on the passive side, indigo.

547.

In order to make these materials available in use, it is necessary that the colouring quality in them should be intimately condensed, and the tinging substance refined, practically speaking, to an infinite divisibility. This is accomplished in various ways, and particularly by the well-known means of fermentation and decomposition.

548.

These colouring substances now attach themselves again to other bodies. Thus, in the mineral kingdom they adhere to earths and metallic oxydes ; they unite in melting with glasses ; and in this case, as the light is transmitted through them, they appear in the greatest beauty, while an eternal duration may be ascribed to them.

549.

They fasten on vegetable and animal bodies with more or less power, and remain more or less permanently; partly owing to their nature,—as yellow, for instance, is more evanescent than blue,—or owing to the nature of the substance on which they appear. They last less in vegetable than in animal substances, and even within this latter kingdom there are again varieties. Hemp or cotton threads, silk or wool, exhibit very different relations to colouring substances.

550.

Here comes into the account the important operation of employing mordants, which may be considered as the intermediate agents between the colour and the recipient substance; various works on dyeing speak of this circumstantially. Suffice it to have alluded to processes by means of which the colour retains a permanency only to be destroyed with the substance, and which may even increase in brightness and beauty by use.

XLIV.

INTERMIXTURE, REAL.

551.

EVERY intermixture pre-supposes a specific state of colour; and thus when we speak of intermixture, we here understand it in an atomic sense. We must first have before us certain bodies arrested at any given point of the colorific circle, before we can produce gradations by their union.

552.

Yellow, blue, and red, may be assumed as pure elementary colours, already existing ; from these, violet, orange, and green, are the simplest combined results.

553.

Some persons have taken much pains to define these intermixtures more accurately, by relations of number, measure, and weight, but nothing very profitable has been thus accomplished.

554.

Painting consists, strictly speaking, in the intermixture of such specific colouring bodies and their infinite possible combinations—combinations which can only be appreciated by the nicest, most practised eye, and only accomplished under its influence.

555.

The intimate combination of these ingredients is effected, in the first instance, through the most perfect comminution of the material by means of grinding, washing, &c., as well as by vehicles or liquid mediums which hold together the pulverized substance, and combine organically, as it were, the unorganic ; such are the oils, resins, &c.—Note V.

556.

If all the colours are mixed together they retain their general character as σκιερὸν, and as they are no longer seen next each other, no completeness, no harmony, is experienced ; the result is grey, which, like apparent colour, always appears somewhat darker than white, and somewhat lighter than black.

557.

This grey may be produced in various ways. By mixing yellow and blue to an emerald green, and then adding pure red, till all three neutralize each other ; or, by placing the primitive and intermediate colours next each other in a certain proportion, and afterwards mixing them.

558.

That all the colours mixed together produce white, is an absurdity which people have credulously been accustomed to repeat for a century, in opposition to the evidence of their senses.

559.

Colours when mixed together retain their

original darkness. The darker the colours, the darker will be the grey resulting from their union, till at last this grey approaches black. The lighter the colours the lighter will be the grey, which at last approaches white.

XLV.

INTERMIXTURE, APPARENT.

560.

THE intermixture, which is only apparent, naturally invites our attention in connexion with the foregoing ; it is in many respects important, and, indeed, the intermixture which we have distinguished as real, might be considered as merely apparent. For the elements of which the combined colour consists are only too small to be considered as distinct parts. Yellow and blue powders mingled together appear green to the naked eye, but through a magnifying glass we can still perceive yellow and blue distinct from each other. Thus yellow and blue stripes seen at a distance, present a green mass; the same observation is applicable with regard to the intermixture of other specific colours.

561.

In the description of our apparatus we shall

have occasion to mention the wheel by means of which the apparent intermixture is produced by rapid movement. Various colours are arranged near each other round the edge of a disk, which is made to revolve with velocity, and thus by having several such disks ready, every possible intermixture can be presented to the eye, as well as the mixture of all colours to grey, darker or lighter, according to the depth of the tints as above explained.

562.

Physiological colours admit, in like manner, of being mixed with others. If, for example, we produce the blue shadow (65) on a light yellow paper, the surface will appear green. The same happens with regard to the other colours if the necessary preparations are attended to.

563.

If, when the eye is impressed with visionary images that last for a while, we look on coloured surfaces, an intermixture also takes place ; the spectrum is determined to a new colour which is composed of the two.

564.

Physical colours also admit of combination. Here might be adduced the experiments in which many-coloured images are seen through the prism, as we have before shown in detail (258, 284).

565.

Those who have prosecuted these inquiries have, however, paid most attention to the appearances which take place when the prismatic colours are thrown on coloured surfaces.

566.

What is seen under these circumstances is quite simple. In the first place it must be remembered that the prismatic colours are much more vivid than the colours of the surface on which they are thrown. Secondly, we have to consider that the prismatic colours may be either homogeneous or heterogeneous, with the recipient surface. In the former case the surface deepens and enhances them, and is itself enhanced in return, as a coloured stone is displayed by a similarly coloured foil. In the opposite case each vitiates, disturbs, and destroys the other.

567.

These experiments may be repeated with coloured glasses, by causing the sun-light to shine through them on coloured surfaces. In every instance similar results will appear.

568.

The same effect takes place when we look on coloured objects through coloured glasses ; the colours being thus according to the same conditions enhanced, subdued, or neutralized.

569

If the prismatic colours are suffered to pass through coloured glasses, the appearances that take place are perfectly analogous ; in these cases more or less force, more or less light and dark, the clearness and cleanness of the glass are all to be allowed for, as they produce many delicate varieties of effect : these will not escape the notice of every accurate observer who takes sufficient interest in the inquiry to go through the experiments.

570.

It is scarcely necessary to mention that several coloured glasses, as well as oiled or transparent papers, placed over each other, may be made to produce and exhibit every kind of intermixture at pleasure.

571.

Lastly, the operation of glazing in painting belongs to this kind of intermixture ; by this means a much more refined union may be produced than that arising from the mechanical, atomic mixture which is commonly employed.

XLVI.

572.

HAVING now provided the colouring materials, as before shown, a further question arises how to communicate these to colourless substances : the answer is of the greatest importance from the connexion of the object with the ordinary wants of men, with useful purposes, and with commercial and technical interests.

573.

Here, again, the dark quality of every colour again comes into the account. From a yellow that is very near to white, through orange, and the hue of minium to pure red and carmine, through all gradations of violet to the deepest blue which is almost identified with black, colour still increases in darkness. Blue once defined, admits of being diluted, made light, united with yellow, and then, as green, it approaches the light side of the scale : but this is by no means according to its own nature.

574.

In the physiological colours we have already seen that they are less than the light, inasmuch as they are a repetition of an impression of light, nay, at last they leave this impression quite as a dark. In physical experiments the employment of semi-transparent mediums, the effect of semi-transparent accessory images, taught us that in such cases we have to do with a subdued light, with a transition to darkness.

575.

In treating of the chemical origin of pigments we found that the same effect was produced on the very first excitement. The yellow tinge which mantles over the steel, already darkens the shining surface. In changing white lead to massicot it is evident that the yellow is darker than white.

576.

This process is in the highest degree delicate; the growing intenseness, as it still increases, tinges the substance more and more intimately and powerfully, and thus indicates the extreme fineness, and the infinite divisibility of the coloured atoms.

577.

The colours which approach the dark side, and consequently, blue in particular, can be made to approximate to black; in fact, a very perfect Prussian blue, or an indigo acted on by vitriolic acid appears almost as a black.

578.

A remarkable appearance may be here adverted to ; pigments, in their deepest and most condensed state, especially those produced from the vegetable kingdom, such as the indigo just mentioned, or madder carried to its intensest hue, no longer show their own colour; on the contrary, a decided metallic shine is seen on their surface, in which the physiological compensatory colour appears.

579.

All good indigo exhibits a copper-colour in its fracture, a circumstance attended to, as a known characteristic, in trade. Again, the indigo which has been acted on by sulphuric acid, if thickly laid on, or suffered to dry so that neither white paper nor the porcelain can appear through, exhibits a colour approaching to orange.

580.

The bright red Spanish rouge, probably prepared from madder, exhibits on its surface a perfectly green, metallic shine. If this colour, or the blue before mentioned, is washed with a pencil on porcelain or paper, it is seen in its real state owing to the bright ground shining through.

581.

Coloured liquids appear black when no light

is transmitted through them, as we may easily see in cubic tin vessels with glass bottoms. In these every transparent-coloured infusion will appear black and colourless if we place a black surface under them.

582.

If we contrive that the image of a flame be reflected from the bottom, the image will appear coloured. If we lift up the vessel and suffer the transmitted light to fall on white paper under it, the colour of the liquid appears on the paper. Every light ground seen through such a coloured medium exhibits the colour of the medium.

583.

Thus every colour, in order to be seen, must have a light within or behind it. Hence the lighter and brighter the grounds are, the more brilliant the colours appear. If we pass lac-varnish over a shining white metal surface, as the so-called foils are prepared, the splendor of the colour is displayed by this internally re-flected light as powerfully as in any prismatic experiment; nay, the force of the physical co-lours is owing principally to the circumstance that light is always acting with and behind them.

584.

Lichtenberg, who of necessity followed the

received theory, owing to the time and circumstances in which he lived, was yet too good an observer, and too acute not to explain and classify, after his fashion, what was evident to his senses. He says, in the preface to Delaval, " It appears to me also, on other grounds, probable, that our organ, in order to be impressed by a colour, must at the same time be impressed by all light (white)."

585.

To procure white as a ground is the chief business of the dyer. Every colour may be easily communicated to colourless earths, especially to alum: but the dyer has especially to do with animal and vegetable products as the ground of his operations.

586.

Everything living tends to colour—to local, specific colour, to effect, to opacity—pervading the minutest atoms. Everything in which life is extinct approximates to white (494), to the abstract, the general state, to clearness,* to transparence.

587.

How this is put in practice in technical operations remains to be adverted to in the chapter on the privation of colour. With regard to the

---

* Verklärung, literally *clarification*.

communication of colour, we have especially to bear in mind that animals and vegetables, in a living state, produce colours, and hence their substances, if deprived of colours, can the more readily re-assume them.

XLVII.

COMMUNICATION, APPARENT.

588.

THE communication of colours, real as well as apparent, corresponds, as may easily be seen, with their intermixture: we need not, therefore, repeat what has been already sufficiently entered into.

589.

Yet we may here point out more circumstantially the importance of an apparent communication which takes place by means of reflection. This phenomenon is well known, but still it is pregnant with inferences, and is of the greatest importance both to the investigator of nature and to the painter.

590.

Let a surface coloured with any one of the positive colours be placed in the sun, and let its reflection be thrown on other colourless objects. This reflection is a kind of subdued light, a half-light, a half-shadow, which, in a subdued state, reflects the colours in question.

591.

If this reflection acts on light surfaces, it is so far overpowered that we can scarcely perceive the colour which accompanies it; but if it acts on shadowed portions, a sort of magical union takes place with the σκιερῷ. Shadow is the proper element of colour, and in this case a subdued colour approaches it, lighting up, tinging, and enlivening it. And thus arises an appearance, as powerful as agreeable, which may render the most pleasing service to the painter who knows how to make use of it. These are the types of the so-called reflexes, which were only noticed late in the history of art, and which have been too seldom employed in their full variety.

592.

The schoolmen called these colours *colores nationales* and *intentionales*, and the history of the doctrine of colours will generally show that the old inquirers already observed the phenomena well enough, and knew how to distinguish them properly, although the whole method of treating such subjects is very different from ours.

XLVIII.

593.

COLOUR may be extracted from substances, whether they possess it naturally or by communication, in various ways. We have thus the power to remove it intentionally for a useful purpose, but, on the other hand, it often flies contrary to our wish.

594.

Not only are the elementary earths in their natural state white, but vegetable and animal substances can be reduced to a white state without disturbing their texture. A pure white is very desirable for various uses, as in the instance of our preferring to use linen and cotton stuffs uncoloured. In like manner some silk stuffs, paper, and other substances, are the more agreeable the whiter they can be. Again, the chief basis of all dyeing consists in white grounds. For these reasons manufacturers, aided by accident and contrivance, have devoted themselves assiduously to discover means of extracting colour : infinite experiments have been made in connexion with this object, and many important facts have been arrived at.

595.

It is in accomplishing this entire extraction of colour that the operation of bleaching consists, which is very generally practised empirically or methodically. We will here shortly state the leading principles.

596.

Light is considered as one of the first means of extracting colour from substances, and not only the sun-light, but the mere powerless day-light : for as both lights—the direct light of the sun, as well as the derived light of the sky— kindle Bologna phosphorus, so both act on coloured surfaces. Whether the light attacks the colour allied to it, and, as it were, kindles and consumes it, thus reducing the definite quality to a general state, or whether some other operation, unknown to us, takes place, it is clear that light exercises a great power on coloured surfaces, and bleaches them more or less. Here, however, the different colours exhibit a different degree of durability; yellow, especially if prepared from certain materials, is, in this case, the first to fly.

597.

Not only light, but air, and especially water, act strongly in destroying colour. It has been even asserted that thread, well soaked and spread on the grass at night, bleaches better than that which is exposed, after soaking, to the sun-light. Thus, in this case, water proves to be a solving and conducting agent, removing the accidental quality, and restoring the substance to a general or colourless state.

598.

The extraction of colour is also effected by re-agents. Spirits of wine has a peculiar tendency to attract the juice which tinges plants, and becomes coloured with it often in a very permanent manner. Sulphuric acid is very efficient in removing colour, especially from wool and silk, and every one is acquainted with the use of sulphur vapours in bleaching.

599.

The strongest acids have been recommended more recently as more expeditious agents in bleaching.

600.

The alkaline re-agents produce the same effects by contrary means—lixiviums alone, oils and fat combined with lixiviums to soap, and so forth.

601.

Before we dismiss this subject, we observe

that it may be well worth while to make certain
delicate experiments as to how far light and air
exhibit their action in the removal of colour.   It
might be possible to expose coloured substances
to the light under glass bells, without air, or
filled with common or particular kinds of air.
The colours might be those of known fugacity,
and it might be observed whether any of the
volatilized colour attached itself to the glass or
was otherwise perceptible as a deposit or preci-
pitate; whether, again, in such a case, this appearance would be perfectly like that which had
gradually ceased to be visible, or whether it had
suffered any change.   Skilful experimentalists
might devise various contrivances with a view
to such researches.

602.

Having thus first considered the operations of
nature as subservient to our purposes, we add a
few observations on the modes in which they
act against us.

603.

The art of painting is so circumstanced that
the most beautiful results of mind and labour are
altered and destroyed in various ways by time.
Hence great pains have been always taken to
find durable pigments, and so to unite them
with each other and with their ground, that their

permanency might be further insured. The technical history of the schools of painting affords sufficient information on this point.

604.

We may here, too, mention a minor art, to which, in relation to dyeing, we are much indebted, namely, the weaving of tapestry. As the manufacturers were enabled to imitate the most delicate shades of pictures, and hence often brought the most variously coloured materials together, it was soon observed that the colours were not all equally durable, but that some faded from the tapestry more quickly than others. Hence the most diligent efforts were made to ensure an equal permanency to all the colours and their gradations. This object was especially promoted in France, under Colbert, whose regulations to this effect constitute an epoch in the history of dyeing. The gay dye which only aimed at a transient beauty, was practised by a particular guild. On the other hand, great pains were taken to define the technical processes which promised durability.

And thus, after considering the artificial extraction, the evanescence, and the perishable nature of brilliant appearances of colour, we are again returned to the desideratum of permanency.

XLIX.

NOMENCLATURE.

605.

AFTER what has been adduced respecting the origin, the increase, and the affinity of colours, we may be better enabled to judge what nomenclature would be desirable in future, and what might be retained of that hitherto in use.

606.

The nomenclature of colours, like all other modes of designation, but especially those employed to distinguish the objects of sense, proceeded in the first instance from particular to general, and from general back again to particular terms. The name of the species became a generic name to which the individual was again referred.

607.

This method might have been followed in consequence of the mutability and uncertainty of ancient modes of expression, especially since, in the early ages, more reliance may be supposed to have been placed on the vivid impressions of sense. The qualities of objects were described indistinctly, because they were impressed clearly on every imagination.

608.

The pure chromatic circle was limited, it is true; but, specific as it was, it appears to have been applied to innumerable objects, while it was circumscribed by qualifying characteristics. If we take a glance at the copiousness of the Greek and Roman terms, we shall perceive how mutable the words were, and how easily each was adapted to almost every point in the colorific circle.—Note W.

609.

In modern ages terms for many new gradations were introduced in consequence of the various operations of dyeing. Even the colours of fashion and their designations, represented an endless series of specific hues. We shall, on occasion, employ the chromatic terminology of modern languages, whence it will appear that the aim has gradually been to introduce more exact definitions, and to individualise and arrest a fixed and specific state by language equally distinct.

610.

With regard to the German terminology, it has the advantage of possessing four monosyllabic names no longer to be traced to their origin, viz., yellow (Gelb), blue, red, green. They represent the most general idea of colour to the imagination, without reference to any very specific modification.

611.

If we were to add two other qualifying terms
to each of these four, as thus—red-yellow, and
yellow-red, red-blue and blue-red, yellow-green
and green-yellow, blue-green and green-blue,*
we should express the gradations of the chromatic circle with sufficient distinctness; and if
we were to add the designations of light and
dark, and again define, in some measure, the
degree of purity or its opposite by the mono-
syllables black, white, grey, brown, we should
have a tolerably sufficient range of expressions
to describe the ordinary appearances presented
to us, without troubling ourselves whether they
were produced dynamically or atomically.

612.

The specific and proper terms in use might,
however, still be conveniently employed, and we
have thus made use of the words orange and
violet. We have in like manner employed the
word "*purpur*" to designate a pure central red,
because the secretion of the murex or "*purpura*"
is to be carried to the highest point of culmination by the action of the sun-light on fine linen
saturated with the juice.

---

* This description is suffered to remain because it accounts for
the terminology employed throughout.—T.

L.

613.

THE colours of minerals are all of a chemical nature, and thus the modes in which they are produced may be explained in a general way by what has been said on the subject of chemical colours.

614.

Among the external characteristics of minerals, the description of their colours occupies the first place; and great pains have been taken, in the spirit of modern times, to define and arrest every such appearance exactly : by this means, however, new difficulties, it appears to us, have been created, which occasion no little inconvenience in practice.

615.

It is true, this precision, when we reflect how it arose, carries with it its own excuse. The painter has at all times been privileged in the use of colours. The few specific hues, in themselves, admitted of no change; but from these, innumerable gradations were artificially produced which imitated the surface of natural objects. It was, therefore, not to be wondered at that these gradations should also be adopted as criterions, and that the artist should be invited to produce tinted patterns with which the objects of nature might be compared, and according to which they were to receive their designations.

616.

But, after all, the terminology of colours which has been introduced in mineralogy, is open to many objections. The terms, for instance, have not been borrowed from the mineral kingdom, as was possible enough in most cases, but from all kinds of visible objects. Too many specific terms have been adopted ; and in seeking to establish new definitions by combining these, the nomenclators have not reflected that they thus altogether efface the image from the imagination, and the idea from the understanding. Lastly, these individual designations of colours, employed to a certain extent as elementary definitions, are not arranged in the best manner as regards their respective derivation from each other : hence, the scholar must learn every single designation, and impress an almost lifeless but positive language on his memory. The further consideration of this would be too foreign to our present subject.*

---

* These remarks have reference to the German mineralogical terminology.—T.

LI.

PLANTS.

617.

THE colours of organic bodies in general may be considered as a higher kind of chemical operation, for which reason the ancients employed the word concoction, πέψις, to designate the process. All the elementary colours, as well as the combined and secondary hues, appear on the surface of organic productions, while on the other hand, the interior, if not colourless, appears, strictly speaking, negative when brought to the light. As we propose to communicate our views respecting organic nature, to a certain extent, in another place, we only insert here what has been before connected with the doctrine of colours, while it may serve as an introduction to the further consideration of the views alluded to : and first, of plants.

618.

Seeds, bulbs, roots, and what is generally shut out from the light, or immediately surrounded by the earth, appear, for the most part, white.

619.

Plants reared from seed, in darkness, are white, or approaching to yellow. Light, on the other hand, in acting on their colours, acts at the same time on their form.

620.

Plants which grow in darkness make, it is true, long shoots from joint to joint : but the stems between two joints are thus longer than they should be; no side stems are produced, and the metamorphosis of the plant does not take place.

621.

Light, on the other hand, places it at once in an active state; the plant appears green, and the course of the metamorphosis proceeds uninterruptedly to the period of reproduction.

622.

We know that the leaves of the stem are only preparations and pre-significations of the instruments of florification and fructification, and accordingly we can already see colours in the leaves of the stem which, as it were, announce the flower from afar, as is the case in the amaranthus.

623.

There are white flowers whose petals have wrought or refined themselves to the greatest purity ; there are coloured ones, in which the elementary hues may be said to fluctuate to and fro. There are some which, in tending to the higher state, have only partially emancipated themselves from the green of the plant.

624.

Flowers of the same genus, and even of the same kind, are found of all colours. Roses, and particularly mallows, for example, vary through a great portion of the colorific circle from white to yellow, then through red-yellow to bright red, and from thence to the darkest hue it can exhibit as it approaches blue.

625.

Others already begin from a higher degree in the scale, as, for example, the poppy, which is yellow-red in the first instance, and which afterwards approaches a violet hue.

626.

Yet the same colours in species, varieties, and even in families and classes, if not constant, are still predominant, especially the yellow colour: blue is throughout rarer.

627.

A process somewhat similar takes place in the juicy capsule of the fruit, for it increases in colour from the green, through the yellowish

and yellow, up to the highest red, the colour of
the rind thus indicating the degree of ripeness.
Some are coloured all round, some only on the
sunny side, in which last case the augmentation
of the yellow into red,— the gradations crowd-
ing in and upon each other,— may be very well
observed.

628.

Many fruits, too, are coloured internally;
pure red juices, especially, are common.

629.

The colour which is found superficially in the
flower and penetratingly in the fruit, spreads
itself through all the remaining parts, colouring
the roots and the juices of the stem, and this
with a very rich and powerful hue.

630.

So, again, the colour of the wood passes from
yellow through the different degrees of red up
to pure red and on to brown.   Blue woods are
unknown to me; and thus in this degree of organisation the active side exhibits itself powerfully, although both principles appear balanced
in the general green of the plant.

631.

We have seen above that the germ pushing

from the earth is generally white and yellowish, but that by means of the action of light and air it acquires a green colour. The same happens with young leaves of trees, as may be seen, for example, in the birch, the young leaves of which are yellowish, and if boiled, yield a beautiful yellow juice : afterwards they become greener, while the leaves of other trees become gradually blue-green.

632.

Thus a yellow ingredient appears to belong more essentially to leaves than a blue one ; for this last vanishes in the autumn, and the yellow of the leaf appears changed to a brown colour. Still more remarkable, however, are the particular cases where leaves in autumn again become pure yellow, and others increase to the brightest red.

633.

Other plants, again, may, by artificial treatment be entirely converted to a colouring matter, which is as fine, active, and infinitely divisible as any other. Indigo and madder, with which so much is effected, are examples : lichens are also used for dyes.

634.

To this fact another stands immediately opposed; we can, namely, extract the colouring part of plants, and, as it were, exhibit it apart, while the organisation does not on this account appear to suffer at all. The colours of flowers may be extracted by spirits of wine, and tinge it; the petals meanwhile becoming white.

635.

There are various modes of acting on flowers and their juices by re-agents. This has been done by Boyle in many experiments. Roses are bleached by sulphur, and may be restored to their first state by other acids; roses are turned green by the smoke of tobacco.

LII.

WORMS, INSECTS, FISHES.

636.

With regard to creatures belonging to the lower degrees of organisation, we may first observe that worms, which live in the earth and remain in darkness and cold moisture, are imperfectly negatively coloured; worms bred in warm moisture and darkness are colourless; light seems expressly necessary to the definite exhibition of colour.

637.

Creatures which live in water, which, although a very dense medium, suffers sufficient light to pass through it, appear more or less coloured. Zoophytes, which appear to animate the purest calcareous earth, are mostly white; yet we find corals deepened into the most beautiful yellow-red: in other cells of worms this colour increases nearly to bright red.

638.

The shells of the crustaceous tribe are beautifully designed and coloured, yet it is to be remarked that neither land-snails nor the shells of crustacea of fresh water, are adorned with such bright colours as those of the sea.

639.

In examining shells, particularly such as are spiral, we find that a series of animal organs, similar to each other, must have moved increasingly forward, and in turning on an axis produced the shell in a series of chambers, divisions, tubes, and prominences, according to a plan for ever growing larger. We remark, however, that a tinging juice must have accompanied the development of these organs, a juice which marked the surface of the shell, probably through the immediate co-operation of the sea-water, with coloured lines, points, spots, and shadings:

this must have taken place at regular intervals, and thus left the indications of increasing growth lastingly on the exterior; meanwhile the interior is generally found white or only faintly coloured.

640.

That such a juice is to be found in shell-fish is, besides, sufficiently proved by experience; for the creatures furnish it in its liquid and colouring state: the juice of the ink-fish is an example. But a much stronger is exhibited in the red juice found in many shell-fish, which was so famous in ancient times, and has been employed with advantage by the moderns. There is, it appears, in the entrails of many of the crustaceous tribe a certain vessel which is filled with a red juice; this contains a very strong and durable colouring substance, so much so that the entire creature may be crushed and boiled, and yet out of this broth a sufficiently strong tinging liquid may be extracted. But the little vessel filled with colour may be separated from the animal, by which means of course a concentrated juice is gained.

641.

This juice has the property that when exposed to light and air it appears first yellowish, then greenish; it then passes to blue, then to a violet, gradually growing redder ; and lastly, by the action of the sun, and especially if transferred to cambric, it assumes a pure bright red colour.

642.

Thus we should here have an augmentation, even to culmination, on the *minus* side, which we cannot easily meet with in inorganic cases ; indeed, we might almost call this example a passage through the whole scale, and we are persuaded that by due experiments the entire revolution of the circle might really be effected, for there is no doubt that by acids duly employed, the pure red may be pushed beyond the culminating point towards scarlet.

643.

This juice appears on the one hand to be connected with the phenomena of reproduction, eggs being found, the embryos of future shellfish, which contain a similar colouring principle. On the other hand, in animals ranking higher in the scale of being, the secretion appears to bear some relation to the development of the blood. The blood exhibits similar properties in regard to colour ; in its thinnest state it appears yellow ; thickened, as it is found in the veins, it appears red ; while the arterial blood exhibits a brighter red, probably owing to the oxydation which takes place by means of breathing. The venous blood approaches more to violet, and by this mutability denotes the tendency to that augmentation and progression which are now familiar to us.

644.

Before we quit the element whence we derived the foregoing examples, we may add a few observations on fishes, whose scaly surface is coloured either altogether in stripes, or in spots, and still oftener exhibits a certain iridescent appearance, indicating the affinity of the scales with the coats of shell-fish, mother-of-pearl, and even the pearl itself. At the same time it should not be forgotten that warmer climates, the influence of which extends to the watery regions, produce, embellish, and enhance these colours in fishes in a still greater degree.

645.

In Otaheite, Forster observed fishes with beautifully iridescent surfaces, and this effect was especially apparent at the moment when the fish died. We may here call to mind the hues of the chameleon, and other similar appearances; for when similar facts are presented together, we are better enabled to trace them.

646.

Lastly, although not strictly in the same

class, the iridescent appearance of certain mo-
luscæ may be mentioned, as well as the phos-
phorescence which, in some marine creatures,
it is said becomes iridescent just before it
vanishes.

647.

We now turn our attention to those creatures
which belong to light, air and dry warmth, and
it is here that we first find ourselves in the
living region of colours. Here, in exquisitely
organised parts, the elementary colours present
themselves in their greatest purity and beauty.
They indicate, however, that the creatures they
adorn, are still low in the scale of organisation, precisely because these colours can thus
appear, as it were, unwrought. Here, too,
heat seems to contribute much to their development.

648.

We find insects which may be considered
altogether as concentrated colouring matter;
among these, the cochineals especially are celebrated; with regard to these we observe that
their mode of settling on vegetables, and even
nestling in them, at the same time produces
those excrescences which are so useful as mordants in fixing colours.

649.

But the power of colour, accompanied by regular organisation, exhibits itself in the most striking manner in those insects which require a perfect metamorphosis for their development —in scarabæi, and especially in butterflies.

650.

These last, which might be called true productions of light and air, often exhibit the most beautiful colours, even in their chrysalis state, indicating the future colours of the butterfly ; a consideration which, if pursued further hereafter, must undoubtedly afford a satisfactory insight into many a secret of organised being.

651.

If, again, we examine the wings of the butterfly more accurately, and in its net-like web discover the rudiments of an arm, and observe further the mode in which this, as it were, flattened arm is covered with tender plumage and constituted an organ of flying ; we believe we recognise a law according to which the great variety of tints is regulated. This will be a subject for further investigation hereafter.

652.

That, again, heat generally has an influence

on the size of the creature, on the accomplish-
ment of the form, and on the greater beauty of
the colours, hardly needs to be remarked.

LIII.

BIRDS.

653.

THE more we approach the higher organisations,
the more it becomes necessary to limit ourselves
to a few passing observations ; for all the natural
conditions of such organised beings are the result of so many premises, that, without having
at least hinted at these, our remarks would only
appear daring, and at the same time insufficient.

654.

We find in plants, that the consummate
flower and fruit are, as it were, rooted in the
stem, and that they are nourished by more perfect juices than the original roots first afforded ;
we remark, too, that parasitical plants which
derive their support from organised structures,
exhibit themselves especially endowed as to
their energies and qualities. We might in some
sense compare the feathers of birds with plants
of this description ; the feathers spring up as a
last structural result from the surface of a body

which has yet much in reserve for the completion of the external economy, and thus are very
richly endowed organs.

655.

The quills not only grow proportionally to a
considerable size, but are throughout branched,
by which means they properly become feathers,
and many of these feathered branches are again
subdivided ; thus, again, recalling the structure
of plants.

656.

The feathers are very different in shape and
size, but each still remains the same organ,
forming and transforming itself according to
the constitution of the part of the body from
which it springs.

657.

With the form, the colour also becomes
changed, and a certain law regulates the general
order of hues as well as that particular dis-
tribution by which a single feather becomes
party coloured. It is from this that all combination of variegated plumage arises, and
whence, at last, the eyes in the peacock's tail
are produced. It is a result similar to that which
we have already unfolded in treating of the
metamorphosis of plants, and which we shall
take an early opportunity to prove.

658.

Although time and circumstances compel us here to pass by this organic law, yet we are bound to refer to the chemical operations which commonly exhibit themselves in the tinting of feathers in a mode now sufficiently known to us.

659.

Plumage is of all colours, yet, on the whole, yellow deepening to red is commoner than blue.

660.

The operation of light on the feathers and their colours, is to be remarked in all cases. Thus, for example, the feathers on the breast of certain parrots, are strictly yellow; the scale-like anterior portion, which is acted on by the light, is deepened from yellow to red. The breast of such a bird appears bright-red, but if we blow into the feathers the yellow appears.

661.

The exposed portion of the feathers is in all cases very different from that which, in a quiet state, is covered; it is only the exposed portion, for instance, in ravens, which exhibits the iridescent appearance; the covered portion does not : from which indication, the feathers of the tail when ruffled together, may be at once placed in the natural order again.

LIV.

MAMMALIA AND HUMAN BEINGS.

662.

HERE the elementary colours begin to leave us altogether. We are arrived at the highest degree of the scale, and shall not dwell on its characteristics long.

663.

An animal of this class is distinguished among the examples of organised being. Every thing that exhibits itself about him is living. Of the internal structure we do not speak, but confine ourselves briefly to the surface. The hairs are already distinguished from feathers, inasmuch as they belong more to the skin, inasmuch as they are simple, thread-like, not branched. They are however, like feathers, shorter, longer, softer, and firmer, colourless or coloured, and all this in conformity to laws which might be defined.

664.

White and black, yellow, yellow-red and brown, alternate in various modifications, but they never appear in such a state as to remind us of the elementary hues. On the contrary, they are all broken colours subdued by organic concoction, and thus denote, more or less, the perfection of life in the being they belong to.

665.

One of the most important considerations connected with morphology, so far as it relates to surfaces, is this, that even in quadrupeds the spots of the skin have a relation with the parts underneath them. Capriciously as nature here appears, on a hasty examination, to operate, she nevertheless consistently observes a secret law. The development and application of this, it is true, are reserved only for accurate and careful investigation and sincere co-operation.

666.

If in some animals portions appear variegated with positive colours, this of itself shows how far such creatures are removed from a perfect organisation ; for, it may be said, the nobler a creature is, the more all the mere material of which he is composed, is disguised by being wrought together ; the more essentially his surface corresponds with the internal organisation, the less can it exhibit the elementary colours. Where all tends to make up a perfect whole, any detached specific developments cannot take place.

667.

Of man we have little to say, for he is entirely distinct from the general physiological results of which we now treat. So much in this case is in affinity with the internal structure, that the surface can only be sparingly endowed.

668.

When we consider that brutes are rather en-cumbered than advantageously provided with intercutaneous muscles; when we see that much that is superfluous tends to the surface, as, for instance, large ears and tails, as well as hair, manes, tufts; we see that nature, in such cases, had much to give away and to lavish.

669.

On the contrary, the general surface of the human form is smooth and clean, and thus in the most perfect examples the beautiful forms are apparent; for it may be remarked in pass-ing, that a superfluity of hair on the chest, arms, and lower limbs, rather indicates weakness than strength. Poets only have sometimes been in-duced, probably by the example of the ferine nature, so strong in other respects, to extol similar attributes in their rough heroes.

670.

But we have here chiefly to speak of colour, and observe that the colour of the human skin, in all its varieties, is never an elementary colour, but presents, by means of organic concoction, a highly complicated result.—Note X.

671.

That the colour of the skin and hair has relation with the differences of character, is beyond question ; and we are led to conjecture that the circumstance of one or other organic system predominating, produces the varieties we see. A similar hypothesis may be applied to nations, in which case it might perhaps be observed, that certain colours correspond with certain confirmations, which has always been observed of the negro physiognomy.

672.

Lastly, we might here consider the problematical question, whether all human forms and hues are not equally beautiful, and whether custom and self-conceit are not the causes why one is preferred to another? We venture, however, after what has been adduced, to assert that the white man, that is, he whose surface varies from white to reddish, yellowish, brownish, in short, whose surface appears most neutral in hue and least inclines to any particular or positive colour, is the most beautiful. On the same principle a similar point of perfection in human conformation may be defined hereafter, when the question relates to form. We do not imagine that this long-disputed question is to be thus, once for all, settled, for there are persons enough who have reason to leave this significancy of the exterior in doubt ; but we thus express a conclusion, derived from observation and reflection, such as might suggest itself to a mind aiming at a satisfactory decision. We subjoin a few observations connected with the elementary chemical doctrine of colours.—Note Y.

LV.

PHYSICAL AND CHEMICAL EFFECTS OF THE TRANSMISSION OF LIGHT THROUGH COLOURED MEDIUMS.

673.

THE physical and chemical effects of colourless light are known, so that it is unnecessary here to describe them at length. Colourless light exhibits itself under various conditions as exciting warmth, as imparting a luminous quality to certain bodies, as promoting oxydation and de-oxydation. In the modes and degrees of these effects many varieties take place, but no difference is found indicating a principle of contrast such as we find in the transmission of coloured light. We proceed briefly to advert to this.

674.

Let the temperature of a dark room be observed by means of a very sensible air-thermometer; if the bulb is then brought to the direct sun light as it shines into the room, nothing is more natural than that the fluid should indicate a much higher degree of warmth. If upon this we interpose coloured glasses, it follows again quite naturally that the degree of warmth must be lowered ; first, because the operation of the direct light is already somewhat impeded by the glass, and again, more especially, because a coloured glass, as a dark medium, admits less light through it.

675.

But here a difference in the excitation of warmth exhibits itself to the attentive observer, according to the colour of the glass. The yellow and the yellow-red glasses produce a higher temperature than the blue and blue-red, the difference being considerable.

676.

This experiment may be made with the prismatic spectrum. The temperature of the room being first remarked on the thermometer, the blue coloured light is made to fall on the bulb, when a somewhat higher degree of warmth is exhibited, which still increases as the other colours are gradually brought to act on the mercury. If the experiment is made with the water-prism, so that the white light can be retained in the centre, this, refracted indeed, but not yet coloured light, is the warmest; the other colours, stand in relation to each other as before.

677.

As we here merely describe, without undertaking to deduce or explain this phenomenon, we only remark in passing, that the pure light is by no means abruptly and entirely at an end with the red division in the spectrum, but that a refracted light is still to be observed deviating from its course and, as it were, insinuating itself beyond the prismatic image, so that on closer examination it will hardly be found necessary to take refuge in invisible rays and their refraction.

678.

The communication of light by means of coloured mediums exhibits the same difference. The light communicates itself to Bologna phosphorus through blue and violet glasses, but by no means through yellow and yellow-red glasses. It has been even remarked that the phosphori which have been rendered luminous under violet and blue glasses, become sooner extinguished when afterwards placed under yellow and yellow-red glasses than those which have been suffered to remain in a dark room without any further influence.

679.

These experiments, like the foregoing, may also be made by means of the prismatic spectrum, when the same results take place.

680.

To ascertain the effect of coloured light on oxydation and de-oxydation, the following means may be employed:—Let moist, perfectly white muriate of silver* be spread on a strip of paper; place it in the light, so that it may become to a certain degree grey, and then cut it in three portions. Of these, one may be preserved in a book, as a specimen of this state; let another be placed under a yellow-red, and the third under a blue-red glass. The last will become a darker grey, and exhibit a de-oxydation; the other, under the yellow-red glass, will, on the contrary, become a lighter grey, and thus approach nearer to the original state of more perfect oxydation. The change in both may be ascertained by a comparison with the unaltered specimen.

681.

An excellent apparatus has been contrived to

---

* Now generally called chloride of silver: the term in the original is Hornsilber.—T.

perform these experiments with the prismatic image. The results are analogous to those already mentioned, and we shall hereafter give the particulars, making use of the labours of an accurate observer, who has been for some time carefully prosecuting these experiments.*

LVI.

CHEMICAL EFFECT IN DIOPTRICAL ACHROMATISM.

682.

WE first invite our readers to turn to what has been before observed on this subject (285, 298), to avoid unnecessary repetition here.

683.

We can thus give a glass the property of producing much wider coloured edges without refracting more strongly than before, that is, without displacing the object much more perceptibly.

684.

This property is communicated to the glass by means of metallic oxydes. Minium, melted and thoroughly united with a pure glass, pro-

---

* The individual alluded to was Seebeck: the result of his experiments was published in the second volume.—T.

duces this effect, and thus flint-glass (291) is prepared with oxyde of lead. Experiments of this kind have been carried farther, and the so-called butter of antimony, which, according to a new preparation, may be exhibited as a pure fluid, has been made use of in hollow lenses and prisms, producing a very strong appearance of colour with a very moderate refraction, and presenting the effect which we have called hyperchromatism in a very vivid manner.

685.

In common glass, the alkaline nature obviously preponderates, since it is chiefly composed of sand and alkaline salts ; hence a series of experiments, exhibiting the relation of perfectly alkaline fluids to perfect acids, might lead to useful results.

686.

For, could the maximum and minimum be found, it would be a question whether a refracting medium could not be discovered, in which the increasing and diminishing appearance of colour, (an effect almost independent of refraction,) could not be done away with altogether, while the displacement of the object would be unaltered.

687.

How desirable, therefore, it would be with

regard to this last point, as well as for the elucidation of the whole of this third division of our work, and, indeed, for the elucidation of the doctrine of colours generally, that those who are occupied in chemical researches, with new views ever opening to them, should take this subject in hand, pursuing into more delicate combinations what we have only roughly hinted at, and prosecuting their inquiries with reference to science as a whole.

PART IV.

GENERAL CHARACTERISTICS.

688.

WE have hitherto, in a manner forcibly, kept phenomena asunder, which, partly from their nature, partly in accordance with our mental habits, have, as it were, constantly sought to be reunited. We have exhibited them in three divisions. We have considered colours, first, as transient, the result of an action and re-action in the eye itself; next, as passing effects of colourless, light-transmitting, transparent, or opaque mediums on light; especially on the luminous image; lastly, we arrived at the point where we could securely pronounce them as permanent, and actually inherent in bodies.

689.

In following this order we have as far as possible endeavoured to define, to separate, and to class the appearances. But now that we need no longer be apprehensive of mixing or confounding them, we may proceed, first, to state the general nature of these appearances considered abstractedly, as an independent circle of facts, and, in the next place, to show how this particular circle is connected with other classes of analogous phenomena in nature.

690.

We have observed that colour under many conditions appears very easily. The susceptibility of the eye with regard to light, the constant re-action of the retina against it, produce instantaneously a slight iridescence. Every subdued light may be considered as coloured, nay, we ought to call any light coloured, inasmuch as it is seen. Colourless light, colourless surfaces, are, in some sort, abstract ideas ; in actual experience we can hardly be said to be aware of them.—Note Z.

691.

If light impinges on a colourless body, is reflected from it or passes through it, colour immediately appears ; but it is necessary here to remember what has been so often urged by us, namely, that the leading conditions of refraction, reflection, &c., are not of themselves sufficient to produce the appearance. Sometimes, it is true, light acts with these merely as light, but oftener as a defined, circumscribed appearance, as a luminous image. The semi-opacity of the medium is often a necessary condition ; while half, and double shadows, are required for many coloured appearances. In all cases, however, colour appears instantaneously. We find, again, that by means of pressure, breathing heat (432, 471), by various kinds of motion and alteration on smooth clean surfaces (461), as well as on colourless fluids (470), colour is immediately produced.

692.

The slightest change has only to take place in the component parts of bodies, whether by immixture with other particles or other such effects, and colour either makes its appearance or becomes changed.

THE FORCE OF COLOUR.
693.

The physical colours, and especially those of the prism, were formerly called "*colores emphatici*," on account of their extraordinary beauty and force. Strictly speaking, however, a high degree of effect may be ascribed to all appearances of colour, assuming that they are exhibited under the purest and most perfect conditions.

694.

The dark nature of colour, its full rich quality, is what produces the grave, and at the same time fascinating impression we sometimes experience, and as colour is to be considered a condition of light, so it cannot dispense with light as the co-operating cause of its appearance, as its basis or ground; as a power thus displaying and manifesting colour.

695.

The existence and the relatively definite character of colour are one and the same thing. Light displays itself and the face of nature, as it were, with a general indifference, informing us as to surrounding objects perhaps devoid of interest or importance ; but colour is at all times specific, characteristic, significant.

696.

Considered in a general point of view, colour is determined towards one of two sides. It thus presents a contrast which we call a polarity, and which we may fitly designate by the expressions *plus* and *minus*.

Plus.	*Minus.*
Yellow.	Blue.
Action.	Negation.*
Light.	Shadow.
Brightness.	Darkness.
Force.	Weakness.
Warmth.	Coldness.
Proximity.	Distance.
Repulsion	Attraction.
Affinity with acids	Affinity with alkalis.

* Wirkung, Beraubung; the last would be more literally rendered *privation*. The author has already frequently made use of the terms *active* and *passive* as equivalent to *plus* and *minus*.—T.

COMBINATION OF THE TWO PRINCIPLES.

697.

If these specific, contrasted principles are combined, the respective qualities do not therefore destroy each other : for if in this intermixture the ingredients are so perfectly balanced that neither is to be distinctly recognised, the union again acquires a specific character ; it appears as a quality by itself in which we no longer think of combination. This union we call green.

698.

Thus, if two opposite phenomena springing from the same source do not destroy each other when combined, but in their union present a third appreciable and pleasing appearance, this result at once indicates their harmonious relation. The more perfect result yet remains to be adverted to.

AUGMENTATION TO RED.

699.

Blue and yellow do not admit of increased intensity without presently exhibiting a new appearance in addition to their own. Each colour, in its lightest state, is a dark ; if condensed it must become darker, but this effect no sooner takes place than the hue assumes an appearance which we designate by the word reddish.

700.

This appearance still increases, so that when the highest degree of intensity is attained it predominates over the original hue. A powerful impression of light leaves the sensation of red on the retina. In the prismatic yellow-red which springs directly from the yellow, we hardly recognise the yellow.

701.

This deepening takes place again by means of colourless semi-transparent mediums, and here we see the effect in its utmost purity and extent. Transparent fluids, coloured with any given hues, in a series of glass-vessels, exhibit it very strikingly. The augmentation is unremittingly rapid and constant; it is universal, and obtains in physiological as well as in physical and chemical colours.

JUNCTION OF THE TWO AUGMENTED EXTREMES.

702.

As the extremes of the simple contrast produce a beautiful and agreeable appearance by their union, so the deepened extremes on being united, will present a still more fascinating colour ; indeed, it might naturally be expected that we should here find the acme of the whole phenomenon.

703.

And such is the fact, for pure red appears; a colour to which, from its excellence, we have appropriated the term "purpur."*

704.

There are various modes in which pure red may appear. By bringing together the violet edge and yellow-red border in prismatic experiments, by continued augmentation in chemical operations, and by the organic contrast in physiological effects.

705.

As a pigment it cannot be produced by intermixture or union, but only by arresting the hue in substances chemically acted on, at the high culminating point. Hence the painter is justified in assuming that there are *three* primitive colours from which he combines all the others. The natural philosopher, on the other hand, assumes only *two* elementary colours, from which he, in like manner, developes and combines the rest.

COMPLETENESS THE RESULT OF VARIETY IN COLOUR.

706.

The various appearances of colour arrested in

---

* Wherever this word occurs incidentally it is translated *pure red*, the English word *purple* being generally employed to denote a colour similar to violet.—T.

their different degrees, and seen in juxtaposition, produce a whole.   This totality is harmony
to the eye.

707.

The chromatic circle has been gradually presented to us; the various relations of its progression are apparent to us.   Two pure original
principles in contrast, are the foundation of the
whole;   an   augmentation   manifests   itself   by
means of which both approach a third state;
hence there exists on both sides a lowest and
highest, a simplest and most qualified state.
Again, two combinations present themselves;
first that of the simple primitive contrasts, then
that of the deepened contrasts.

HARMONY OF THE COMPLETE STATE.

708.

The whole ingredients of the chromatic scale,
seen in juxtaposition, produce an harmonious
impression on the eye.   The difference between
the physical contrast and harmonious opposition
in all its extent should not be overlooked.   The
first resides in the pure restricted original dualism, considered in its antagonizing elements;
the other results from the the fully developed
effects of the complete state.

709.

Every single opposition in order to be harmonious must comprehend the whole.   The

physiological experiments are sufficiently convincing on this point. A development of all the possible contrasts of the chromatic scale will be shortly given.*

FACILITY WITH WHICH COLOUR MAY BE MADE TO TEND EITHER TO THE PLUS OR MINUS SIDE.

710.

We have already had occasion to take notice of the mutability of colour in considering its socalled augmentation and progressive variations round the whole circle ; but the hues even pass and repass from one side to the other, rapidly and of necessity.

711.

Physiological colours are different in appearance as they happen to fall on a dark or on a light ground. In physical colours the combination of the objective and subjective experiments is very remarkable. The epoptical colours, it appears, are contrasted according as the light shines through or upon them. To what extent the chemical colours may be changed by fire and alkalis, has been sufficiently shown in its proper place.

EVANESCENCE OF COLOUR.

712.

All that has been adverted to as subsequent

---

* No diagram or table of this kind was ever given by the author.—T.

to the rapid excitation and definition of colour, immixture, augmentation, combination, separation, not forgetting the law of compensatory harmony, all takes place with the greatest rapidity and facility ; but with equal quickness colour again altogether disappears.

713.

The physiological appearances are in no wise to be arrested ; the physical last only as long as the external condition lasts ; even the chemical colours have great mutability, they may be made to pass and repass from one side to the other by means of opposite re-agents, and may even be annihilated altogether.

PERMANENCE OF COLOUR.
714.

The chemical colours afford evidence of very great duration. Colours fixed in glass by fusion, and by nature in gems, defy all time and re-action.

715.

The art of dyeing again fixes colour very powerfully. The hues of pigments which might otherwise be easily rendered mutable by re-agents, may be communicated to substances in the greatest permanency by means of mordants.

PART V.

716.

THE investigator of nature cannot be required
to be a philosopher, but it is expected that he
should so far have attained the habit of philo-
sophizing, as to distinguish himself essentially
from the world, in order to associate himself
with it again in a higher sense. He should
form to himself a method in accordance with
observation, but he should take heed not to reduce observation to mere notion, to substitute
words for this notion, and to use and deal with
these words as if they were things. He should
be acquainted with the labours of philosophers,
in order to follow up the phenomena which have
been the subject of his observation, into the
philosophic region.

717.

It cannot be required that the philosopher
should be a naturalist, and yet his co-operation
in physical researches is as necessary as it is
desirable. He needs not an acquaintance with
details for this, but only a clear view of those
conclusions where insulated facts meet.

718.

We have before (175) alluded to this important consideration, and repeat it here where it is in its place. The worst that can happen to physical science as well as to many other kinds of knowledge is, that men should treat a secondary phenomenon as a primordial one, and (since it is impossible to derive the original fact from the secondary state), seek to explain what is in reality the cause by an effect made to usurp its place. Hence arises an endless confusion, a mere verbiage, a constant endeavour to seek and to find subterfuges whenever truth presents itself and threatens to be overpowering.

719.

While the observer, the investigator of nature, is thus dissatisfied in finding that the appearances he sees still contradict a received theory, the philosopher can calmly continue to operate in his abstract department on a false result, for no result is so false but that it can be made to appear valid, as form without substance, by some means or other.

720.

If, on the other hand, the investigator of nature can attain to the knowledge of that which we have called a primordial phenomenon, he is safe ; and the philosopher with him. The inves-

tigator of nature is safe, since he is persuaded
that he has here arrived at the limits of his
science, that he finds himself at the height of
experimental research ; a height whence he can
look back upon the details of observation in all
its steps, and forwards into, if he cannot enter,
the regions of theory. The philosopher is safe,
for he receives from the experimentalist an
ultimate fact, which, in his hands, now becomes
an elementary one. He now justly pays little
attention to appearances which are understood
to be secondary, whether he already finds them
scientifically arranged, or whether they present
themselves to his casual observation scattered
and confused. Should he even be inclined to
go over this experimental ground himself, and
not be averse to examination in detail, he does
this conveniently, instead of lingering too long
in the consideration of secondary and intermediate circumstances, or hastily passing them
over without becoming accurately acquainted
with them.

721.

To place the doctrine of colours nearer, in this
sense, within the philosopher's reach, was the
author's wish ; and although the execution of
his purpose, from various causes, does not correspond with his intention, he will still keep
this object in view in an intended recapitula-

tion, as well as in the polemical and historical
portions of his work ; for he will have to return
to the consideration of this point hereafter, on
an occasion where it will be necessary to speak
with less reserve.

RELATION TO MATHEMATICS.

722.

It may be expected that the investigator of
nature, who proposes to treat the science of
natural philosophy in its entire range, should
be a mathematician. In the middle ages, mathematics was the chief organ by means of
which men hoped to master the secrets of nature,
and even now, geometry in certain departments
of physics, is justly considered of first importance.

723.

The author can boast of no attainments of
this kind, and on this account confines himself
to departments of science which are independent of geometry ; departments which in modern times have been opened up far and wide.

724.

It will be universally allowed that mathematics, one of the noblest auxiliaries which can
be employed by man, has, in one point of view,
been of the greatest use to the physical sciences;
but that, by a false application of its methods,

it has, in many respects, been prejudicial to them, is also not to be denied ; we find it here and there reluctantly admitted.

725.

The theory of colours, in particular, has suffered much, and its progress has been incalculably retarded by having been mixed up with optics generally, a science which cannot dispense with mathematics; whereas the theory of colours, in strictness, may be investigated quite independently of optics.

726.

But besides this there was an additional evil. A great mathematician was possessed with an entirely false notion on the physical origin of colours ; yet, owing to his great authority as a geometer, the mistakes which he committed as an experimentalist long became sanctioned in the eyes of a world ever fettered in prejudices.

727.

The author of the present inquiry has endeavoured throughout to keep the theory of colours distinct from the mathematics, although there are evidently certain points where the assistance of geometry would be desirable. Had not the unprejudiced mathematicians, with whom he has had, or still has, the good fortune to be acquainted, been prevented by other occupations from making common cause with him, his work would not have wanted some merit in this respect. But this very want may be in the end advantageous, since it may now become the object of the enlightened mathematician to ascertain where the doctrine of colours is in need of his aid, and how he can contribute the means at his command with a view to the complete elucidation of this branch of physics.

728.

In general it were to be wished that the Germans, who render such good service to science, while they adopt all that is good from other nations, could by degrees accustom themselves to work in concert. We live, it must be confessed, in an age, the habits of which are directly opposed to such a wish. Every one seeks, not only to be original in his views, but to be independent of the labours of others, or at least to persuade himself that he is so, even in the course of his life and occupation. It is very often remarked that men who undoubtedly have accomplished much, quote themselves only, their own writings, journals, and compendiums ; whereas it would be far more advantageous for the individual, and for the world, if many were devoted to a common pursuit. The conduct of our neighbours the French is, in this respect, worthy of imitation; we have a pleasing instance in Cuvier's preface to his "Tableau Elémentaire de l'Histoire Naturelle des Animaux."

729.

He who has observed science and its progress with an unprejudiced eye, might even ask whether it is desirable that so many occupations and aims, though allied to each other, should be united in one person, and whether it would not be more suitable for the limited powers of the human mind to distinguish, for example, the investigator and inventor, from him who employs and applies the result of experiment? Astronomers, who devote themselves to the observation of the heavens and the discovery or enumeration of stars, have in modern times formed, to a certain extent, a distinct class from those who calculate the orbits, consider the universe in its connexion, and more accurately define its laws. The history of the doctrine of colours will often lead us back to these considerations.

RELATION TO THE TECHNICAL OPERATIONS OF THE DYER.

730.

If in our labours we have gone out of the province of the mathematician, we have, on the other hand, endeavoured to meet the practical views of the dyer; and although the chapter which treats of colour in a chemical point of view is not the most complete and circumstantial, yet in that portion, as well as in our general observations respecting colour, the dyer will find his views assisted far more than by the theory hitherto in vogue, which failed to afford him any assistance.

731.

It is curious, in this view, to take a glance at the works containing directions on the art of dyeing. As the Catholic, on entering his temple, sprinkles himself with holy water, and after bending the knee, proceeds perhaps to converse with his friends on his affairs, without any especial devotion; so all the treatises on dyeing begin with a respectful allusion to the accredited theory, without afterwards exhibiting a single trace of any principle deduced from this theory, or showing that it has thrown light on any part of the art, or that it offers any useful hints in furtherance of practical methods.

732.

On the other hand, there are men who, after having become thoroughly and experimentally acquainted with the nature of dyes, have not been able to reconcile their observations with the received theory; who have, in short, discovered its weak points, and sought for a general view more consonant to nature and experience. When we come to the names of Castel and Gülich, in our historical review, we shall have occasion to enter into this more fully, and an opportunity will then present itself to show that an assiduous experience in taking advantage of every accident may, in fact, be said almost to exhaust the knowledge of the province to which it is confined. The high and complete result is then submitted to the theorist, who, if he examines facts with accuracy, and reasons with candour, will find such materials eminently useful as a basis for his conclusions.—Note A A.

RELATION TO PHYSIOLOGY AND PATHOLOGY.

733.

If the phenomena adduced in the chapter where colours were considered in a physiological and pathological view are for the most part generally known, still some new views, mixed up with them, will not be unacceptable to the physiologist. We especially hope to have given him cause to be satisfied by classing certain phenomena which stood alone, under analogous facts, and thus, in some measure, to have prepared the way for his further investigations.

734.

The appendix on pathological colours, again,

is admitted to be scanty and unconnected. We reflect, however, that Germany can boast of men who are not only highly experienced in this department, but are likewise so distinguished for general cultivation, that it can cost them but little to revise this portion, to complete what has been sketched, and at the same time to connect it with the higher facts of organisation.

RELATION TO NATURAL HISTORY.

735.

If we may at all hope that natural history will gradually be modified by the principle of deducing the ordinary appearances of nature from higher phenomena, the author believes he may have given some hints and introductory views bearing on this object also. As colour, in its infinite variety, exhibits itself on the surface of living beings, it becomes an important part of the outward indications, by means of which we can discover what passes underneath.

736.

In one point of view it is certainly not to be too much relied on, on account of its indefinite and mutable nature; yet even this mutability, inasmuch as it exhibits itself as a constant quality, again becomes a criterion of a mutable vitality; and the author wishes nothing more than that time may be granted him to develop the results of his observations on this subject more fully; here they would not be in their place.

RELATION TO GENERAL PHYSICS.

737.

The state in which general physics now is, appears, again, particularly favourable to our labours; for natural philosophy, owing to indefatigable and variously directed research, has gradually attained such eminence, that it appears not impossible to refer a boundless empiricism to one centre.

738.

Without referring to subjects which are too far removed from our own province, we observe that the formulæ under which the elementary appearances of nature are expressed, altogether tend in this direction; and it is easy to see that through this correspondence of expression, a correspondence in meaning will necessarily be soon arrived at.

739.

True observers of nature, however they may differ in opinion in other respects, will agree that all which presents itself as appearance, all that we meet with as phenomenon, must either indicate an original division which is capable of union, or an original unity which admits of division, and that the phenomenon will present itself accordingly. To divide the united, to unite the divided, is the life of nature; this is the eternal systole and diastole, the eternal collapsion and expansion, the inspiration and expiration of the world in which we live and move.

740.

It is hardly necessary to observe that what we here express as number and restrict to dualism is to be understood in a higher sense; the appearance of a third, a fourth order of facts progressively developing themselves is to be similarly understood; but actual observation should, above all, be the basis of all these expressions.

741.

Iron is known to us as a peculiar substance, different from other substances: in its ordinary state we look upon it as a mere material remarkable only on account of its fitness for various uses and applications. How little, however, is necessary to do away with the comparative insignificancy of this substance. A two-fold power is called forth,* which, while it tends again to a

---

* Eine Entzweyung geht vor; literally, *a division takes place.* According to some, the two magnetic powers are previously in the bar, and are then separated at the ends.—T.

state of union, and, as it were, seeks itself, acquires a kind of magical relation with its like, and propagates this double property, which is in fact but a principle of reunion, throughout all bodies of the same kind. We here first observe the mere substance, iron ; we see the division that takes place in it propagate itself and disappear, and again easily become re-excited. This, according to our mode of thinking, is a primordial phenomenon in immediate relation with its idea, and which acknowledges nothing earthly beyond it.

742.

Electricity is again peculiarly characterised. As a mere quality we are unacquainted with it; for us it is a nothing, a zero, a mere point, which, however, dwells in all apparent existences, and at the same time is the point of origin whence, on the slightest stimulus, a double appearance presents itself, an appearance which only manifests itself to vanish. The conditions under which this manifestation is excited are infinitely varied, according to the nature of particular bodies. From the rudest mechanical friction of very different substances with one another, to the mere contiguity of two entirely similar bodies, the phenomenon is present and stirring, nay, striking and powerful, and so decided and specific, that when we employ the terms or formulæ polarity, plus and minus, for north and south, for glass and resin, we do so justifiably and in conformity with nature.

743.

This phenomenon, although it especially affects the surface, is yet by no means superficial. It influences the tendency or determination of material qualities, and connects itself in immediate co-operation with the important double phenomenon which takes place so universally in chemistry,—oxydation, and de-oxydation.

744.

To introduce and include the appearances of colour in this series, this circle of phenomena was the object of our labours. What we have not succeeded in others will accomplish. We found a primordial vast contrast between light and darkness, which may be more generally expressed by light and its absence. We looked for the intermediate state, and sought by means of it to compose the visible world of light, shade, and colour. In the prosecution of this we employed various terms applicable to the development of the phenomena, terms which we adopted from the theories of magnetism, of electricity, and of chemistry. It was necessary, however, to extend this terminology, since we found ourselves in an abstract region, and had to express more complicated relations.

745.

If electricity and galvanism, in their general character, are distinguished as superior to the more limited exhibition of magnetic phenomena, it may be said that colour, although coming under similar laws, is still superior ; for since it addresses itself to the noble sense of vision, its perfections are more generally displayed. Compare the varied effects which result from the augmentation of yellow and blue to red, from the combination of these two higher extremes to pure red, and the union of the two inferior extremes to green. What a far more varied scheme is apparent here than that in which magnetism and electricity are comprehended. These last phenomena may be said to be inferior again on another account; for though they penetrate and give life to the universe, they cannot address themselves to man in a higher sense in order to his employing them æsthetically. The general, simple, physical law must first be elevated and diversified itself in order to be available for elevated uses.

746.

If the reader, in this spirit, recalls what has been stated by us throughout, generally and in detail, with regard to colour, he will himself pursue and unfold what has been here only lightly hinted at. He will augur well for science, technical processes, and art, if it should prove possible to rescue the attractive subject of the doctrine of colours from the atomic restriction and isolation in which it has been banished, in order to restore it to the general dynamic flow of life and action which the present age loves to recognise in nature. These considerations will press upon us more strongly when, in the historical portion, we shall have to speak of many an enterprising and intelligent man who failed to possess his contemporaries with his convictions.

RELATION TO THE THEORY OF MUSIC.

747.

Before we proceed to the moral associations of colour, and the æsthetic influences arising from them, we have here to say a few words on its relation to melody. That a certain relation exists between the two, has been always felt; this is proved by the frequent comparisons we meet with, sometimes as passing· allusions, sometimes as circumstantial parallels. The error which writers have fallen into in trying to establish this analogy we would thus define:

748.

Colour and sound do not admit of being directly compared together in any way, but both are referable to a higher formula, both are derivable, although each for itself, from this higher law. They are like two rivers which have their source in one and the same mountain, but sub-sequently pursue their way under totally different conditions in two totally different regions, so that throughout the whole course of both no two points can be compared. Both are general, elementary effects acting according to the general law of separation and tendency to union, of undulation and oscillation, yet acting thus in wholly different provinces, in different modes, on different elementary mediums, for different senses.—Note B B.

749.

Could some investigator rightly adopt the method in which we have connected the doctrine of colours with natural philosophy generally, and happily supply what has escaped or been missed by us, the theory of sound, we are persuaded, might be perfectly connected with general physics : at present it stands, as it were, isolated within the circle of science.

750.

It is true it would be an undertaking of the greatest difficulty to do away with the positive character which we are now accustomed to attribute to music—a character resulting from the achievements of practical skill, from accidental, mathematical, æsthetical influences—and to substitute for all this a merely physical inquiry tending to resolve the science into its first elements. Yet considering the point at which science and art are now arrived, considering the many excellent preparatory investigations that have been made relative to this subject, we may perhaps still see it accomplished.

CONCLUDING OBSERVATIONS ON TERMINOLOGY.

751.

We never sufficiently reflect that a language, strictly speaking, can only be symbolical and figurative, that it can never express things directly, but only, as it were, reflectedly. This is especially the case in speaking of qualities which are only imperfectly presented to observation, which might rather be called powers than objects, and which are ever in movement throughout nature. They are not to be arrested, and yet we find it necessary to describe them; hence we look for all kinds of formulæ in order, figuratively at least, to define them.

752.

Metaphysical formulæ have breadth as well as depth, but on this very account they require a corresponding import; the danger here is vagueness. Mathematical expressions may in many cases be very conveniently and happily employed, but there is always an inflexibility in them, and we presently feel their inadequacy; for even in elementary cases we are very soon conscious of an incommensurable idea; they are, besides, only intelligible to those who are especially conversant in the sciences to which such formulæ are appropriated. The terms of the science of mechanics are more addressed to the ordinary mind, but they are ordinary in other senses, and always have something unpolished; they destroy the inward life to offer from without an insufficient substitute for it. The formulæ of the corpuscular theories are nearly allied to the last; through them the mutable becomes rigid, description and expression uncouth : while, again, moral terms, which undoubtedly can express nicer relations, have the effect of mere symbols in the end, and are in danger of being lost in a play of wit.

753.

If, however, a writer could use all these modes of description and expression with perfect command, and thus give forth the result of his observations on the phenomena of nature in a diversified language; if he could preserve himself from predilections, still embodying a lively meaning in as animated an expression, we might look for much instruction communicated in the most agreeable of forms.

754.

Yet, how difficult it is to avoid substituting the sign for the thing ; how difficult to keep the essential quality still living before us, and not to kill it with the word. With all this, we are exposed in modern times to a still greater danger by adopting expressions and terminologies from all branches of knowledge and science to embody our views of simple nature. Astronomy, cosmology, geology, natural history, nay religion and mysticism, are called in in aid ; and how often do we not find a general idea and an elementary state rather hidden and obscured than elucidated and brought nearer to us by the employment of terms, the application of which is strictly specific and secondary. We are quite aware of the necessity which led to the introduction and general adoption of such a language, we also know that it has become in a certain sense indispensable ; but it is only a moderate, unpretending recourse to it, with an internal conviction of its fitness, that can recommend it.

755.

After all, the most desirable principle would be that writers should borrow the expressions employed to describe the details of a given province of investigation from the province itself ; treating the simplest phenomenon as an elementary formula, and deriving and developing the more complicated designations from this.

756.

The necessity and suitableness of such a conventional language where the elementary sign expresses the appearance itself, has been duly appreciated by extending, for instance, the application of the term polarity, which is borrowed from the magnet to electricity, &c. The *plus* and *minus* which may be substituted for this, have found as suitable an application to many phenomena ; even the musician, probably without troubling himself about these other departments, has been naturally led to express the leading difference in the modes of melody by *major* and *minor*.

757.

For ourselves we have long wished to introduce the term polarity into the doctrine of colours ; with what right and in what sense, the present work may show. Perhaps we may hereafter find room to connect the elementary phenomena together according to our mode, by a similar use of symbolical terms, terms which must at all times convey the directly corresponding idea; we shall thus render more explicit what has been here only alluded to generally, and perhaps too vaguely expressed.

PART VI.

EFFECT OF COLOUR WITH REFERENCE TO MORAL ASSOCIATIONS.

758.

SINCE colour occupies so important a place in the series of elementary phenomena, filling as it does the limited circle assigned to it with fullest variety, we shall not be surprised to find that its effects are at all times decided and significant, and that they are immediately associated with the emotions of the mind. We shall not be surprised to find that these appearances presented singly, are specific, that in combination they may produce an harmonious, characteristic, often even an inharmonious effect on the eye, by means of which they act on the mind; producing this impression in their most general elementary character, without relation to the nature or form of the object on whose surface they are apparent. Hence, colour considered as an element of art, may be made subservient to the highest æsthetical ends.—Note C C.

759.

People experience a great delight in colour, generally. The eye requires it as much as it requires light. We have only to remember the refreshing sensation we experience, if on a cloudy day the sun illumines a single portion of the scene before us and displays its colours. That healing powers were ascribed to coloured gems, may have arisen from the experience of this indefinable pleasure.

760.

The colours which we see on objects are not qualities entirely strange to the eye ; the organ is not thus merely habituated to the impression ; no, it is always predisposed to produce colour of itself, and experiences a sensation of delight if something analogous to its own nature is offered to it from without ; if its susceptibility is distinctly determined towards a given state.

761.

From some of our earlier observations we can conclude, that general impressions produced by single colours cannot be changed, that they act specifically, and must produce definite, specific states in the living organ.

762.

They likewise produce a corresponding influence on the mind. Experience teaches us that particular colours excite particular states of feeling. It is related of a witty Frenchman, " Il prétendoit que son ton de conversation avec

Madame étoit changé depuis qu'elle avoit changé en cramoisi le meuble de son cabinet, qui étoit bleu."

763.

In order to experience these influences completely, the eye should be entirely surrounded with one colour; we should be in a room of one colour, or look through a coloured glass. We are then identified with the hue, it attunes the eye and mind in mere unison with itself.

764.

The colours on the *plus* side are yellow, red-yellow (orange), yellow-red (minium, cinnabar). The feelings they excite are quick, lively, aspiring.

YELLOW.

765.

This is the colour nearest the light. It appears on the slightest mitigation of light, whether by semi-transparent mediums or faint reflection from white surfaces. In prismatic experiments it extends itself alone and widely in the light space, and while the two poles remain separated from each other, before it mixes with blue to produce green it is to be seen in its utmost purity and beauty. How the chemical yellow developes itself in and upon the white, has been circumstantially described in its proper place.

766.

In its highest purity it always carries with it the nature of brightness, and has a serene, gay, softly exciting character.

767.

In this state, applied to dress, hangings, carpeting, &c., it is agreeable. Gold in its perfectly unmixed state, especially when the effect of polish is superadded, gives us a new and high idea of this colour; in like manner, a strong yellow, as it appears on satin, has a magnificent and noble effect.

768.

We find from experience, again, that yellow excites a warm and agreeable impression. Hence in painting it belongs to the illumined and emphatic side.

769.

This impression of warmth may be experienced in a very lively manner if we look at a landscape through a yellow glass, particularly on a grey winter's day. The eye is gladdened, the heart expanded and cheered, a glow seems at once to breathe towards us.

770.

If, however, this colour in its pure and bright

state is agreeable and gladdening, and in its utmost power is serene and noble, it is, on the other hand, extremely liable to contamination, and produces a very disagreeable effect if it is sullied, or in some degree tends to the *minus* side. Thus, the colour of sulphur, which inclines to green, has a something unpleasant in it.

771.

When a yellow colour is communicated to dull and coarse surfaces, such as common cloth, felt, or the like, on which it does not appear with full energy, the disagreeable effect alluded to is apparent. By a slight and scarcely perceptible change, the beautiful impression of fire and gold is transformed into one not undeserving the epithet foul ; and the colour of honour and joy reversed to that of ignominy and aversion. To this impression the yellow hats of bankrupts and the yellow circles on the mantles of Jews, may have owed their origin.

RED-YELLOW.

772.

As no colour can be considered as stationary, so we can very easily augment yellow into reddish by condensing or darkening it. The colour increases in energy, and appears in red-yellow more powerful and splendid.

773.

All that we have said of yellow is applicable here in a higher degree. The red-yellow gives an impression of warmth and gladness, since it represents the hue of the intenser glow of fire, and of the milder radiance of the setting sun. Hence it is agreeable around us, and again, as clothing, in greater or less degrees is cheerful and magnificent. A slight tendency to red immediately gives a new character to yellow, and while the English and Germans content themselves with bright pale yellow colours in leather, the French, as Castel has remarked, prefer a yellow enhanced to red; indeed, in general, everything in colour is agreeable to them which belongs to the active side.

YELLOW-RED.

774.

As pure yellow passes very easily to red-yellow, so the deepening of this last to yellow-red is not to be arrested. The agreeable, cheerful sensation which red-yellow excites, increases to an intolerably powerful impression in bright yellow-red.

775.

The active side is here in its highest energy, and it is not to be wondered at that impetuous, robust, uneducated men, should be especially pleased with this colour. Among savage nations the inclination for it has been universally remarked, and when children, left to themselves, begin to use tints, they never spare vermilion and minium.

776.

In looking steadfastly at a perfectly yellow-red surface, the colour seems actually to penetrate the organ. It produces an extreme excitement, and still acts thus when somewhat darkened. A yellow-red cloth disturbs and enrages animals. I have known men of education to whom its effect was intolerable if they chanced to see a person dressed in a scarlet cloak on a grey, cloudy day.

777.

The colours on the *minus* side are blue, red-blue, and blue-red. They produce a restless, susceptible, anxious impression.

BLUE.

778.

As yellow is always accompanied with light, so it may be said that blue still brings a principle of darkness with it.

779.

This colour has a peculiar and almost indescribable effect on the eye. As a hue it is powerful, but it is on the negative side, and in its highest purity is, as it were, a stimulating negation. Its appearance, then, is a kind of contradiction between excitement and repose.

780.

As the upper sky and distant mountains appear blue, so a blue surface seems to retire from us.

781.

But as we readily follow an agreeable object that flies from us, so we love to contemplate blue, not because it advances to us, but because it draws us after it.

782.

Blue gives us an impression of cold, and thus, again, reminds us of shade. We have before spoken of its affinity with black.

783.

Rooms which are hung with pure blue, appear in some degree larger, but at the same time empty and cold.

784.

The appearance of objects seen through a blue glass is gloomy and melancholy.

785.

When blue partakes in some degree of the *plus* side, the effect is not disagreeable. Sea-green is rather a pleasing colour.

RED-BLUE.

786.

We found yellow very soon tending to the intense state, and we observe the same progression in blue.

787.

Blue deepens very mildly into red, and thus acquires a somewhat active character, although it is on the passive side. Its exciting power is, however, of a very different kind from that of the red-yellow. It may be said to disturb rather than enliven.

788.

As augmentation itself is not to be arrested, so we feel an inclination to follow the progress of the colour, not, however, as in the case of the red-yellow, to see it still increase in the active sense, but to find a point to rest in.

789.

In a very attenuated state, this colour is known to us under the name of lilac ; but even in this degree it has a something lively without gladness.

790.

This unquiet feeling increases as the hue progresses, and it may be safely assumed, that a carpet of a perfectly pure deep blue-red would be intolerable. On this account, when it is used for dress, ribbons, or other ornaments, it is employed in a very attenuated and light state, and thus displays its character as above defined, in a peculiarly attractive manner.

791.

As the higher dignitaries of the church have appropriated this unquiet colour to themselves, we may venture to say that it unceasingly aspires to the cardinal's red through the restless degrees of a still impatient progression.

RED.

792.

We are here to forget everything that borders on yellow or blue. We are to imagine an absolutely pure red, like fine carmine suffered to dry on white porcelain. We have called this colour "purpur" by way of distinction, although we are quite aware that the purple of the ancients inclined more to blue.

793.

Whoever is acquainted with the prismatic

origin of red, will not think it paradoxical if we assert that this colour partly *actu*, partly *potentiâ*, includes all the other colours.

794.

We have remarked a constant progress or augmentation in yellow and blue, and seen what impressions were produced by the various states; hence it may naturally be inferred that now, in the junction of the deepened extremes, a feeling of satisfaction must succeed; and thus, in physical phenomena, this highest of all appearances of colour arises from the junction of two contrasted extremes which have gradually prepared themselves for a union.

795.

As a pigment, on the other hand, it presents itself to us already formed, and is most perfect as a hue in cochineal; a substance which, however, by chemical action may be made to tend to the *plus* or the *minus* side, and may be considered to have attained the central point in the best carmine.

796.

The effect of this colour is as peculiar as its nature. It conveys an impression of gravity and dignity, and at the same time of grace and attractiveness. The first in its dark deep state,

the latter in its light attenuated tint ; and thus
the dignity of age and the amiableness of youth
may adorn itself with degrees of the same hue.

797.

History relates many instances of the jealousy
of sovereigns with regard to the quality of red.
Surrounding accompaniments of this colour
have always a grave and magnificent effect.

798.

The red glass exhibits a bright landscape in
so dreadful a hue as to inspire sentiments of awe.

799.

Kermes and cochineal, the two materials
chiefly employed in dyeing to produce this
colour, incline more or less to the *plus* or *minus*
state, and may be made to pass and repass the
culminating point by the action of acids and
alkalis : it is to be observed that the French
arrest their operations on the active side, as is
proved by the French scarlet, which inclines to
yellow. The Italians, on the other hand, remain
on the passive side, for their scarlet has a tinge
of blue.

800.

By means of a similar alkaline treatment, the
so-called crimson is produced ; a colour which
the French must be particularly prejudiced

against, since they employ the expressions—
"Sot en cramoisi, méchant en cramoisi," to
mark the extreme of the silly and the repre-
hensible.

801.

If yellow and blue, which we consider as the
most fundamental and simple colours, are united
as they first appear, in the first state of their
action, the colour which we call green is the
result.

802.

The eye experiences a distinctly grateful impression from this colour. If the two elementary
colours are mixed in perfect equality so that
neither predominates, the eye and the mind repose on the result of this junction as upon a
simple colour. The beholder has neither the
wish nor the power to imagine a state beyond
it. Hence for rooms to live in constantly, the
green colour is most generally selected.

COMPLETENESS AND HARMONY.

803.

We have hitherto assumed, for the sake of
clearer explanation, that the eye can be compelled to assimilate or identify itself with a
single colour; but this can only be possible for
an instant.

804.

For when we find ourselves surrounded by a given colour which excites its corresponding sensation on the eye, and compels us by its presence to remain in a state identical with it, this state is soon found to be forced, and the organ unwillingly remains in it.

805.

When the eye sees a colour it is immediately excited, and it is its nature, spontaneously and of necessity, at once to produce another, which with the original colour comprehends the whole chromatic scale. A single colour excites, by a specific sensation, the tendency to universality.

806.

To experience this completeness, to satisfy itself, the eye seeks for a colourless space next every hue in order to produce the complemental hue upon it.

807.

In this resides the fundamental law of all harmony of colours, of which every one may convince himself by making himself accurately acquainted with the experiments which we have described in the chapter on the physiological colours.

808.

If, again, the entire scale is presented to the eye externally, the impression is gladdening, since the result of its own operation is presented to it in reality. We turn our attention therefore, in the first place, to this harmonious juxtaposition.

809.

As a very simple means of comprehending the principle of this, the reader has only to imagine a moveable diametrical index in the colorific circle.* The index, as it revolves round the whole circle, indicates at its two extremes the complemental colours, which, after all, may be reduced to three contrasts.

810.

Yellow demands Red-blue,
Blue   ,,   Red-yellow,
Red   ,,   Green,

and contrariwise.

811.

In proportion as one end of the supposed index deviates from the central intensity of the colours, arranged as they are in the natural order, so the opposite end changes its place in the contrasted gradation, and by such a simple

---

* Plate 1, fig. 3.

contrivance the complemental colours may be indicated at any given point. A chromatic circle might be made for this purpose, not confined, like our own, to the leading colours, but exhibiting them with their transitions in an unbroken series. This would not be without its use, for we are here considering a very important point which deserves all our attention.*

812.

We before stated that the eye could be in some degree pathologically affected by being long confined to a single colour; that, again, definite moral impressions were thus produced, at one time lively and aspiring, at another susceptible and anxious—now exalted to grand associations, now reduced to ordinary ones. We now observe that the demand for completeness, which is inherent in the organ, frees us from this restraint; the eye relieves itself by producing the opposite of the single colour forced upon it, and thus attains the entire impression which is so satisfactory to it.

813.

Simple, therefore, as these strictly harmonious contrasts are, as presented to us in the narrow circle, the hint is important, that nature tends to emancipate the sense from confined

---

* See Note C.

impressions by suggesting and producing the whole, and that in this instance we have a natural phenomenon immediately applicable to æsthetic purposes.

814.

While, therefore, we may assert that the chromatic scale, as given by us, produces an agreeable impression by its ingredient hues, we may here remark that those have been mistaken who have hitherto adduced the rainbow as an example of the entire scale; for the chief colour, pure red, is deficient in it, and cannot be produced, since in this phenomenon, as well as in the ordinary prismatic series, the yellow-red and blue-red cannot attain to a union.

815.

Nature perhaps exhibits no general phenomenon where the scale is in complete combination. By artificial experiments such an appearance may be produced in its perfect splendour. The mode, however, in which the entire series is connected in a circle, is rendered most intelligible by tints on paper, till after much experience and practice, aided by due susceptibility of the organ, we become penetrated with the idea of this harmony, and feel it present in our minds.

816.

Besides these pure, harmonious, self-developed combinations, which always carry the conditions of completeness with them, there are others which may be arbitrarily produced, and which may be most easily described by observing that they are to be found in the colorific circle, not by diameters, but by chords, in such a manner that an intermediate colour is passed over.

817.

We call these combinations characteristic because they have all a certain significancy and tend to excite a definite impression; an impression, however, which does not altogether satisfy, inasmuch as every characteristic quality of necessity presents itself only as a part of a whole, with which it has a relation, but into which it cannot be resolved.

818.

As we are acquainted with the impressions produced by the colours singly as well as in their harmonious relations, we may at once conclude that the character of the arbitrary combinations will be very different from each other as regards their significancy. We proceed to review them separately.

YELLOW AND BLUE.

819.

This is the simplest of such combinations. It may be said that it contains too little, for since every trace of red is wanting in it, it is defective as compared with the whole scale. In this view it may be called poor, and as the two contrasting elements are in their lowest state, may be said to be ordinary; yet it is recommended by its proximity to green—in short, by containing the ingredients of an ultimate state.

YELLOW AND RED.

820.

This is a somewhat preponderating combination, but it has a serene and magnificent effect. The two extremes of the active side are seen together without conveying any idea of progression from one to the other. As the result of their combination in pigments is yellow-red, so they in some degree represent this colour.

BLUE AND RED.

821.

The two ends of the passive side with the excess of the upper end of the active side. The effect of this juxtaposition approaches that of the blue-red produced by their union.

822.

These, when placed together, as the deepened extremes of both sides, have something exciting, elevated : they give us a presentiment of red, which in physical experiments is produced by their union.

823.

These four combinations have also the common quality of producing the intermediate colour of our colorific circle by their union, a union which actually takes place if they are opposed to each other in small quantities and seen from a distance. A surface covered with narrow blue and yellow stripes appears green at a certain distance.

824.

If, again, the eye sees blue and yellow next each other, it finds itself in a peculiar disposition to produce green without accomplishing it, while it neither experiences a satisfactory sensation in contemplating the detached colours, nor an impression of completeness in the two.

825.

Thus it will be seen that it was not without reason we called these combinations characteristic ; the more so, since the character of each combination must have a relation to that of the single colours of which it consists.

COMBINATIONS NON-CHARACTERISTIC.

826.

We now turn our attention to the last kind of combinations. These are easily found in the circle ; they are indicated by shorter chords, for in this case we do not pass over an entire intermediate colour, but only the transition from one to the other.

827.

These combinations may justly be called non-characteristic, inasmuch as the colours are too nearly alike for their impression to be significant. Yet most of these recommend themselves to a certain degree, since they indicate a progressive state, though its relations can hardly be appreciable.

828.

Thus yellow and yellow-red, yellow-red and red, blue and blue-red, blue-red and red, represent the nearest degrees of augmentation and culmination, and in certain relations as to quantity may produce no unpleasant effect.

829.

The juxtaposition of yellow and green has

always something ordinary, but in a cheerful sense; blue and green, on the other hand, is ordinary in a repulsive sense. Our good forefathers called these last fool's colours.

RELATION OF THE COMBINATIONS TO LIGHT AND DARK.

830.

These combinations may be very much varied by making both colours light or both dark, or one light and the other dark; in which modifications, however, all that has been found true in a general sense is applicable to each particular case. With regard to the infinite variety thus produced, we merely observe:

831.

The colours of the active side placed next to black gain in energy, those of the passive side lose. The active conjoined with white and brightness lose in strength, the passive gain in cheerfulness. Red and green with black appear dark and grave; with white they appear gay.

832.

To this we may add that all colours may be more or less broken or neutralised, may to a certain degree be rendered nameless, and thus combined partly together and partly with pure colours; but although the relations may thus be varied to infinity, still all that is applicable with regard to the pure colours will be applicable in these cases.

CONSIDERATIONS DERIVED FROM THE EVIDENCE OF EXPERIENCE AND HISTORY.

833.

The principles of the harmony of colours having been thus far defined, it may not be irrelevant to review what has been adduced in connexion with experience and historical examples.

834.

The principles in question have been derived from the constitution of our nature and the constant relations which are found to obtain in chromatic phenomena. In experience we find much that is in conformity with these principles, and much that is opposed to them.

835.

Men in a state of nature, uncivilised nations, children, have a great fondness for colours in their utmost brightness, and especially for yellow-red: they are also pleased with the motley. By this expression we understand the juxtaposition of vivid colours without an harmonious balance; but if this balance is observed, through instinct or accident, an agreeable effect may be produced. I remember a Hessian officer, returned from America, who had painted his face with the positive colours, in the manner of the Indians; a kind of completeness or due balance was thus produced, the effect of which was not disagreeable.

836.

The inhabitants of the south of Europe make use of very brilliant colours for their dresses. The circumstance of their procuring silk stuffs at a cheap rate is favourable to this propensity. The women, especially, with their bright-coloured bodices and ribbons, are always in harmony with the scenery, since they cannot possibly surpass the splendour of the sky and landscape.

837.

The history of dyeing teaches us that certain technical conveniences and advantages have had great influence on the costume of nations. We find that the Germans wear blue very generally because it is a permanent colour in cloth; so in many districts all the country people wear green twill, because that material takes a green dye well. If a traveller were to pay attention to these circumstances, he might collect some amusing and curious facts.

838.

Colours, as connected with particular frames

of mind, are again a consequence of peculiar character and circumstances. Lively nations, the French for instance, love intense colours, especially on the active side; sedate nations, like the English and Germans, wear straw-coloured or leather-coloured yellow accompanied with dark blue. Nations aiming at dignity of appearance, the Spaniards and Italians for instance, suffer the red colour of their mantles to incline to the passive side.

839.

In dress we associate the character of the colour with the character of the person. We may thus observe the relation of colours singly, and in combination, to the colour of the complexion, age, and station.

840.

The female sex in youth is attached to rose-colour and sea-green, in age to violet and dark-green. The fair-haired prefer violet, as opposed to light yellow, the brunettes, blue, as opposed to yellow-red, and all on good grounds. The Roman emperors were extremely jealous with regard to their purple. The robe of the Chinese Emperor is orange embroidered with red; his attendants and the ministers of religion wear citron-yellow.

841.

People of refinement have a disinclination to colours. This may be owing partly to weakness of sight, partly to the uncertainty of taste, which readily takes refuge in absolute negation. Women now appear almost universally in white and men in black.

842.

An observation, very generally applicable, may not be out of place here, namely, that man, desirous as he is of being distinguished, is quite as willing to be lost among his fellows.

843.

Black was intended to remind the Venetian noblemen of republican equality.

844.

To what degree the cloudy sky of northern climates may have gradually banished colour may also admit of explanation.

845.

The scale of positive colours is obviously soon exhausted ; on the other hand, the neutral, sub-dued, so-called fashionable colours present infinitely varying degrees and shades, most of which are not unpleasing.

846.

It is also to be remarked that ladies, in wearing positive colours, are in danger of making a complexion which may not be very bright still less so, and thus to preserve a due balance with such brilliant accompaniments, they are induced to heighten their complexions artificially.

847.

An amusing inquiry might be made which would lead to a critique of uniforms, liveries, cockades, and other distinctions, according to the principles above hinted at. It might be observed, generally, that such dresses and insignia should not be composed of harmonious colours. Uniforms should be characteristic and dignified ; liveries might be ordinary and striking to the eye. Examples both good and bad would not be wanting, since the scale of colours usually employed for such purposes is limited, and its varieties have been often enough tried.*

ÆSTHETIC INFLUENCE.

848.

From the moral associations connected with the appearance of colours, single or combined, their æsthetic influence may now be deduced

---

* Some early Italian writers, Sicillo, Occolti, Rinaldi, and others, have treated this subject in connexion with the supposed signification of colours.—T.

for the artist. We shall touch the most essential points to be attended to after first considering the general condition of pictorial representation, light and shade, with which the appearance of colour is immediately connected.

CHIARO-SCURO.

849.

We apply the term chiaro-scuro (Helldunkel) to the appearance of material objects when the mere effect produced on them by light and shade is considered.—Note **D D**.

850.

In a narrower sense a mass of shadow lighted by reflexes is often thus designated; but we here use the expression in its first and more general sense.

851.

The separation of light and dark from all appearance of colour is possible and necessary. The artist will solve the mystery of imitation sooner by first considering light and dark independently of colour, and making himself acquainted with it in its whole extent.

852.

Chiaro-scuro exhibits the substance as substance, inasmuch as light and shade inform us as to degrees of density.

853.

We have here to consider the highest light, the middle tint, and the shadow, and in the last the shadow of the object itself, the shadow it casts on other objects, and the illumined shadow or reflexion.

854.

The globe is well adapted for the general exemplification of the nature of chiaro-scuro, but it is not altogether sufficient. The softened unity of such complete rotundity tends to the vapoury, and in order to serve as a principle for effects of art, it should be composed of plane surfaces, so as to define the gradations more.

855.

The Italians call this manner "il piazzoso;" in German it might be called "das Flächenhafte."* If, therefore, the sphere is a perfect example of natural chiaro-scuro, a polygon would exhibit the artist-like treatment in which all kinds of lights, half-lights, shadows, and reflexions, would be appreciable.—Note E E.

856.

The bunch of grapes is recognised as a good example of a picturesque completeness in chiaro-scuro, the more so as it is fitted, from its form, to represent a principal group; but it is only

* The English technical expressions "flat" and "square" have an association of mannerism.—T.

available for the master who can see in it what he has the power of producing.

857.

In order to make the first idea intelligible to the beginner, (for it is difficult to consider it abstractedly even in a polygon,) we may take a cube, the three sides of which that are seen represent the light, the middle tint, and the shadow in distinct order.

858.

To proceed again to the chiaro-scuro of a more complicated figure, we might select the example of an open book, which presents a greater diversity.

859.

We find the antique statues of the best time treated very much with reference to these effects. The parts intended to receive the light are wrought with simplicity, the portion originally in shade is, on the other hand, in more distinct surfaces to make them susceptible of a variety of reflexions ; here the example of the polygon will be remembered.—Note **F F**.

860.

The pictures of Herculaneum and the Aldo-brandini marriage are examples of antique painting in the same style.

861.

Modern examples may be found in single figures by Raphael, in entire works by Correggio, and also by the Flemish masters, especially Rubens.

TENDENCY TO COLOUR.

862.

A picture in black and white seldom makes its appearance; some works of Polidoro are examples of this kind of art. Such works, inasmuch as they can attain form and keeping, are estimable, but they have little attraction for the eye, since their very existence supposes a violent abstraction.

863.

If the artist abandons himself to his feeling, colour presently announces itself. Black no sooner inclines to blue than the eye demands yellow, which the artist instinctively modifies, and introduces partly pure in the light, partly reddened and subdued as brown, in the reflexes, thus enlivening the whole.—Note G G.

864.

All kinds of *camayeu*, or colour on similar colour, end in the introduction either of a complemental contrast, or some variety of hue. Thus, Polidoro in his black and white frescoes sometimes introduced a yellow vase, or something of the kind.

865.

In general it may be observed that men have at all times instinctively striven after colour in the practice of the art. We need only observe daily, how soon amateurs proceed from colourless to coloured materials. Paolo Uccello painted coloured landscapes to colourless figures. —Note **H H.**

866.

Even the sculpture of the ancients could not be exempt from the influence of this propensity. The Egyptians painted their bas-reliefs ; statues had eyes of coloured stones. Porphyry draperies were added to marble heads and extremities, and variegated stalactites were used for the pedestals of busts. The Jesuits did not fail to compose the statue of their S. Luigi, in Rome, in this manner, and the most modern sculpture distinguishes the flesh from the drapery by staining the latter.

KEEPING.

867.

If linear perspective displays the gradation of objects in their apparent size as affected by distance, aërial perspective shows us their gradation in greater or less distinctness, as affected by the same cause.

868.

Although from the nature of the organ of sight, we cannot see distant objects so distinctly as nearer ones, yet aërial perspective is grounded strictly on the important fact that all mediums called transparent are in some degree dim.

869.

The atmosphere is thus always, more or less, semi-transparent. This quality is remarkable in southern climates, even when the barometer is high, the weather dry, and the sky cloudless, for a very pronounced gradation is observable between objects but little removed from each other.

870.

The appearance on a large scale is known to every one; the painter, however, sees or believes he sees, the gradation in the slightest varieties of distance. He exemplifies it practically by making a distinction, for instance, in the features of a face according to their relative position as regards the plane of the picture. The direction of the light is attended to in like manner. This is considered to produce a gradation from side to side, while keeping has reference to depth, to the comparative distinctness of near and distant things.

COLOURING.

871.

In proceeding to consider this subject, we assume that the painter is generally acquainted with our sketch of the theory of colours, and that he has made himself well acquainted with certain chapters and rubrics which especially concern him. He will thus be enabled to make use of theory as well as practice in recognising the principles of effect in nature, and in employing the means of art.

COLOUR IN GENERAL NATURE.

872.

The first indication of colour announces itself in nature together with the gradations of aerial perspective ; for aerial perspective is intimately connected with the doctrine of semi-transparent mediums. We see the sky, distant objects and even comparatively near shadows, blue. At the same moment, the illuminating and illuminated objects appear yellow, gradually deepening to red. In many cases the physiological suggestion of contrasts comes into the account, and an entirely colourless landscape, by means of these assisting and counteracting tendencies, appears to our eyes completely coloured.

873.

Local colours are composed of the general elementary colours; but these are determined or specified according to the properties of substances and surfaces on which they appear: this specification is infinite.

874.

Thus, there is at once a great difference between silk and wool similarly dyed. Every kind of preparation and texture produces corresponding modifications. Roughness, smoothness, polish, all are to be considered.

875.

It is therefore one of the pernicious prejudices of art that the skilful painter must never attend to the material of draperies, but always represent, as it were, only abstract folds. Is not all characteristic variety thus done away with, and is the portrait of Leo X. less excellent because velvet, satin, and moreen, are imitated in their relative effect?

876.

In the productions of nature, colours appear more or less modified, specified, even individualised: this may be readily observed in minerals and plants, in the feathers of birds and the skins of beasts.

877.

The chief art of the painter is always to imitate the actual appearance of the definite hue, doing away with the recollection of the elementary ingredients of colour. This difficulty is in no instance greater than in the imitation of the surface of the human figure.

878.

The colour of flesh, as a whole, belongs to the active side, yet the bluish of the passive side mingles with it. The colour is altogether removed from the elementary state and neutralised by organisation.

879.

To bring the colouring of general nature into harmony with the colouring of a given object, will perhaps be more attainable for the judicious artist after the consideration of what has been pointed out in the foregoing theory. For the most fancifully beautiful and varied appearances may still be made true to the principles of nature.

CHARACTERISTIC COLOURING.

880.

The combination of coloured objects, as well as the colour of their ground, should depend on considerations which the artist pre-establishes for himself. Here a reference to the effect of colours singly or combined, on the feelings, is especially necessary. On this account the painter should possess himself with the idea of the general dualism, as well as of particular contrasts, not forgetting what has been adverted to with regard to the qualities of colours.

881.

The characteristic in colour may be comprehended under three leading rubrics, which we here define as the powerful, the soft, and the splendid.

882.

The first is produced by the preponderance of the active side, the second by that of the passive side, and the third by completeness, by the exhibition of the whole chromatic scale in due balance.

883.

The powerful impression is attained by yellow, yellow-red, and red, which last colour is to be arrested on the plus side. But little violet and blue, still less green, are admissible. The soft effect is produced by blue, violet, and red, which in this case is arrested on the minus side; a moderate addition of yellow and yellow-red, but much green may be admitted.

884.

If it is proposed to produce both these effects in their full significancy, the complemental colours may be excluded to a minimum, and only so much of them may be suffered to appear as is indispensable to convey an impression of completeness.

HARMONIOUS COLOURING.

885.

Although the two characteristic divisions as above defined may in some sense be also called harmonious, the harmonious effect, properly so called, only takes place when all the colours are exhibited together in due balance.

886.

In this way the splendid as well as the agreeable may be produced; both of these, however, have of necessity a certain generalised effect, and in this sense may be considered the reverse of the characteristic.

887.

This is the reason why the colouring of most modern painters is without character, for, while they follow their general instinctive feeling only, the last result of such a tendency must be mere completeness; this, they more or less attain, but thus at the same time neglect the characteristic impression which the subject might demand.

888.

But if the principles before alluded to are kept in view, it must be apparent that a distinct style of colour may be adopted on safe grounds for every subject. The application requires, it is true, infinite modifications, which can only succeed in the hands of genius.

GENUINE TONE.

889.

If the word tone, or rather tune, is to be still borrowed in future from music, and applied to colouring, it might be used in a better sense than heretofore.

890.

For it would not be unreasonable to compare a painting of powerful effect, with a piece of music in a sharp key ; a painting of soft effect with a piece of music in a flat key, while other equivalents might be found for the modifications of these two leading modes.

FALSE TONE.

891.

The word tone has been hitherto understood to mean a veil of a particular colour spread over the whole picture ; it was generally yellow, for the painter instinctively pushed the effect towards the powerful side.

892.

If we look at a picture through a yellow glass it will appear in this tone. It is worth while to make this experiment again and again, in order to observe what takes place in such an operation. It is a sort of artificial light, deepening, and at the same time darkening the *plus* side, and neutralising the *minus* side.

893.

This spurious tone is produced instinctively through uncertainty as to the means of attaining a genuine effect; so that instead of completeness, monotony is the result.

WEAK COLOURING.

894.

It is owing to the same uncertainty that the colours are sometimes so much broken as to have the effect of a grey camayeu, the handling being at the same time as delicate as possible.

895.

The harmonious contrasts are often found to be very happily felt in such pictures, but without spirit, owing to a dread of the motley.

896.

A picture may easily become party-coloured or motley, when the colours are placed next each other in their full force, as it were only mechanically and according to uncertain impressions.

897.

If, on the other hand, weak colours are combined, even although they may be dissonant, the effect, as a matter of course, is not striking. The uncertainty of the artist is communicated to the spectator, who, on his side, can neither praise nor censure.

898.

It is also important to observe that the colours may be disposed rightly in themselves, but that a work may still appear motley, if they are falsely arranged in relation to light and shade.

899.

This may the more easily occur as light and shade are already defined in the drawing, and are, as it were, comprehended in it, while the colour still remains open to selection.

DREAD OF THEORY.

900.

A dread of, nay, a decided aversion for all

theoretical views respecting colour and everything belonging to it, has been hitherto found to
exist among painters ; a prejudice for which,
after all, they were not to be blamed ; for what
has been hitherto called theory was groundless,
vacillating, and akin to empiricism.   We hope
that our labours may tend to diminish this prejudice, and stimulate the artist practically to
prove and embody the principles that have been
explained.

ULTIMATE AIM.

901.

But without a comprehensive view of the
whole of our theory, the ultimate object will not
be attained.   Let the artist penetrate himself
with all that we have stated.   It is only by
means of harmonious relations in light and
shade, in keeping, in true and characteristic
colouring, that a picture can be considered complete, in the sense we have now learnt to attach
to the term.

GROUNDS.

902.

It was the practice of the earlier artists to
paint on light grounds.   This ground consisted
of gypsum, and was thickly spread on linen or
panel, and then levigated.   After the outline
was drawn, the subject was washed in with a

blackish or brownish colour. Pictures prepared in this manner for colouring are still in existence, by Leonardo da Vinci, and Fra Bartolomeo; there are also several by Guido.— Note I I.

903.

When the artist proceeded to colour, and had to represent white draperies, he sometimes suffered the ground to remain untouched. Titian did this latterly when he had attained the greatest certainty in practice, and could accomplish much with little labour. The whitish ground was left as a middle tint, the shadows painted in, and the high lights touched on.— Note K K.

904.

In the process of colouring, the preparation merely washed as it were underneath, was always effective. A drapery, for example, was painted with a transparent colour, the white ground shone through it and gave the colour life, so the parts previously prepared for shadows exhibited the colour subdued, without being mixed or sullied.

905.

This method had many advantages; for the painter had a light ground for the light portions of his work and a dark ground for the shadowed portions. The whole picture was prepared; the artist could work with thin colours in the shadows, and had always an internal light to give value to his tints. In our own time painting in water colours depends on the same principles.

906.

Indeed a light ground is now generally employed in oil-painting, because middle tints are thus found to be more transparent, and are in some degree enlivened by a bright ground ; the shadows, again, do not so easily become black.

907.

It was the practice for a time to paint on dark grounds. Tintoret probably introduced them. Titian's best pictures are not painted on a dark ground.

908.

The ground in question was red-brown, and when the subject was drawn upon it, the strongest shadows were laid in ; the colours of the lights impasted very thickly in the bright parts, and scumbled towards the shadows, so that the dark ground appeared through the thin colour as a middle tint. Effect was attained in finishing by frequently going over the bright parts and touching on the high lights.

909.

If this method especially recommended itself
in practice on account of the rapidity it allowed
of, yet it had pernicious consequences. The
strong ground increased and became darker,
and the light colours losing their brightness by
degrees, gave the shadowed portions more and
more preponderance. The middle tints became
darker and darker, and the shadows at last quite
obscure. The strongly impasted lights alone
remained bright, and we now see only light
spots on the painting. The pictures of the
Bolognese school, and of Caravaggio, afford
sufficient examples of these results.

910.

We may here in conclusion observe, that
glazing derives its effect from treating the prepared colour underneath as a light ground. By
this operation colours may have the effect of
being mixed to the eye, may be enhanced, and
may acquire what is called tone ; but they thus
necessarily become darker.

PIGMENTS.

911.

We receive these from the hands of the chemist and the investigator of nature. Much has
been recorded respecting colouring substances,

which is familiar to all by means of the press. But such directions require to be revised from time to time. The master meanwhile communicates his experience in these matters to his scholar, and artists generally to each other.

912.

Those pigments which according to their nature are the most permanent, are naturally much sought after, but the mode of employing them also contributes much to the duration of a picture. The fewest possible colouring materials are to be employed, and the simplest methods of using them cannot be sufficiently recommended.

913.

For from the multitude of pigments colouring has suffered much. Every pigment has its peculiar nature as regards its effect on the eye; besides this it has its peculiar quality, requiring a corresponding technical method in its application. The former circumstance is a reason why harmony is more difficult of attainment with many materials than with few, the latter, why chemical action and re-action may take place among the colouring substances.

914.

We may refer, besides, to some false tendencies which the artists suffer themselves to be led away with. Painters are always looking for new colouring substances, and believe when such a substance is discovered that they have made an advance in the art. They have a great curiosity to know the practical methods of the old masters, and lose much time in the search. Towards the end of the last century we were thus long tormented with wax-painting. Others turn their attention to the discovery of new methods, through which nothing new is accomplished; for, after all, it is the feeling of the artist only that informs every kind of technical process.

ALLEGORICAL, SYMBOLICAL, MYSTICAL APPLICATION OF COLOUR.

915.

It has been circumstantially shown above, that every colour produces a distinct impression on the mind, and thus addresses at once the eye and feelings. Hence it follows that colour may be employed for certain moral and æsthetic ends.

916.

Such an application, coinciding entirely with nature, might be called symbolical, since the colour would be employed in conformity with its effect, and would at once express its meaning. If, for example, pure red were assumed to

designate majesty, there can be no doubt that
this would be admitted to be a just and expressive symbol. All this has been already sufficiently entered into.

917.

Another application is nearly allied to this ;
it might be called the allegorical application. In this there is more of accident and
caprice, inasmuch as the meaning of the sign
must be first communicated to us before we
know what it is to signify ; what idea, for instance, is attached to the green colour, which
has been appropriated to hope ?

918.

That, lastly, colour may have a mystical allusion, may be readily surmised, for since every
diagram in which the variety of colours may be
represented points to those primordial relations
which belong both to nature and the organ of
vision, there can be no doubt that these may be
made use of as a language, in cases where it is
proposed to express similar primordial relations
which do not present themselves to the senses
in so powerful and varied a manner. The mathematician extols the value and applicability
of the triangle ; the triangle is revered by the
mystic ; much admits of being expressed in it
by diagrams, and, among other things, the law

of the phenomena of colours; in this case, indeed, we presently arrive at the ancient mysterious hexagon.

919.

When the distinction of yellow and blue is duly comprehended, and especially the augmentation into red, by means of which the opposite qualities tend towards each other and become united in a third; then, certainly, an especially mysterious interpretation will suggest itself, since a spiritual meaning may be connected with these facts; and when we find the two separate principles producing green on the one hand and red in their intenser state, we can hardly refrain from thinking in the first case on the earthly, in the last on the heavenly, generation of the Elohim.—Note L L.

920.

But we shall do better not to expose ourselves, in conclusion, to the suspicion of enthusiasm; since, if our doctrine of colours finds favour, applications and allusions, allegorical, symbolical, and mystical, will not fail to be made, in conformity with the spirit of the age.

CONCLUDING OBSERVATIONS.

In reviewing this labour, which has occupied me long, and which at last I give but as a sketch, I am reminded of a wish once expressed by a careful writer, who observed that he would gladly see his works printed at once as he conceived them, in order then to go to the task with a fresh eye; since everything defective presents itself to us more obviously in print than even in the cleanest manuscript. This feeling may be imagined to be stronger in my case, since I had not even an opportunity of going through a fair transcript of my work before its publication, these pages having been put together at a time when a quiet, collected state of mind was out of the question.*

Some of the explanations I was desirous of giving are to be found in the introduction, but in the portion of my work to be devoted to the history of the doctrine of colours, I hope to give a more detailed account of my investigations and the vicissitudes they underwent. One inquiry, however, may not be out of place here; the consideration, namely, of the question, what can a man accomplish who cannot devote his whole life to scientific pursuits? what can he perform as a temporary guest on an estate not his own, for the advantage of the proprietor?

When we consider art in its higher character, we might wish that masters only had to do with

---

* Towards the close of 1806, when Weimar was occupied by Napoleon after the battle of Jena.—T.

it, that scholars should be trained by the severest study, that amateurs might feel themselves happy in reverentially approaching its precincts. For a work of art should be the effusion of genius, the artist should evoke its substance and form from his inmost being, treat his materials with sovereign command, and make use of external influences only to accomplish his powers.

But if the professor in this case has many reasons for respecting the dilettante, the man of science has every motive to be still more indulgent, since the amateur here is capable of contributing what may be satisfactory and useful. The sciences depend much more on experiment than art, and for mere experiment many a votary is qualified. Scientific results are arrived at by many means, and cannot dispense with many hands, many heads. Science may be communicated, the treasure may be inherited, and what is acquired by one may be appropriated by many. Hence no one perhaps ought to be reluctant to offer his contributions. How much do we not owe to accident, to mere practice, to momentary observation. All who are endowed only with habits of attention, women, children, are capable of communicating striking and true remarks.

In science it cannot therefore be required, that he who endeavours to furnish something in its aid should devote his whole life to it, should survey and investigate it in all its extent; for this, in most cases, would be a severe condition even for the initiated. But if we look through the history of science in general, especially the history of physics, we shall find that many important acquisitions have been made by single inquirers, in single departments, and very often by unprofessional observers.

To whatever direction a man may be determined by inclination or accident, whatever class of phenomena especially strike him, excite his interest, fix his attention, and occupy him, the result will still be for the advantage of science: for every new relation that comes to light, every new mode of investigation, even the imperfect attempt, even error itself is available; it may stimulate other observers and is never without its use as influencing future inquiry.

With this feeling the author himself may look back without regret on his endeavours. From this consideration he can derive some encouragement for the prosecution of the remainder of his task; and although not satisfied with the result of his efforts, yet re-assured by the sincerity of his intentions, he ventures to recommend his past and future labours to the interest of his contemporaries and posterity.

Multi pertransibunt et augebitur scientia.

NOTES.

NOTE A.—Par. 18.

LEONARDO DA VINCI observes that "a light object relieved on a dark ground appears magnified;" and again, "Objects seen at a distance appear out of proportion; this is because the light parts transmit their rays to the eye more powerfully than the dark. A woman's white head-dress once appeared to me much wider than her shoulders, owing to their being dressed in black."* "It is now generally admitted that the excitation produced by light is propagated on the retina a little beyond the outline of the image. Professor Plateau, of Ghent, has devoted a very interesting special memoir to the description and explanation of phenomena of this nature. See his 'Mémoire sur l'Irradiation,' published in the 11th vol. of the Transactions of the Royal Academy of Sciences at Brussels."†—S. F.

NOTE B.—Par. 23.

"The duration of ocular spectra produced by strongly exciting the retina, may be conveniently measured by minutes and seconds; but to ascertain the duration of more evanescent phenomena, recourse must be had to other means. The Chevalier d'Arcy (Mem. de l'Acad. des Sc.

---

* "Trattato della Pittura, Roma, 1817," p. 143—223. This edition, published from a Vatican MS., contains many observations not included in former editions.

† A few notes (marked with inverted commas and with the signature S. F.) have been kindly furnished by a scientific friend.

1765,) endeavoured to ascertain the duration of the impression produced by a glowing coal in the following manner. He attached it to the circumference of a wheel, the velocity of which was gradually increased until the apparent trace of the object formed a complete circle, and then measured the duration of a revolution, which was obviously that of the impression. To ascertain the duration of a revolution it is sufficient merely to know the number of revolutions described in a given time. Recently more refined experiments of the same kind have been made by Professors Plateau and Wheatstone."—S. F.

NOTE C.—Par. 50.

Every treatise on the harmonious combination of colours contains the diagram of the chromatic circle more or less elaborately constructed. These diagrams, if intended to exhibit the contrasts produced by the action and re-action of the retina, have one common defect. The opposite colours are made equal in intensity ; whereas the complemental colour pictured on the retina is always less vivid, and always darker or lighter than the original colour. This variety undoubtedly accords more with harmonious effects in painting.

The opposition of two pure hues of equal intensity, differing only in the abstract quality of colour, would immediately be pronounced crude and inharmonious. It would not, however, be strictly correct to say that such a contrast is too violent ; on the contrary, it appears the contrast is not carried far enough, for though differing in colour, the two hues may be exactly similar in purity and intensity. Complete contrast, on the other hand, supposes dissimilarity in all respects.

In addition to the mere difference of hue, the eye, it seems, requires difference in the lightness or darkness of the hue. The spectrum of a colour relieved as a dark on a light ground, is a light colour on a dark ground, and *vice versâ*. Thus, if we look at a bright red wafer on the whitest surface, the complemental image will be still lighter than the white surface; if the same wafer is placed on a black surface, the complemental image will be still darker. The colour of both these spectra may be called greenish, but it is evident that a colour must be scarcely appreciable as such, if it is lighter than white and darker than black. It is, however, to be remarked, that the white surface round the light greenish image seems tinged with a reddish hue, and the black surface round the dark image becomes slightly illuminated with the same colour, thus in both cases assisting to render the image apparent (58).

The difficulty or impossibility of describing degrees of colour in words, has also had a tendency to mislead, by conveying the idea of more positive hues than the physiological contrast warrants. Thus, supposing scarlet to be relieved as a dark, the complemental colour is so light in degree and so faint in colour, that it should be called a pearly grey; whereas the theorists, looking at the quality of colour abstractedly, would call it a green-blue, and the diagram would falsely present such a hue equal in intensity to scarlet, or as nearly equal as possible.

Even the difference of mass which good taste requires may be suggested by the physiological phenomena, for unless the complemental image is suffered to fall on a surface precisely as near to the eye as that on which the original colour was displayed, it appears larger or smaller than the original object (22), and this in a rapidly increasing proportion. Lastly, the shape itself soon becomes changed (26).

That vivid colour demands the comparative absence of colour, either on a lighter or darker scale, as its contrast, may be inferred again from the fact that bright colourless objects produce strongly coloured spectra. In darkness, the spectrum which is first white, or nearly white, is followed by red: in light, the spectrum which is first black, is followed by green (39—44). All colour, as the author observes (259), is to be considered as half-light, inasmuch as it

is in every case lighter than black and darker than white.
Hence no contrast of colour with colour, or even of colour
with black or white, can be so great (as regards lightness or
darkness) as the contrast of black and white, or light and
dark abstractedly. This distinction between the differences
of degree and the differences of kind is important, since a
just application of contrast in colour may be counteracted
by an undue difference in lightness or darkness. The mere
contrast of colour is happily employed in some of Guido's
lighter pictures, but if intense darks had been opposed to his
delicate carnations, their comparative whiteness would have
been unpleasantly apparent. On the other hand, the flesh-
colour in Giorgione, Sebastian del Piombo (his best imi-
tator), and Titian, was sometimes so extremely glowing* that
the deepest colours, and black, were indispensable accompaniments. The manner of Titian as distinguished from
his imitation of Giorgione, is golden rather than fiery, and
his biographers are quite correct in saying that he was fond
of opposing red (lake) and blue to his flesh.† The correspondence of these contrasts with the physiological phenomena will be immediately apparent, while the occasional
practice of Rubens in opposing bright red to a still cooler
flesh-colour, will be seen to be equally consistent.

The effect of white drapery (the comparative absence of
colour) in enhancing the glow of Titian's flesh-colour, has
been frequently pointed out :‡ the shadows of white thus
opposed to flesh, often present, again, the physiological contrast, however delicately, according to the hue of the carna-

---

* " Ardito veramente alquanto, sanguigno, e quasi fiammeggiante."
—*Zanetti della Pittura Veneziana*, Ven. 1771, p. 90. Warm as the flesh
colour of the colourists is, it still never approaches a positive hue, if we except
some examples in frescoes and other works intended to be seen at a great
distance. Zanetti, speaking of a fresco by Giorgione, now almost obliterated,
compares the colour to " un vivo raggio di cocente sole."—*Varie Pitture a
fresco dei Principali Maestri Veneziani.* Ven. 1760.

† Ridolfi.

‡ Zanetti, l. ii.

tion. The lights, on the other hand, are not, and probably never were, quite white, but from the first, partook of the quality of depth, a quality assumed by the colourists to pervade every part of a picture more or less.*

It was before observed that the description of colours in words may often convey ideas of too positive a nature, and it may be remarked generally that the colours employed by the great masters are, in their ultimate effect, more or less subdued or broken. The physiological contrasts are, however, still applicable in the most comparatively neutral scale.

Again, the works of the colourists show that these oppositions are not confined to large masses (except perhaps in works to be seen only at a great distance) ; on the contrary, they are more or less apparent in every part, and when at last the direct and intentional operations of the artist may have been insufficient to produce them in their minuter degrees, the accidental results of glazing and other methods may be said to extend the contrasts to infinity. In such productions, where every smallest portion is an epitome of the whole, the eye still appreciates the fascinating effect of contrast, and the work is pronounced to be true and complete, in the best sense of the words.

The Venetian method of scumbling and glazing exhibits these minuter contrasts within each other, and is thus generally considered more refined than the system of breaking the colours, since it ensures a fuller gradation of hues, and produces another class of contrasts, those, namely, which result from degrees of transparence and opacity. In some of the Flemish and Dutch masters, and sometimes in Reynolds, the two methods are combined in great perfection.

---

* Two great authorities, divided by more than three centuries, Leon Battista Alberti and Reynolds, have recommended this subdued treatment of white. " It is to be remembered," says the first, " that no surface should be made so white that it cannot be made more so. In white dresses again, it is necessary to stop far short of the last degree of whiteness."—*Della Pittura*, l. ii., compare with Reynolds, vol. i. dis. 8.

The chromatic diagram does not appear to be older than the last century. It is one of those happy adaptations of exacter principles to the objects of taste which might have been expected from Leonardo da Vinci. That its true principle was duly felt is abundantly evident from the works of the colourists, as well as from the general observations of early writers.* The more practical directions occasionally to be met with in the treatises of Leon Battista Alberti, Leonardo da Vinci and others, are conformable to the same system. Some Italian works, not written by painters, which pretend to describe this harmony, are, however, very imperfect.† A passage in Lodovico Dolce's Dialogue on Colours is perhaps the only one worth quoting. "He," says that writer, "who wishes to combine colours that are agreeable to the eye, will put grey next dusky orange; yellow-green next rose-colour; blue next orange; dark purple, black, next dark-green; white next black, and white next flesh-colour."‡ The Dialogue on Painting, by the same author, has the reputation of containing some of Titian's precepts: if the above passage may be traced to the same source, it must be confessed that it is almost the only one of the kind in the treatise from which it is taken.

NOTE D.—Par. 66.

In some of these cases there can be no doubt that Goethe

---

* Vasari observes, " L'unione nella pittura è una discordanza di colori diversi accordati insième."—Vol. i. c. 18. This observation is repeated by various writers on art in nearly the same words, and at last appears in Sandrart : " Concordia, potissimum picturæ decus, in discordiâ consistit, et quasi litigio colorum."—P. i. c. 5. The source, perhaps, is Aristotle : he observes, " We are delighted with harmony, because it is the union of contrary principles having a ratio to each other."—*Problem.*

† See " Occolti Trattato de' Colori." Parma, 1568.

‡ " Volendo l'uomo accoppiare insième colori che all'occhio dilettino— porrà insième il berrettino col leonato ; il verde-giallo con l'incarnato e rosso ; il turchino con l'arangi ; il morello col verde oscuro ; il nero col bianco ; il bianco con l'incarnato."—*Dialogo di M. Lodovico Dolce nel quale si ragiona della qualità, diversità, e proprietà de' colori.* Venezia, 1565.

attributes the contrast too exclusively to the physiological cause, without making sufficient allowance for the actual difference in the colour of the lights. The purely physical nature of some coloured shadows was pointed out by Pohlmann; and Dr. Eckermann took some pains to convince Goethe of the necessity of making such a distinction. Goethe at first adhered to his extreme view, but some time afterwards confessed to Dr. Eckermann, that in the case of the blue shadows of snow (74), the reflection of the sky was undoubtedly to be taken into the account. "Both causes may, however, operate together," he observed, "and the contrast which a warm yellow light demands may heighten the effect of the blue." This was all his opponent contended.*

With a few such exceptions, the general theory of Goethe with regard to coloured shadows is undoubtedly correct; the experiments with two candles (68), and with coloured glass and fluids (80), as well as the observations on the shadows of snow (75), are conclusive, for in all these cases only one light is actually changed in colour, while the other still assumes the complemental hue. "Coloured shadows," Dr. J. Müller observes, "are usually ascribed to the physiological influence of contrast; the complementary colour presented by the shadow being regarded as the effect of internal causes acting on that part of the retina, and not of the impression of coloured rays from without. This explanation is the one adopted by Rumford, Goethe, Grotthuss, Brandes, Tourtual, Pohlmann, and most authors who have studied the subject."†

In the Historical Part the author gives an account of a scarce French work, " Observations sur les Ombres Colorées," Paris, 1782. The writer‡ concludes that " the colour

---

* Eckermann's " Gespräche mit Goethe," vol. ii. p. 76 and 280.

† " Elements of Physiology," by J. Müller, M.D., translated from the German by William Baly, M.D. London, 1839.

‡ Anonymous, having only given the initials H. F. T.

of shadows is as much owing to the light that causes them as to that which (more faintly) illumines them."

NOTE E.—Par. 69.

This opinion of the author is frequently repeated (201, 312, 591), and as it seems at first sight to be at variance with a received principle of art, it may be as well at once to examine it.

In order to see the general proposition in its true point of view, it will be necessary to forget the arbitrary distinctions of light and shade, and to consider all such modifications between highest brightness and absolute darkness only as so many lesser degrees of light.* The author, indeed, by the word shadow, always understands a lesser light.

The received notion, as stated by Du Fresnoy,† is much too positive and unconditional, and is only true when we understand the "displaying" light to comprehend certain degrees of half or reflected light, and the "destroying" shade to mean the intensest degree of obscurity.

There are degrees of brightness which destroy colour as well as degrees of darkness.‡ In general, colour resides in a mitigated light, but a very little observation shows us that different colours require different degrees of light to display them. Leonardo da Vinci frequently inculcates the general principle above alluded to, but he as frequently qualifies it; for he not only remarks that the highest light may be com-

---

* Leonardo da Vinci observes : " L'ombra è diminuzione di luce, tenebre è privazione di luce." And again : " Sempre il minor lume è ombra del lume maggiore."—*Trattato della Pittura*, pp. 274-299.

N. B. The same edition before described has been consulted throughout.

† " Lux varium vivumque dabit, nullum umbra colorem."

De Arte Graphicâ.

" Know first that light displays and shade destroys

Refulgent nature's variegated dies."—MASON's *Translation.*

‡ A Spanish writer, Diego de Carvalho e Sampayo, quoted by Goethe (" Farbenlehre," vol. ii.), has a similar observation. This destroying effect of light is striking in climates where the sun is powerful, and was not likely to escape the notice of a Spaniard.

parative privation of colour, but observes, with great truth, that some hues are best displayed in their fully illumined parts, some in their reflections, and some in their half-lights; and again, that every colour is most beautiful when lit by reflections from its own surface, or from a hue similar to its own.*

The Venetians went further than Leonardo in this view and practice; and he seems to allude to them when he criticises certain painters, who, in aiming at clearness and fulness of colour, neglected what, in his eyes, was of superior importance, namely, gradation and force of chiaroscuro.†

That increase of colour supposes increase of darkness, as so often stated by Goethe, may be granted without difficulty. To what extent, on the other hand, increase of darkness, or rather diminution of light, is accompanied by increase of colour, is a question which has been variously answered by various schools. Examples of the total negation of the principle are not wanting, nor are they confined to the infancy of the art. Instances, again, of the opposite tendency are frequent in Venetian and early Flemish pictures resembling the augmenting richness of gems or of stained glass :‡

---

* Trattato, pp. 103, 121, 123, 324, &c.

† Ib. pp. 85, 134.

‡ Absolute opacity, to judge from the older specimens of stained glass, seems to have been considered inadmissible. The window was to admit light, however modified and varied, in the form prescribed by the architect, and that form was to be preserved. This has been unfortunately lost sight of in some modern glass-painting, which, by excluding the light in large masses, and adopting the opacity of pictures (the reverse of the influence above alluded to), has interfered with the architectural symmetry in a manner far from desirable. On the other hand, if we suppose painting at any period to have aimed at the imitation of stained glass, such an imitation must of necessity have led to extreme force; for the painter sets out by substituting a mere white ground for the real light of the sky, and would thus be compelled to subdue every tone accordingly. In such an imitation his colour would soon deepen to its intensest state; indeed, considerable portions of the darker hues would be lost in obscurity. The early Flemish pictures seldom err on the side of a gay superabundance of colour; on the contrary, they are generally re-

indeed, it is not impossible that the increase of colour in shade, which is so remarkable in the pictures alluded to, may have been originally suggested by the rich and fascinating effect of stained glass; and the Venetians, in this as in many other respects, may have improved on a hint borrowed from the early German painters, many of whom painted on glass.*

At all events, the principle of still increasing in colour in certain hues seems to have been adopted in Flanders and in Venice at an early period;† while Giorgione, in carrying the style to the most daring extent, still recommended it by corresponding grandeur of treatment in other respects.

The same general tendency, except that the technical methods are less transparent, is, however, very striking in some of the painters of the school of Umbria, the instructors or early companions of Raphael.‡ The influence of

---

markable for comparatively cool lights, for extreme depth, and a certain subdued splendour, qualities which would necessarily result from the imitation or influence in question.

* See Langlois, " Peinture sur Verre." Rouen, 1832 ; Descamps, " La Vie des Peintres Flamands ;" and Gessert, " Geschichte der Glasmalerei." Stutgard, 1839. The antiquity of the glass manufactory of Murano (Venice) is also not to be forgotten. Vasari objects to the Venetian glass, because it was darker in colour than that of Flanders, France, and England ; but this very quality was more likely to have an advantageous influence on the style of the early oil-painters. The use of stained glass was, however, at no period very general in Italy.

† Zanetti, " Della Pittura Veneziana," marks the progress of the early Venetian painters by the gradual use of the warm outline. There are some mosaics in St. Mark's which have the effect of flesh-colour, but on examination, the only red colour used is found to be in the outlines and markings. Many of the drawings of the old masters, heightened with red in the shadows, have the same effect. In these drawings the artists judiciously avoided colouring the lips and cheeks much, for this would only have betrayed the want of general colour, as is observable when statues are so treated.

‡ Andrea di Luigi, called L'Ingegno, and Niccolo di Fuligno, are cited as the most prominent examples. See Rumohr, " Italienische Forschungen." Perugino himself occasionally adopted a very glowing colour.

The early Italian schools which adhered most to the Byzantine types appear to have been also the most remarkable for depth, or rather darkness, of colour. This fidelity to customary representation was sometimes, as in the schools of these examples, as well as that of Fra Bartolommeo, in Florence, is distinctly to be traced in the works of the great artist just named, but neither is so marked as the effect of his emulation of a Venetian painter at a later period. The glowing colour, sometimes bordering on exaggeration, which Raphael adopted in Rome, is undoubtedly to be attributed to the rivalry of Sebastian del Piombo. This painter, the best of Giorgione's imitators, arrived in Rome, invited by Agostini Chigi, in 1511, and the most powerful of Raphael's frescoes, the Heliodorus and Mass of Bolsena, as well as some portraits in the same style, were painted in the two following years. In the hands of some of Raphael's scholars, again, this extreme warmth was occasionally carried to excess, particularly by Pierino del Vaga, with whom it often degenerated into redness. The representative of the glowing manner in Florence was Fra Bartolommeo, and, in the same quality, considered abstractedly, some painters of the school of Ferrara were second to none.

In another Note (par. 177) some further considerations

Umbria, and to a certain extent in those of Siena and Bologna, the result of a religious veneration for the ancient examples ; in others, as in Venice, the circumstance of frequent intercourse with the Levant is also to be taken into the account. The Greek pictures of the Madonna, not to mention other representations, were extremely dark, in exaggerated conformity, it is supposed, with the tradition respecting her real complexion (see D'Agincourt, vol. iv. p. 1) ; a belief which obtained so late as Lomazzo's time, for, speaking of the Madonna, he observes, " Leggesi però che fu alquanto bruna." Giotto, who with the independence of genius betrayed a certain contempt for these traditions, failed perhaps to unite improvement with novelty when he substituted a pale white flesh-colour for the traditional brown. Some specimens of his works, still existing at Padua, present a remarkable contrast in this respect with the earliest productions of the Venetian and Paduan artists. His works at Florence differ as widely from those of the earlier painters of Tuscany. This peculiarity was inherited by his imitators, and at one time almost characterised the Florentine school. Leon Battista Alberti was not perhaps the first who objected to it (" Vorrei io che dai pittori fosse comperato il color bianco assai più caro che le preziosissime gemme."—*Della Pittura*, l. ii.) The attachment of Fra Bartolommeo to the grave character of the Christian types is exemplified in his deep colouring, as well as in other respects.

are offered, which may partly explain the prevalence of this style in the beginning of the sixteenth century; here we merely add, that the conditions under which the appearance itself is most apparent in nature are perhaps more obvious in Venice than elsewhere. The colour of general nature may be observed in all places with almost equal convenience, but with regard to an important quality in living nature, namely, the colour of flesh, perhaps there are no circumstances in which its effects at different distances can be so conveniently compared as when the observer and the observed gradually approach and glide past each other on so smooth an element and in so undisturbed a manner as on the canals and in the gondolas of Venice;* the complexions, from the peculiar mellow carnations of the Italian women to the sun-burnt features and limbs of the mariners, presenting at the same time the fullest variety in another sense.

At a certain distance—the colour being always assumed to be unimpaired by interposed atmosphere—the reflections appear kindled to intenser warmth; the fiery glow of Giorgione is strikingly apparent; the colour is seen in its largest relation; the *macchia*,† an expression so emphatically used by Italian writers, appears in all its quantity, and the reflections being the focus of warmth, the hue seems to deepen in shade.

A nearer view gives the detail of cooler tints more perceptibly,‡ and the forms are at the same time more distinct. Hence Lanzi is quite correct when, in distinguishing the style of Titian from that of Giorgione, he says that Titian's

---

* Holland might be excepted, and in Holland similar causes may have had a similar influence.

† Local colour; literally, the *blot*.

‡ Zanetti ventures to single out the picture of Tobit and the Angel in S. Marziale as the first example of Titian's own manner, and in which a direct imitation of Giorgione is no longer apparent. In this picture the lights are cool and the blood-tint very effective.

was at once more defined and less fiery.* In a still nearer observation the eye detects the minute lights which Leonardo da Vinci says are incompatible with effects such as those we have described,† and which, accordingly, we never find in Giorgione and Titian. This large impression of colour, which seems to require the condition of comparative distance for its full effect, was most fitly employed by the same great artists in works painted in the open air or for large altar-pieces. Their celebrated frescoes on the exterior of the Fondaco de' Tedeschi at Venice, to judge from their faint remains and the descriptions of earlier writers, were remarkable for extreme warmth in the shadows. The old frescoes in the open air throughout Friuli have often the same character, and, owing to the fulness of effect which this treatment ensures, are conspicuous at a very great distance.‡

In assuming that the Venetian painters may have acquired a taste for this breadth§ of colour under the circumstances above alluded to, it is moreover to be remembered that the time for this agreeable study was the evening; when the sun had already set behind the hills of Bassano; when the light was glowing but diffused; when shadows

---

* " Meno sfumato, men focoso."—*Storia Pittorica.*

† " La prima cosa che de' colori si perde nelle distanze è il lustro, loro minima parte."—*Trattato,* p. 213; and elsewhere, " I lumi principali in picciol luogo son quelli che in picciola distanza sono i primi che si perdono all' occhio." —p. 128.

‡ A colossal St. Christopher, the usual subject, is frequently seen occupying the whole height of the external wall of a church. We have here an example of the influence of religion, such as it was, even on the style of colouring and practical methods of the art. The mere sight of the image of St. Christopher, the type of strength, was considered sufficient to reinvigorate those who were exhausted by the labours of husbandry. The following is a specimen of the inscriptions inculcating this belief :—

" Christophori Sancti speciem quicumque tuetur,
    Illo namque die nullo languore tenetur."

Hence the practice of painting the figure on the outside of churches, hence its colossal size, and hence the powerful qualities in colour above described. See Maniago, " Storia delle Belle Arti Friulane."

§ The authority of Fuseli sufficiently warrants the application of the term breadth to colour ; he speaks of Titian's " breadth of local tint."

were soft—conditions all agreeing with the character of
their colouring :* above all, when the hour invited the
fairer portion of the population to betake themselves in
their gondolas to the lagunes. The scene of this "prome-
nade" was to the north of Venice, the quarter in which
Titian at one time lived. A letter exists written by Francesco Priscianese, giving an account of his supping with
the great painter in company with Jacopo Nardi, Pietro
Aretino, the sculptor Sansovino, and others. The writer
speaks of the beauty of the garden, where the table was
prepared, looking over the lagunes towards Murano, "which
part of the sea," he continues, "as soon as the sun was
down, was covered with a thousand gondolas, graced with
beautiful women, and enlivened by the harmony of voices
and instruments, which lasted till midnight, forming a
pleasing accompaniment to our cheerful repast."†

To return to Goethe : perhaps the foregoing remarks may
warrant the conclusion that his idea of colour in shadow is
not irreconcileable with the occasional practice of the best
painters. The highest examples of the style thus defined
are, or were, to be found in the works of Giorgione‡ and
Titian, and hence the style itself, though "within that circle"

---

* Zanetti quotes an opinion of the painters of his time to the same effect :—
"Teneano essi (alcuni maestri) per cosa certa, che in molte opere Tiziano
volesse fingere il lume—quale si vede nell' inclinarsi del sole verso la sera.
Gli orizzonti assai luminosi dietro le montagne, le ombre incerte e più le car-
nagioni brunette e rosseggianti delle figure, gl'induceano a creder questo."—
Lib. ii. Leonardo da Vinci observes, "Quel corpo che si troverà in mediocre
lume fia in lui poca differenza da' lumi all' ombre. E questo accade sul far
della sera—e queste opere sono dolci ed hacci grazia ogni qualità di volto,"
&c.—p. 336. Elsewhere, "Le ombre fatte dal sole od altri lumi particolari
sono senza grazia."—p. 357 ; see also p. 247.

† See "Francesco Priscianese De' Primi Principii della Lingua Latina,"
Venice, 1550. The letter is at the end of the work. It is quoted in Ticozzi's
"Vite de' Pittori Vecelli," Milan, 1817.

‡ The works of Giorgione are extremely rare. The pictures best calculated
to give an idea of the glowing manner for which he is celebrated, are the
somewhat early works and several of the altar-pieces of Titian, the best
specimens of Palma Vecchio, and the portraits of Sebastian del Piombo.

few "dare walk," is to be considered the grandest and most perfect. Its possible defects or abuse are not to be dissembled : in addition to the danger of exaggeration* it is seldom united with the plenitude of light and shade, or with roundness ; yet, where fine examples of both modes of treatment may be compared, the charm of colour has perhaps the advantage.† The difficulty of uniting qualities so different in their nature, is proved by the very rare instances in which it has been accomplished. Tintoret in endeavouring to add chiaro-scuro to Venetian colour, in almost every instance fell short of the glowing richness of Titian.‡

---

* Zanetti and Lodovico Dolce mention Lorenzo Lotto as an instance of the excess of Giorgione's style. Titian himself sometimes overstepped the mark, as his biographers confess, and as appears, among other instances, from the head of St. Peter in the picture (now in the Vatican) in which the celebrated St. Sebastian is introduced. Raphael was criticised by some cardinals for a similar defect. See " Castiglione, Il Cortigiano," l. ii.

In the same paragraph to which the present observations refer, the authority of Kircher is quoted ; his treatise, " Ars magna lucis et umbræ," was published in Rome in 1646. In a portrait of Nicholas Poussin, engraved by Clouet, the painter is represented holding a book, which, from the title and the circumstance of Poussin having lived in Rome in Kircher's time, Goethe supposes to be the work in question. The abuse of the principle above alluded to, is perhaps exemplified in the red half-tints observable in some of Poussin's figures.

The augmentation of colour in subdued light was still more directly taught by Lomazzo. He composes the half-tints of flesh merely by diminishing the quantity of white, the proportions of the other colours employed (for he enters into minute details) remaining unaltered. See his " Trattato della arte della Pittura," Milan, 1584, p. 301.

† In the Dresden Gallery, a picture attributed to Titian—at all events a lucid Venetian picture—hangs next the St. George of Correggio. After looking at the latter, the Venetian work appears glassy and unsubstantial, but on reversing the order of comparison, the Correggio may be said to suffer more, and for a moment its fine transitions of light and shade seem changed to heaviness.

‡ The finest works of Tintoret—the Crucifixion and the Miracolo del Servo (considered here merely with reference to their colour,) may be said to combine the excellences of Titian and Giacomo Bassan, on a grand scale ; the sparkling clearness of the latter is one of the prominent characteristics of these pictures. Tintoret is reported to have once said that a union of his own knowledge of form with Bassan's colour would be the perfection of painting. See " Verci Notizie de' Pittori di Bassano ;" Ven. 1775, p. 61.

Giacomo Bassan and his imitators, even in their dark effects, still had the principle of the gem in view : their light, in certain hues, is the minimum of colour, their lower tones are rich, their darks intense, and all is sparkling.* Of the great painters who, beginning, on the other hand, with chiaroscuro, sought to combine with it the full richness of colour, Correggio, in the opinion of many, approached perfection nearest ; but we may perhaps conclude with greater justice that the desired excellence was more completely attained by Rembrandt than by any of the Italians.

NOTE F.—Par. 83.

The author, in these instances, seems to be anticipating his subsequent explanations on the effect of semi-transparent mediums. For an explanation of the general view contained in these paragraphs respecting the gradual increase of colour from high light, see the last Note.

The anonymous French work before alluded to, among other interesting examples, contains a chapter on shadows cast by the upper light of the sky and coloured by the setting sun. The effect of this remarkable combination is, that the light on a wall is most coloured immediately under a projecting roof, and becomes comparatively neutralised in proportion to its distance from the edge of the darkest shade.

NOTE G.—Par. 98.

" The simplest case of the phenomenon, which Goethe calls a subjective halo, and one which at once explains its cause, is the following. Regard a red wafer on a sheet of white paper, keeping the eye stedfastly fixed on a point at

---

* That this last quality, the characteristic of Bassan's best pictures, was held in high estimation by Paul Veronese, is not only evident from that painter's own works, but from the circumstance of his preferring to place his sons with Bassan rather than with any other painter. (See " Boschini Carta del Navegar," p. 280.) The Baptism of Sta. Lucilla, in Boschini's time considered the finest of Giacomo's works, is still in the church of S. Valentino, at Bassano, and may be considered the type of the lucid and sparkling manner.

its center. When the retina is fatigued, withdraw the head a little from the paper, and a green halo will appear to surround the wafer. By this slight increase of distance the image of the wafer itself on the retina becomes smaller, and the ocular spectrum which before coincided with the direct image, being now relatively larger, is seen as a surrounding ring."—S. F. Goethe mentions cases of this kind, but does not class them with subjective halos. See Par. 30.

NOTE H.—Par. 113.

" Cases of this kind are by no means uncommon. Several interesting ones are related in Sir John Herschell's article on Light in the Encyclopædia Metropolitana. Careful investigation has, however, shown that this defect of vision arises in most, if not in all cases, from an inability to perceive the red, not the blue rays. The terms are so confounded by the individuals thus affected, that the comparison of colours in their presence is the only criterion."—S. F.

NOTE I.—Par. 135.

The author more than once admits that this chapter on " Pathological Colours" is very incomplete, and expresses a wish (Par. 734) that some medical physiologists would investigate the subject further. This was afterwards in a great degree accomplished by Dr. Johannes Müller, in his memoir " Uber die Phantastischen Gesichtserscheinungen." Coblentz, 1826. Similar phenomena have been also investigated with great labour and success by Purkinje. For a collection of extraordinary facts of the kind recorded by these writers, the reader may consult Scott's Letters on Demonology and Witchcraft.* The instances adduced by Müller and others are, however, intended to prove the inherent capacity of the organ of vision to produce light and colours. In some maladies of the eye, the patient, it seems,

---

* See also a curious passage on the beatific vision of the monks of Mount Athos, in Gibbon, chap. 63.

suffers the constant presence of light without external light. The exciting principle in this case is thus proved to be within, and the conclusion of the physiologists is that external light is only one of the causes which produce luminous and coloured impressions. That this view was anticipated by Newton may be gathered from the concluding " query" in the third book of his Optics.

NOTE K.—Par. 140.

" Catoptrical colours. The colours included under this head are principally those of fibres and grooved surfaces ; they can be produced artificially by cutting parallel grooves on a surface of metal from 2000 to 10,000 in the inch. See ' Brewster's Optics,' p 120. The colours called by Goethe *paroptical,* correspond with those produced by the diffraction or inflection of light in the received theory.—See Brewster, p. 95. The phenomena included under the title ' Epoptical Colours,' are generally known as the colours of thin plates. They vary with the thickness of the film, and the colour seen by reflection always differs from that seen by transmission. The laws of these phenomena have been thoroughly investigated. See Nobili, and Brewster, p. 100." —S. F.

The colours produced by the transmission of polarised light through chrystalised mediums, were described by Goethe, in his mode, subsequently to the publication of his general theory, under the name of Entoptic Colours. See note to Par. 485.

NOTE L.—Par. 150.

We have in this and the next paragraph the outline of Goethe's system. The examples that follow seem to establish the doctrine here laid down, but there are many cases which it appears cannot be explained on such principles : hence, philosophers generally prefer the theory of absorption, according to which it appears that certain mediums " have the property of absorbing some of the component rays of white light, while they allow the passage of others."*

Whether all the facts adduced by Goethe—for instance, that recorded in Par. 172, are to be explained by this doctrine, we leave to the investigators of nature to determine. Dr. Eckermann, in conversing with Goethe, thus described the two leading phenomena (156, 158) as seen by him in the Alps. " At a distance of eighteen or twenty miles at midday in bright sunshine, the snow appeared yellow or even reddish, while the dark parts of the mountain, free from snow, were of the most decided blue. The appearances did not surprise me, for I could have predicted that the mass of the interposed medium would give a deep yellow tone to the white snow, but I was pleased to witness the effect, since it so entirely contradicted the erroneous views of some philosophers, who assert that the air has a blue-tinging quality. The observation, said Goethe, is of importance, and contradicts the error you allude to completely."†

The same writer has some observations to the same effect on the colour of the Rhone at Geneva. A circumstance of an amusing nature which he relates in confirmation of Goethe's theory, deserves to be inserted. " Here (at Strasburg), passing by a shop, I saw a little glass bust of Napoleon, which, relieved as it was against the dark in-

---

* See " Muller's Elements of Physiology," translated from the German by William Baly, M.D. " The laws of absorption," it has been observed, " have not been studied with so much success as those of other phenomena of physical optics, but some excellent observations on the subject will be found in Herschell's Treatise on Light in the Encyclopædia Metropolitana, § III."

† " Eckermann's Gespräche mit Goethe," vol. ii. p. 280. Leonardo da Vinci had made precisely the same observation. " A distant mountain will appear of a more beautiful blue in proportion as it is dark in colour. The illumined air, interposed between the eye and the dark mass, being thinner towards the summit of the mountain, will exhibit the darkness as a deeper blue and *vice versâ*."—*Trattato della Pittura*, p. 143. Elsewhere—" The air which intervenes between the eye and dark mountains becomes blue ; but it does not become blue in (before) the light part, and much less in (before) the portion that is covered with snow."—p. 244.

terior of the room, exhibited every gradation of blue, from
milky light blue to deep violet. I foresaw that the bust
seen from within the shop with the light behind it, would
present every degree of yellow, and I could not resist walking in and addressing the owner, though perfectly unknown
to me. My first glance was directed to the bust, in which,
to my great joy, I saw at once the most brilliant colours of
the warmer kind, from the palest yellow to dark ruby red.
I eagerly asked if I might be allowed to purchase the bust;
the owner replied that he had only lately brought it with
him from Paris, from a similar attachment to the emperor
to that which I appeared to feel, but, as my ardour seemed
far to surpass his, I deserved to possess it. So invaluable
did this treasure seem in my eyes, that I could not help
looking at the good man with wonder as he put the bust into
my hands for a few franks. I sent it, together with a curious
medal which I had bought in Milan, as a present to Goethe,
and when at Frankfort received the following letter from
him." The letter, which Dr. Eckermann gives entire, thus
concludes—" When you return to Weimar you shall see
the bust in bright sunshine, and while the transparent
countenance exhibits a quiet blue,* the thick mass of the
breast and epaulettes glows with every gradation of warmth,
from the most powerful ruby-red downwards; and as the
granite statue of Memnon uttered harmonious sounds, so the
dim glass image displays itself in the pomp of colours. The
hero is victorious still in supporting the Farbenlehre."†

One effect of Goethe's theory has been to invite the attention of scientific men to facts and appearances which
had before been unnoticed or unexplained. To the above
cases may be added the very common, but very important,
fact in painting, that a light warm colour, passed in a semi-

---

* This supposes either that the mass was considerably thicker, or that there
was a dark ground behind the head, and a light ground behind the rest of the
figure.

† " Eckermann's Gespräche mit Goethe," vol. ii. p. 242.

transparent state over a dark one, produces a cold, bluish hue, while the operation reversed, produces extreme warmth. On the judicious application of both these effects, but especially of the latter, the richness and brilliancy of the best-coloured pictures greatly depends. The principle is to be recognised in the productions of schools apparently opposite in their methods. Thus the practice of leaving the ground, through which a light colour is apparent, as a means of ensuring warmth and depth, is very common among the Dutch and Flemish painters. The Italians, again, who preferred a solid under-painting, speak of internal light as the most fascinating quality in colour. When the ground is entirely covered by solid painting, as in the works of some colourists, the warmest tints in shadows and reflections have been found necessary to represent it. This was the practice of Rembrandt frequently, and of Reynolds universally, but the glow of their general colour is still owing to its being repeatedly or ultimately enriched on the above principle. Lastly, the works of those masters who were accustomed to paint on dark grounds are often heavy and opaque; and even where this influence of the ground was overcome, the effects of time must be constantly diminishing the warmth of their colouring as the surface becomes rubbed and the dark ground more apparent through it. The practice of painting on dark grounds was intended by the Carracci to compel the students of their school to aim at the direct imitation of the model, and to acquire the use of the brush; for the dark ground could only be overcome by very solid painting. The result answered their expectations as far as dexterity of pencil was concerned, but the method was fatal to brilliancy of colour. An intelligent writer of the seventeenth century* relates that Guido adopted his extremely light style from seeing the rapid change in some works of the Carracci soon after they were done It

---

* Scanelli, " Microcosmo della Pittura," Cesena, 1657, p. 114.

is important, however, to remark, that Guido's remedy was external rather than internal brilliancy; and it is evident that so powerless a brightness as white paint can only acquire the splendour of light by great contrast, and, above all, by being seen through external darkness. The secret of Van Eyck and his contemporaries is always assumed to consist in the vehicle (varnish or oils) he employed; but a far more important condition of the splendour of colour in the works of those masters was the careful preservation of internal light by painting thinly, but ultimately with great force, on white grounds. In some of the early Flemish pictures in the Royal Gallery at Munich, it may be observed, that wherever an alteration was made by the painter, so that a light colour is painted over a dark one, the colour is as opaque as in any of the more modern pictures which are generally contrasted with such works. No quality in the vehicle could prevent this opacity under such circumstances; and on the other hand, provided the internal splendour is by any means preserved, the vehicle is comparatively unimportant.

It matters not (say the authorities on these points) whether the effect in question is attained by painting thinly over the ground, in the manner of the early Flemish painters and sometimes of Rubens, or by painting a solid light preparation to be afterwards toned to richness in the manner of the Venetians. Among the mechanical causes of the clearness of colours superposed on a light preparation may be mentioned that of careful grinding. All writers on art who have descended to practical details have insisted on this. From the appearance of some Venetian pictures it may be conjectured that the colours of the solid under-painting were sometimes less perfectly ground than the scumbling colours (the light having to pass through the one and to be reflected from the other). The Flemish painters appear to have used carefully-ground pigments universally. This is very evident in Flemish copies from Raphael, which, though equally impasted with the originals, are to be detected, among other indications, by the finely-ground colours employed.

NOTE M.—Par. 177.

Without entering further into the scientific merits or demerits of this chapter on the "First Class of Dioptrical Colours," it is to be observed that several of the examples correspond with the observations of Leonardo da Vinci, and again with those of a much older authority, namely, Aristotle. Goethe himself admits, and it has been remarked by others, that his theory, in many respects, closely resembles that of Aristotle: indeed he confesses* that at one time he had an intention of merely paraphrasing that philosopher's Treatise on Colours.†

We have already remarked (Note on par. 150) that Goethe's notion with regard to the production of warm colours, by the interposition of dark transparent mediums before a light ground, agrees with the practice of the best schools in colouring; and it is not impossible that the same reasons which may make this part of the doctrine generally acceptable to artists now, may have recommended the very similar theory of Aristotle to the painters of the fifteenth and sixteenth centuries: at all events, it appears that the ancient theory was known to those painters.

It is unnecessary to dwell on the fact that the doctrines of Aristotle were enthusiastically embraced and generally inculcated at the period in question;‡ but it has not been

---

* "Geschichte der Farbenlehre," in the "Nachgelassene Werke." Cotta, 1833.

† The treatise in question is ascribed by Goethe to Theophrastus, but it is included in most editions of Aristotle, and even attributed to him in those which contain the works of both philosophers; for instance, in the Aldine Princeps edition, 1496. Calcagnini says, the treatise is made up of two separate works on the subject, both by Aristotle.

‡ His authority seems to have been equally great on subjects connected with the phenomena of vision: the Italian translator of a Latin treatise, by Portius, on the structure and colours of the eye, thus opens his dedication to the Cardinal Ercole Gonzaga, of Mantua:—"Grande anzi quasi infinito è

observed that the Italian writers who translated, para-
phrased, and commented on Aristotle's Treatise on Colours
in particular, were in several instances the personal friends
of distinguished painters. Celio Calcagnini* had the highest
admiration for Raphael ; Lodovico Dolce† was the eulogist
of Titian ; Portius,‡ whose amicable relations with the Florentine painters may be inferred from various circumstances,
lectured at Florence on the Aristotelian doctrines early in
the sixteenth century. The Italian translations were later,
but still prove that these studies were undertaken with reference to the arts, for one of them is dedicated to the
painter Cigoli.§

---

l'obligo che ha il mondo con quel più divino che umano spirito di Aristo-
tile."

* In a letter to Ziegler the mathematician, Calcagnini speaks of Raphael
as " the first of painters in the theory as well as in the practice of his art."
This expression may, however, have had reference to a remarkable circumstance mentioned in the same letter, namely, that Raphael entertained the
learned Fabius of Ravenna as a constant guest, and employed him to translate
Vitruvius into Italian. This MS. translation, with marginal notes, written
by Raphael, is now in the library at Munich. " Passavant, Rafael von Urbino."

† Lodovico Dolce's Treatise on Colours (1565) is in the form of a dialogue,
like his " Aretino." The abridged theory of Aristotle is followed by a translation of the Treatise of Antonius Thylesius on Colours ; this is adapted to the
same colloquial form, and the author is not acknowledged : the book ends
with an absurd catalogue of emblems. The " Somma della Filosofia d'Aris-
totile," published earlier by the same author, is a very careless performance.

‡ A Latin translation of Aristotle's Treatise on Colours, with comments by
Simon Portius, was first published, according to Goethe, at Naples in 1537.
In a later Florentine edition, 1548, dedicated to Cosmo I., Portius alludes to
his having lectured at an earlier period in Florence on the doctrines of Aristotle, at which time he translated the treatise in question. Another Latin
translation, with notes, was published later in the same century at Padua—
" Emanuele Marguino Interprete :" but by far the clearest view of the Aristotelian theory is to be found in the treatise of Antonio Vidi Scarmiglione of
Fuligno (" De Coloribus," Marpurgi, 1591). It is dedicated to the Emperor
Rudolph II. Of all the paraphrases of the ancient doctrine this comes nearest
to the system of Goethe ; but neither this nor any other of the works alluded
to throughout this Note are mentioned by the author in his History of the
Doctrine of Colours, except that of Portius.

§ An earlier Italian translation appeared in Rome, 1535. See " Argelatus
Biblioteca degli Volgarizzatori."

The writers on art, from Leon Battista Alberti to Borghini, without mentioning later authorities, either tacitly coincide with the Aristotelian doctrine, or openly profess to explain it. It is true this is not always done in the clearest manner, and some of these writers might say with Lodovico Dolce, " I speak of colours, not as a painter, for that would be the province of the divine Titian."

Leonardo da Vinci in his writings, as in everything else, appears as an original genius. He now and then alludes generally to opinions of " philosophers," but he quotes no authority ancient or modern. Nevertheless, a passage on the nature of colours, particularly where he speaks of the colours of the elements, appears to be copied from Leon Battista Alberti,* and from the mode in which some of Leonardo's propositions are stated, it has been supposed †️ that he had been accustomed at Florence to the form of the Aristotelian philosophy. At all events, some of the most important of his observations respecting light and colours, have a great analogy with those contained in the treatise in question. The following examples will be sufficient to prove this coincidence ; the corresponding passages in Goethe are indicated, as usual, by the numbers of the paragraphs ; the references to Leonardo's treatise are given at the bottom of the page.

Aristotle.

" A vivid and brilliant red appears when the weak rays of the sun are tempered by subdued and shadowy white."— 154.

Leonardo.

" The air which is between the sun and the earth at sun-

---

* " Della Pittura e della Statua," Lib. 1, p. 16, Milan edition, 1804. Compare with the " Trattato della Pittura," p. 141. Other points of resemblance are to be met with. The notion of certain colours appropriated to the four elements, occurs in Aristotle, and is indeed attributed to older writers.

† See the notes to the Roman edition of the " Trattato della Pittura."

rise or sun-set, always invests what is beyond it more than any other (higher) portion of the air : this is because it is whiter."*

A bright object loses its whiteness in proportion to its distance from the eye much more when it is illuminated by the sun, for it partakes of the colour of the sun mingled with the colour (tempered by the mass) of the air interposed between the eye and the brightness.†

ARISTOTLE.

" If light is overspread with much obscurity, a red colour appears ; if the light is brilliant and vivid, this red changes to a flame-colour."‡—150, 160.

LEONARDO.

" This (the effect of transparent colours on various grounds) is evident in smoke, which is blue when seen against black, but when it is opposed to the (light) blue sky, it appears brownish and reddening."§

ARISTOTLE.

" White surfaces as a ground for colours, have the effect of making the pigments‖ appear in greater splendour."— 594, 902.

---

* Page 237.

† Page 301

‡ In the Treatise *De Igne*, by Theophrastus, we find the same notion thus pressed : "Brightness (τὸ λευκὸν) seen through a dark coloured medium (διὰ τῦ μέλανος) appears red ; as the sun seen through smoke or soot : hence the coal is redder than the flame." Scarmiglione, from whom Kircher seems to have copied, observes :—"Itaque color realis est lux opaca ; licet id e plurimis apparentiis colligere. Luna enim in magnâ solis eclipsi rubra conspicitur, quia tenebris lux præpeditur ac veluti tegitur."—*De Coloribus.*

§ Page 122.

‖ Tὰ ἄνϑη : translated *flores* by Calcagnini and the rest, by Goethe, *die Blüthe*, the bloom. That the word sometimes signified pigments is sufficiently apparent from the following passage of Suidas (quoted by Emeric David, " Discours Historiques sur la Peinture Moderne") ἄνϑεσι κεκοσμημέναι, οιον ψιμμυϑιώ,

LEONARDO.

" To exhibit colours in their beauty, the whitest ground should be prepared. I speak of colours that are (more or less) transparent."*

ARISTOTLE.

"The air near us appears colourless; but when seen in depth, owing to its thinness it appears blue;† for where the light is deficient (beyond it), the air is affected by the darkness and appears blue : in a very accumulated state, however, it appears, as is the case with water, quite white."— 155, 158.

LEONARDO.

" The blue of the atmosphere is owing to the mass of illuminated air interposed between the darkness above and the earth. The air in itself has no colour, but assumes qualities according to the nature of the objects which are beyond it. The blue of the atmosphere will be the more intense in proportion to the degree of darkness beyond it :" elsewhere—" if the air had not darkness beyond it, it would be white."‡

ARISTOTLE.

" We see no colour in its pure state, but every hue is variously intermingled with others : even when it is uninfluenced by other colours, the effect of light and shade modifies it in various ways, so that it undergoes alterations and appears unlike itself. Thus, bodies seen in shade or in

---

φύκει καὶ τοῖς ὁμοίοις. Variis pigmentis ornatæ, ut cerussâ, fuco, et aliis similibus. (Suid. in voc. 'Εξηνθεσμέναι.) A panel prepared for painting, with a white ground consolidated with wax, and perhaps mastic, was found in Herculaneum.

* Page 114.

† 'Εν βάθει δὲ θεωρουμένου ἐγγυτάτω φαίνεται τῶ χρώματι κυανοειδὴς διὰ τὴν ἀραιότητα. " But when seen in depth, it appears (even) in its nearest colour, blue, owing to its thinness." The Latin interpretations vary very much throughout. The point which is chiefly important is however plain enough, viz. that darkness seen through a light medium is blue.

‡ Page 136—430.

light, in more pronounced or softer sun-shine, with their surfaces inclined this way or that, with every change exhibit a different colour."

LEONARDO.

" No substance will ever exhibit its own hue unless the light which illumines it is entirely similar in colour. It very rarely happens that the shadows of opaque bodies are really similar (in colour) to the illumined parts. The surface of every substance partakes of as many hues as are reflected from surrounding objects."*

ARISTOTLE.

" So, again, with regard to the light of fire, of the moon, or of lamps, each has a different colour, which is variously combined with differently coloured objects."

LEONARDO.

" We can scarcely ever say that the surface of illumined bodies exhibits the real colour of those bodies. Take a white band and place it in the dark, and let it receive light by means of three apertures from the sun, from fire, and from the sky : the white band will be tricoloured."†

ARISTOTLE.

" When the light falls on any object and assumes (for example) a red or green tint, it is again reflected on other substances, thus undergoing a new change But this effect, though it really takes place, is not appreciable by the eye : though the light thus reflected to the eye is composed of a variety of colours, the principal of these only are distinguishable."

LEONARDO.

" No colour reflected on the surface of another colour, tinges that surface with its own colour (merely), but will be

---

* Page 121, 306, 326, 387.   † Page 306.

mixed with various other reflections impinging on the same surface :" but such effects, he observes elsewhere, "are scarcely, if at all, distinguishable in a very diffused light."*

ARISTOTLE.

" Thus, all combinations of colours are owing to three causes ; the light, the medium through which the light appears, such as water or air, and lastly the local colour from which the light happens to be reflected."

LEONARDO.

" All illumined objects partake of the colour of the light they receive.

" Every opaque surface partakes of the colour of the intervening transparent medium, according to the density of such medium and the distance between the eye and the object.

" The medium is of two kinds ; either it has a surface, like water, &c., or it is without a common surface, like the air."†

In the observations on trees and plants more points of resemblance might be quoted ; the passages corresponding with Goethe's views are much more numerous.

It is remarkable that Leonardo, in opposition, it seems to some authorities,‡ agrees with Aristotle in reckoning black and white as colours, placing them at the beginning and end of the scale.§ Like Aristotle, again, he frequently makes use of the term black, for obscurity ; he even goes further,

---

* Page 104, 369.

† Page 236, 260, 328.

‡ " De' semplici colori il primo è il bianco : benchè i filosofi non accettano nè il bianco nè il nero nel numero de' colori."—p. 125, 141.   Elsewhere, however, he sometimes adopts the received opinion.

§ Leon Battista Alberti, in like manner observes :—" Affermano (i filosofi) che le spezie de' colori sono sette, cioè, che il bianco ed il nero sono i duoi estremi, infra i quali ve n'è uno nel mezzo (rosso) e che infra ciascuno di questi duoi estremi e quel del mezzo, da ogni parte ve ne sono due altri."   An absurd statement of Lomazzo, p. 190, is copied verbatim from Lodovico Dolce

for he seems to consider that blue may be produced by the actual mixture of black and white, provided they are pure.*
The ancient author, however, explains himself on this point as follows—" We must not attempt to make our observations on these effects by mixing colours as painters mix them, but by remarking the appearances as produced by the rays of light mingling with each other."†

When we consider that Leonardo's Treatise professes to embrace the subject of imitation in painting, and that Aristotle's briefly examines the physical nature and appearance of colours, it must be admitted that the latter sustains the above comparison with advantage; and it is somewhat extraordinary that observations indicating so refined a knowledge of nature, as regards the picturesque, should not have been taken into the account, for such appears to be the fact, in the various opinions and conjectures that have been expressed from time to time on the painting of the Greeks. The treatise in question must have been written when Apelles painted, or immediately before; and as a proof

---

(Somma della Filos. d'Arist.); but elsewhere, p. 306, Lomazzo agrees with Alberti. Aristotle seems to have misled the two first, for after saying there are seven colours, he appears only to mention six : he says—"There are seven colours, if brown is to be considered equivalent to black, which seems reasonable. Yellow, again, may be said to be a modification of white. Between these we find red, purple, green, and blue."—*De Sensu et Sensili.* Perhaps it is in accordance with this passage that Leonardo da Vinci reckons eight colours.—*Trattato*, p. 126.

* Page 122, 142, 237.

† On the authority of this explanation the word μέλαν has sometimes been translated in the foregoing extracts *obscurity, darkness.*

Raffaello Borghini, in his attempt to describe the doctrine of Aristotle with a view to painting, observes—"There are two principles which concur in the production of colour, namely, light and transparence." But he soon loses this clue to the best part of the ancient theory, and when he has to speak of the derivation of colours from white and black, he evidently understands it in a mere atomic sense, and adds—"I shall not at present pursue the opinion of Aristotle, who assumes black and white as principal colours, and considers all the rest as intermediate between them."—*Il Riposo,* l. ii. Accordingly, like Lodovico Dolce, he proceeds to a subject where he was more at home, namely, the symbolical meaning of colours.

that Aristotle's remarks on the effect of semi-transparent mediums were not lost on the artists of his time, the following passage from Pliny is subjoined, for, though it is well known, it acquires additional interest from the foregoing extracts.

" He (Apelles) passed a dark colour over his pictures when finished, so thin that it increased the splendour of the tints, while it protected the surface from dust and dirt : it could only be seen on looking into the picture. The effect of this operation, judiciously managed, was to prevent the colours from being too glaring, and to give the spectator the impression of looking through a transparent crystal. At the same time it seemed almost imperceptibly to add a certain dignity of tone to colours that were too florid."
" This," says Reynolds, " is a true and artist-like description of glazing or scumbling, such as was practised by Titian and the rest of the Venetian painters."

The account of Pliny has, in this instance, internal evidence of truth, but it is fully confirmed by the following passage in Aristotle :—" Another mode in which the effect of colours is exhibited is when they appear through each other, as painters employ them when they glaze (ἐπαλεί-φοντες)* a (dark) colour over a lighter one ; just as the sun, which is in itself white, assumes a red colour when seen through darkness and smoke. This operation also ensures a variety of colours, for there will be a certain ratio between those which are on the surface and those which are in depth."—*De Sensu et Sensili.*

Aristotle's notion respecting the derivation of colours from white and black may perhaps be illustrated by the following opinion on the very similar theory of Goethe.

" Goethe and Seebeck regard colour as resulting from the mixture of white and black, and ascribe to the different

---

* This word is only strictly applied to unctuous substances, and may confirm the views of those writers who have conjectured that asphaltum was a chief ingredient in the *atramentum* of the ancients.

colours a quality of darkness (σκιερὸν), by the different de
grees of which they are distinguished, passing from white to
black through the gradations of yellow, orange, red, violet,
and blue, while green appears to be intermediate again between yellow and blue. This remark, though it has no
influence in weakening the theory of colours proposed by
Newton, is certainly correct, having been confirmed experimentally by the researches of Herschell, who ascertained
the relative intensity of the different coloured rays by illuminating objects under the microscope by their means, &c.

" Another certain proof of the difference in brightness of
the different coloured rays is afforded by the phenomena of
ocular spectra. If, after gazing at the sun, the eyes are
closed so as to exclude the light, the image of the sun appears at first as a luminous or white spectrum upon a dark
ground, but it gradually passes through the series of colours
to black, that is to say, until it can no longer be distinguished from the dark field of vision ; and the colours
which it assumes are successively those intermediate between white and black in the order of their illuminating
power or brightness, namely, yellow, orange, red, violet,
and blue. If, on the other hand, after looking for some
time at the sun we turn our eyes towards a white surface,
the image of the sun is seen at first as a black spectrum
upon the white surface, and gradually passes through the
different colours from the darkest to the lightest, and at
last becomes white, so that it can no longer be distinguished
from the white surface "*—See par. 40, 44.

It is not impossible that Aristotle's enumeration of the
colours may have been derived from, or confirmed by, this
very experiment. Speaking of the after-image of colours
he says, " The impression not only exists in the sensorium
in the act of perceiving, but remains when the organ is at
rest. Thus if we look long and intently on any object,

---

* " Elements of Physiology," by J. Muller, M.D., translated from the German by William Baly, M.D. London, 1839.

when we change the direction of the eyes a responding colour follows. If we look at the sun, or any other very bright object, and afterwards shut our eyes, we shall, as if in ordinary vision, first see a colour of the same kind; this will presently be changed to a red colour, then to purple, and so on till it ends in black and disappears."—*De Insomniis.*

NOTE N.—Par. 246.

" The appearance of white in the centre, according to the Newtonian theory, arises from each line of rays forming its own spectrum. These spectra, superposing each other on all the middle part, leave uncorrected (unneutralised) colours only at the two edges."—S. F.*

NOTE O.—Par. 252.

These experiments with grey objects, which exhibit different colours as they are on dark or light grounds, were suggested, Goethe tells us, by an observation of Antonius Lucas, of Lüttich, one of Newton's opponents, and, in the opinion of the author, one of the few who made any well-founded objections. Lucas remarks, that the sun acts merely as a circumscribed image in the prismatic experiments, and that if the same sun had a lighter background than itself, the colours of the prism would be reversed. Thus in Goethe's experiments, when the grey disk is on a dark ground, it is edged with blue on being magnified; when on a light ground it is edged with yellow. Goethe acknowledges that Lucas had in some measure anticipated his own theory.—Vol. ii. p. 440.

NOTE P.—Par. 284.

The earnestness and pertinacity with which Goethe in-

* This was objected to Goethe when his " Beyträge zur Optik" first appeared ; he answered the objection by a coloured diagram in the plates to the " Farbenlehre :" in this he undertakes to show that the assumed gradual " correction" of the colours would produce results different from the actual appearance in nature.

sisted that the different colours are not subject to different
degrees of refrangibility are at least calculated to prove that
he was himself convinced on the subject, and, however extraordinary it may seem, his conviction appears to have been
the result of infinite experiments and the fullest ocular evidence.   He returns to the question in the controversial
division of his work, in the historical part, and again in the
description of the plates.   In the first he endeavours to
show that Newton's experiment with the blue and red paper
depends entirely on the colours being so contrived as to
appear elongated or curtailed by the prismatic borders.
" If," he says, " we take a light-blue instead of a dark one,
the illusion (in the latter case) is at once evident.   According to the Newtonian theory the yellow-red (red) is the
least refrangible colour, the violet the most refrangible.
Why, then, does Newton place a blue paper instead of a
violet next the red?   If the fact were as he states it, the
difference in the refrangibility of the yellow-red and violet
would be greater than in the case of the yellow-red and
blue.   But here comes in the circumstance that a violet
paper conceals the prismatic borders less than a dark-blue
paper, as every observer may now easily convince himself,"
&c.—Polemischer Theil, par. 45.   Desaguliers, in repeating the experiment, confessed that if the ground of the
colours was not black, the effect did not take place so well.
Goethe adds, "not only not so well, but not at all."—Historischer Theil, p. 459.   Lucas of Lüttich, one of Newton's
first opponents, denied that two differently-coloured silks are
different in distinctness when seen in the microscope.
Another experiment proposed by him, to show the unsoundness of the doctrine of various refrangibility, was the
following :—Let a tin plate painted with the prismatic colours in stripes be placed in an empty cubical vessel, so
that from the spectator's point of view the colours may be
just hidden by the rim.   On pouring water into this vessel,
all the colours become visible in the same degree ; whereas,
it was contended, if the Newtonian doctrine were true, some

colours would be apparent before others.—Historischer Theil, p. 434.

Such are the arguments and experiments adduced by Goethe on this subject; they have all probably been answered. In his analysis of Newton's celebrated *Experimentum Crucis*, he shows again that by reversing the prismatic colours (refracting a dark instead of a light object), the colours that are the most refrangible in Newton's experiment become the least so, and *vice versâ*.

Without reference to this objection, it is now admitted that " the difference of colour is not a test of difference of refrangibility, and the conclusion deduced by Newton is no longer admissible as a general truth, that to the same degree of refrangibility ever belongs the same colour, and to the same colour ever belongs the same degree of refrangibility."—Brewster's Optics, p. 72.

NOTE Q.—Par. 387.

With the exception of two very inconclusive letters to Sulpice Boisserée, and some incidental observations in the conclusion of the historical portion under the head of entoptic colours, Goethe never returned to the rainbow. Among the plates he gave the diagram of Antonius de Dominis. An interesting chapter on halos, parhelia, and paraselenæ, will be found in Brewster's Optics, p. 270.

NOTE R.—Par. 478.

The most complete exhibition of the colouring or mantling of metals was attained by the late Cav. Nobili, professor of physical science in Florence. The general mode in which these colours are produced is thus explained by him :*—

" A point of platinum is placed vertically at the distance of about half a line above a lamina of the same metal laid

---

* See "Memorie ed Osservazioni, edite et inedite del Cav. Professor Nobili," Firenze, 1834.

horizontally at the bottom of a vessel of glass or porcelain. Into this vessel a solution of acetate of lead is poured so as to cover not only the lamina of platinum, but two or three lines of the point as well. Lastly, the point is put in communication with the negative pole of a battery, and the lamina with the positive pole. At the moment in which the circuit is completed a series of coloured rings is produced on the lamina under the point similar to those observed by Newton in lenses pressed together."

The scale of colours thus produced corresponds very nearly with that observed by Newton and others in thin plates and films, but it is fuller, for it extends to forty-four tints. The following list, as given by Nobili, is divided by him into four series to agree with those of Newton : the numbers in brackets are those of Newton's scale. The Italian terms are untranslated, because the colours in some cases present very delicate transitions.*

First Series.

1. Biondo argentino (4).†
2. Biondo.
3. Biondo d'oro.
4. Biondo acceso (5).
5. Fulvo.
6. Fulvo acceso.
7. Rosso di rame (6).
8. Ocria.
9. Ocria violacea.
10. Rosso violaceo (7).

Second Series.

11. Violetto (8).
12. Indaco (10).
13. Blu carico.
14. Blu.
15. Blu chiaro (11).
16. Celeste.
17. Celeste-giallognolo.
18. Giallo chiarissimo (12).
19. Giallo.
20. Giallo acceso.
21. Giallo-rancio.
22. Rancio (13).
23. Rancio-rossiccio.
24. Rancio-rosso.
25. Rosso-rancio.
26. Lacca-rancia (14).
27. Lacca.
28. Lacca accesa (15).

* The colours in some of the compound terms are in a manner mutually neutralising ; such terms might, no doubt, be amended.

† The three first numbers in Newton's scale are black, blue, and white.

Third Series.

29. Lacca-purpurea (16).	34. Verde-giallo (20).
30. Lacca-turchiniccia (17).	35. Verde-rancio.
31. Porpora-verdognola (18).	36. Rancio-verde (21).
32. Verde (19).	37. Rancio-roseo.
33. Verde giallognolo.	38. Lacca-rosea (22).

Fourth Series.

39. Lacca-violacea (24).	43. Verde-giallo rossiccio
40. Violaceo-verdognolo (25).	(28).
41. Verde (26).	44. Lacca-rosea (30).
42. Verde-giallo (27).	

" These tints," Professor Nobili observes, " are disposed according to the order of the thin mantlings which occasion them; the colour of the thinnest film is numbered 1; then follow in order those produced by a gradual thickening of the medium. I cannot deceive myself in this arrangement, for the thin films which produce the colours are all applied with the same electro-chemical process. The battery, the solution, the distances, &c., are always the same; the only difference is the time the effect is suffered to last. This is a mere instant for the colour of No. 1, a little longer for No. 2, and so on, increasing for the succeeding numbers. Other criterions, however, are not wanting to ascertain the place to which each tint belongs."

The scale differs from that of Newton, inasmuch as there is no blue in Nobili's first series and no green in the second: green only appears in the third and fourth series. " The first series," says the Professor, " is remarkable for the fire and metallic appearance of its tints, the second for clearness and brilliancy, the third and fourth for force and richness." The fourth, he observes, has the qualities of the third in a somewhat lesser degree, but the two greens are very nearly alike.

It is to be observed, that red and green are the principal

ingredients in the third and fourth series, blue and yellow in the second and first.

NOTE S.—Par. 485.

A chapter on entoptic colours, contained in the supplement to Goethe's works, was translated with the intention of inserting it among the notes, but on the whole it was thought most advisable to omit it. Like many other parts of the "Doctrine of Colours" it might have served as a specimen of what may be achieved by accurate observation unassisted by a mathematical foundation. The whole theory of the polarization of light has, however, been so fully investigated since Goethe's time, that the chapter in question would probably have been found to contain very little to interest scientific readers, for whom it seems chiefly to have been intended. One observation occurs in it which indeed has more reference to the arts; in order to make this intelligible, the leading experiment must be first described, and for this purpose the following extracts may serve.

3.*

" The experiment, in its simplest form, is to be made as follows:—let a tolerably thick piece of plate-glass be cut into several squares of an inch and a half; let these be heated to a red heat and then suddenly cooled. The squares of glass which do not split in this operation are now fit to produce the entoptic colours.

4.

" In our mode of exhibiting the phenomenon, the observer is, above all, to betake himself, with his apparatus to the open air. All dark rooms, all small apertures (fora-

---

* The numbers, as usual, indicate the corresponding paragraphs in the original.

mina exigua),* are again to be given up. A pure, cloudless sky is the source whence we are to derive a satisfactory insight into these appearances.

5.

" The atmosphere being clear, let the observer lay the squares above described on a black surface, so placing them that two sides may be parallel with the plane of vision. When the sun is low, let him hold the squares so as to reflect to the eye that portion of the sky opposite to the sun, and he will then perceive four dark points in the four corners of a light space. If, after this, he turn towards the quarters of the sky at right angles with that where his first observation was made, he will see four bright points on a dark ground: between the two regions the figures appear to fluctuate.

6.

" From this simple reflection we now proceed to another, which, but little more complicated, exhibits the appearance much more distinctly. A solid cube of glass, or in its stead a cube composed of several plates, is placed on a black mirror, or held a little inclined above it, at sun-rise or sunset. The reflection of the sky being now suffered to fall through the cube on the mirror, the appearance above described will appear more distinctly. The reflection of the sky opposite to the sun presents four dark points on a light ground; the two lateral portions of the sky present the contrary appearance, namely, four light points on a dark ground. The space not occupied by the corner points appears in the first case as a white cross, in the other as a black cross, expressions hereafter employed in describing the phenomena. Before sun-rise or after sun-set, in a very

---

* In the historical part, Goethe has to speak of so many followers of Newton who begin their statements with " Si per foramen exiguum," that the term is a sort of by-word with him.

subdued light, the white cross appears on the side of the sun also.*

" We thus conclude that the direct reflection of the sun produces a light figure, which we call a white cross; the oblique reflection gives a dark figure, which we call a black cross. If we make the experiment all round the sky, we shall find that a fluctuation takes place in the intermediate regions."

We pass over a variety of observations on the modes of exhibiting this phenomenon, the natural transparent substances which exhibit it best, and the detail of the colours seen within† them, and proceed to an instance where the author was enabled to distinguish the " direct" from the "oblique" reflection by means of the entoptic apparatus, in a painter's study.

40.

" An excellent artist, unfortunately too soon taken from us, Ferdinand Jagemann, who, with other qualifications, had a fine eye for light and shade, colour and keeping, had built himself a painting-room for large as well as small works. The single high window was to the north, facing the most open sky, and it was thought that all necessary requisites had been sufficiently attended to.

" But after our friend had worked for some time, it appeared to him, in painting portraits, that the faces he copied were not equally well lighted at all hours of the day, and yet his sitters always occupied the same place, and the serenity of the atmosphere was unaltered.

" The variations of the favourable and unfavourable light had their periods during the day. Early in the morning the light appeared most unpleasantly grey and unsatisfac-

---

* At mid-day on the 24th of June the author observed the white cross reflected from every part of the horizon. At a certain distance from the sun, corresponding, he supposes, with the extent of halos, the black cross appeared.

† Whence the term *entoptic*.

tory; it became better, till at last, about an hour before noon, the objects had acquired a totally different appearance. Everything presented itself to the eye of the artist in its greatest perfection, as he would most wish to transfer it to canvas. In the afternoon this beautiful appearance vanished—the light became worse, even in the brightest day, without any change having taken place in the atmosphere.

" As soon as I heard of this circumstance, I at once connected it in my own mind with the phenomena which I had been so long observing, and hastened to prove, by a physical experiment, what a clear-sighted artist had discovered entirely of himself, to his own surprise and astonishment.

" I had the second* entoptic apparatus brought to the spot, and the effect on this was what might be conjectured from the above statement. At mid-day, when the artist saw his model best lighted, the north, direct reflection gave the white cross; in the morning and evening, on the other hand, when the unfavourable oblique light was so unpleasant to him, the cube showed the black cross; in the intermediate hours the state of transition was apparent."

The author proceeds to recal to his memory instances where works of art had struck him by the beauty of their appearance owing to the light coming from the quarter opposite the sun, in " direct reflection," and adds, " Since these decided effects are thus traceable to their cause, the friends of art, in looking at and exhibiting pictures, may enhance the enjoyment to themselves and others by attending to a fortunate reflection."

---

* Before described : the author describes several others more or less complicated, and suggests a portable one. " Such plates, which need only be an inch and a quarter square, placed on each other to form a cube, might be set in a brass case, open above and below. At one end of this case a black mirror with a hinge, acting like a cover, might be fastened. We recommend this simple apparatus, with which the principal and original experiment may be readily made. With this we could, in the longest days, better define the circle round the sun where the black cross appears," &c.

NOTE T.—Par. 496.

"Since Goethe wrote, all the earths have been decomposed, and have been shown to be metallic bases united with oxygen; but this does not invalidate his statement."—S. F.

NOTE U.—Par. 502.

The cold nature of black and its affinity to blue are assumed by the author throughout; if the quality is opaque, and consequently greyish, such an affinity is obvious, but in many fine pictures, intense black seems to be considered as the last effect of heat, and in accompanying crimson and orange may be said rather to present a difference of degree than a difference of kind. In looking at the great picture of the globe, we find this last result produced in climates where the sun has greatest power, as we find it the immediate effect of fire. The light parts of black animals are often of a mellow colour; the spots and stripes on skins and shells are generally surrounded by a warm hue, and are brown before they are absolutely black. In combustion, the blackness which announces the complete ignition, is preceded always by the same mellow, orange colour. The representation of this process was probably intended by the Greeks in the black and subdued orange of their vases: indeed, the very colours may have been first produced in the kiln. But without supposing that they were retained merely from this accident, the fact that the combination itself is extremely harmonious, would be sufficient to account for its adoption. Many of the remarks of Aristotle* and Theophrastus† on the production of black, are derived from the observation of the action of fire, and on one occasion, the former distinctly alludes to the terracotta kiln. That the above opinion as to the nature of black was prevalent in the sixteenth century, may be in-

* "De Coloribus." † "De Igne."

ferred from Lomazzo, who observes,—" Quanto all' origine e generazione de' colori, la frigidità è la madre della bianchezza : il calore è padre del nero."* The positive coldness of black may be said to begin when it approaches grey. When Leonardo da Vinci says that black is most beautiful in shade, he probably means to define its most intense and transparent state, when it is furthest removed from grey.

NOTE V.—Par. 555.

The nature of vehicles or liquid mediums to combine with the substance of colours, has been frequently discussed by modern writers on art, and may perhaps be said to have received as much attention as it deserves. Reynolds smiles at the notion of our not having materials equal to those of former times, and indeed, although the methods of individuals will always differ, there seems no reason to suppose that any great technical secret has been lost. In these inquiries, however, which relate merely to the mechanical causes of bright and durable colouring, the skill of the painter in the adequate employment of the higher resources of his art is, as if by common consent, left out of the account, and without departing from this mode of considering the question, we would merely repeat a conviction before expressed, viz. that the preservation of internal brightness, a quality compatible with various methods, has had more to do with the splendour and durability of finely coloured pictures than any vehicle. The observations that follow are therefore merely intended to show how far the older written authorities on this subject agree with the results of modern investigation, without at all assuming that the old methods, if known, need be implicitly followed.

On a careful examination of the earlier pictures, it is said

---

* "Trattato," &c. p. 191, the rest of the passage, it must be admitted, abounds with absurdities.

that a resinous substance appears to have been mingled with the colours together with the oil; that the fracture of the indurated pigment is shining, and that the surface resists the ordinary solvents.* This admixture of resinous solutions or varnishes with the solid colours is not alluded to, as far as we have seen, by any of the writers on Italian practice, but as the method corresponds with that now prevalent in England, the above hypothesis is not likely to be objected to for the present.

Various local circumstances and relations might seem to warrant the supposition that the Venetian painters used resinous substances. An important branch of commerce between the mountains of Friuli and Venice still consists in the turpentine or fir-resin.† Similar substances produced from various trees, and known under the common name of balsams,‡ were imported from the East through Venice, for general use, before the American balsams§ in some degree superseded them; and a Venetian painter, Marco Boschini, in his description of the Archipelago, does not omit to speak of the abundance of mastic produced in the island of Scio.||

The testimonies, direct or indirect, against the employ-

---

* See "Marcucci Saggio Analitico-chimico sopra i colori," &c. Rome, 1816, and "Taylor's Translation of Merimée on Oil-painting," London, 1839. The last-named work contains much useful information.

† Italian writers of the 16th century speak of three kinds. Cardanus says, that of the *abies* was esteemed most, that of the *larix* next, and that of the *picea* least. The resin extracted by incision from the last (the pinus abies Linnæi) is known by the name of Burgundy pitch; when extracted by fire it is black. The three varieties occur in Italian treatises on art, under the names of *oglio di abezzo, trementina* and *pece Greca.*

‡ The concrete balsam *benzoe*, called by the Italians *beluzino*, and *belzoino*, is sometimes spoken of as a varnish.

§ Marcucci supposes that balsam of copaiba was mixed with the pigments by the (later) Venetians.

|| "L'Archipelago con tutte le Isole," Ven. 1658. The incidental notices of the remains of antiquity in this work would be curious and important if they could be relied on. In describing the island of Samos, for instance, the author asserts that the temple of Juno was in tolerable preservation, and that the statue was still there.

ment of any such substances by the Venetian painters, in the
solid part of their work, seem, notwithstanding, very conclusive; we begin with the writer just named.   In his principal composition, a poem * describing the practice and the
productions of the Venetian painters, Boschini speaks of
certain colours which they shunned, and adds :—" In like
manner (they avoided) shining liquids and varnishes, which
I should rather call lackers ;† for the surface of flesh, if
natural and unadorned, assuredly does not shine, nature
speaks as to this plainly." After alluding to the possible
alteration of this natural appearance by means of cosmetics,
he continues : " Foreign artists set such great store by these
varnishes, that a shining surface seems to them the only desirable quality in art. What trash it is they prize! fir-resin,
mastic, and sandarach, and larch-resin (not to say treacle),
stuff fit to polish boots.‡   If those great painters of ours
had to represent armour, a gold vase, a mirror, or anything
of the kind, they made it shine with (simple) colours."§

This writer so frequently alludes to the Flemish painters,
of whose great reputation he sometimes seems jealous, that
the above strong expression of opinion may have been
pointed at them.   On the other hand it is to be observed
that the term *forestieri*, strangers, does not necessarily mean
transalpine foreigners, but includes those Italians who were

---

* "La Carta del Navegar Pitoresco," Ven. 1660.   It is in the Venetian
dialect.

† Inveriadure (invetriature), literally the glazing applied to earthenware.

‡ " O de che strazze se fan cavedal !
    D'ogio d'avezzo, mastici e sandraca ;
    E trementina (per no'dir triaca)
    Robe, che ilustrerave ogni stival."—p. 338.

The alliteration of the words *trementina* and *triaca* is of course lost in a
translation.

§ " I li ha fati straluser co' i colori."   Boschini was at least constant in his
opinion.   In the second edition of his " Ricche Minere della Pittura Veneziana," which appeared fourteen years after the publication of his poem, he
repeats that the Venetian painters avoided some colours in flesh " e similmente
i lustri e le vernici."

not of the Venetian state.* The directions given by Raphael Borghini,† and after him by Armenini,‡ respecting the use and preparation of varnishes made from the very materials in question, may thus have been comprehended in the censure, especially as some of these recipes were copied and republished in Venice by Bisagno,§ in 1642—that is, only six years before Boschini's poem appeared.

Ridolfi's Lives of the Venetian Painters‖ (1648) may be mentioned with the two last. His only observation respecting the vehicle is, that Giovanni Bellini, after introducing himself by an artifice into the painting-room of Antonello da Messina, saw that painter dip his brush from time to time in linseed oil. This story, related about two hundred years after the supposed event, is certainly not to be adduced as very striking evidence in any way.¶

Among the next writers, in order of time prior to Bisagno, may be mentioned Canepario** (1619). His work, " De Atramentis" contains a variety of recipes for different purposes : one chapter, *De atramentis diversicoloribus,* has a more direct reference to painting. His observations under this head are by no means confined to the preparation of transparent colours, but he says little on the subject of

---

* Thus, in the introduction to the " Ricche Minere," Boschini calls the Milanese, Florentine, Lombard, and Bolognese painters, *forestieri.*

† " Il Riposo," Firenze, 1584.

‡ " De' Veri Precetti della Pittura," Ravenna, 1587.

§ " Trattato della Pittura fondato nell' autorità di molti eccellenti in questa professione." Venezia, 1642. Bisagno remarks in his preface, that the books on art were few, and that painters were in the habit of keeping them secret. He acknowledges that he has availed himself of the labours of others, but without mentioning his sources : some passages are copied from Lomazzo. He, however, lays claim to some original observations, and says he had seen much and discoursed with many excellent painters.

‖ " Le Meraviglie dell' Arte," Venezia, 1648.

¶ It has been conjectured by some that this story proved the immixture of varnishes with the colours, and that the oil was only used to dilute them. The epitaph on Antonello da Messina which existed in Vasari's time, alludes to his having mixed the colours with oil.

** " Petri Mariæ Caneparii De Atramentis cujuscumque generis," Venet. 1619. It was republished at Rotterdam in 1718.

varnishes. After describing a mode of preserving white of egg, he says, "Others are accustomed to mix colours in liquid varnish and linseed, or nut-oil ; for a liquid and oily varnish binds the (different layers of) colours better together, and thus forms a very fit glazing material."* On the subject of oils he observes, that linseed oil was in great request among painters ; who, however, were of opinion that nut-oil excelled it " in giving brilliancy to pictures, in preserving them better, and in rendering the colours more vivid."†

Lomazzo (a Milanese) says nothing on the subject of vehicles in his principal work, but in his " Idea del Tempio della Pittura,"‡ he speaks of grinding the colours " in nut-oil, and spike-oil, and other things," the " and" here evidently means *or*, and by " other things" we are perhaps to understand other oils, poppy oil, drying oils, &c.

The directions of Raphael Borghini and Vasari § cannot certainly be considered conclusive as to the practice of the Venetians, but they are very clear on the subject of varnish. These writers may be considered the earliest Italian authorities who have entered much into practical methods. In the few observations on the subject of vehicles in Leonardo da Vinci's treatise, "there is nothing," as M. Merimée observes, " to show that he was in the habit of mixing varnish with his colours." Cennini says but little on the subject

* " Ita quod magis ex hiis evadit atramentum picturæ summopere idoneum." Thus, if *atramentum* is to be understood, as usual, to mean a glazing colour, the passage can only refer to the immixture of varnish with the transparent colours applied last in order.

† In a passage that follows respecting the mode of extracting nut-oil, Caneparius appears to mistranslate Galen, c. 7—" De Simplicium Medicamentorum facultatibus." The observations of Galen on this subject, and on the drying property of linseed, may have given the first hint to the inventors of oil-painting. The custom of dating the origin of this art from Van Eyck is like that of dating the commencement of modern painting from Cimabue. The improver is often assumed to be the inventor.

‡ Milan, 1590.

§ The particulars here alluded to are to be found in the first edition of Vasari (1550) as well as the second.—v. i. c. 21, &c.

of oil-painting ; Leon Battista Alberti is theoretical rather than practical, and the published extracts of Lorenzo Ghiberti's MS. chiefly relate to sculpture.

Borghini and Vasari agree in recommending nut-oil in preference to linseed-oil ; both recommend adding varnish to the colours in painting on walls in oil, " because the work does not then require to be varnished afterwards," but in the ordinary modes of painting on panel or cloth, the varnish is omitted. Borghini expressly says, that oil alone (senza più) is to be employed ; he also recommends a very sparing use of it.

The treatise of Armenini (1587) was published at Ravenna, and he himself was of Faenza, so that his authority, again, cannot be considered decisive as to the Venetian practice. After all, he recommends the addition of " common varnish" only for the ground or preparation, as a consolidating medium, for the glazing colours, and for those dark pigments which are slow in drying. Many of his directions are copied from the writers last named ; the recipes for varnishes, in particular, are to be found in Borghini. Christoforo Sorte* (1580) briefly alludes to the subject in question. After speaking of the methods of distemper, he observes that the same colours may be used in oil, except that instead of mixing them with size, they are mixed on the palette with nut-oil, or (if slow in drying) with boiled linseed-oil : he does not mention varnish. The Italian writers next in order are earlier than Vasari, and may therefore be considered original, but they are all very concise.

---

* " Osservazioni nella Pittura." In Venezia, 1580. Sorte, who, it appears, was a native of Verona, had worked in his youth with Giulio Romano, at Mantua, and communicates the methods taught him by that painter, for giving the true effects of perspective in compositions of figures. He is, perhaps, the earliest who describes the process of water-colour painting as distinguished from distemper and as adapted to landscape, if the art he describes deserves the name.

The treatise of Michael Angelo Biondo* (1549), remarkable for its historical mistakes, is not without interest in other respects. The list of colours he gives is, in all probability, a catalogue of those in general use in Venice at the period he wrote. With regard to the vehicle, he merely mentions oil and size as the mediums for the two distinct methods of oil-painting and distemper, and does not speak of varnish. The passages in the Dialogue of Doni† (1549), which relate to the subject in question, are to the same effect. " In colouring in oil," he observes, " the most brilliant colours (that we see in pictures) are prepared by merely mixing them with the end of a knife on the palette." Speaking of the perishable nature of works in oil-painting as compared with sculpture, he says, that the plaster of Paris (gesso) and mastic, with other ingredients of which the ground is prepared, are liable to decay, &c. ; and elsewhere, in comparing painting in general with mosaic, that in the former the colours " must of necessity be mixed with various things, such as oils, gums, white or yolk of egg, and juice of figs, all which tend to impair the beauty of the tints." This catalogue of vehicles is derived from all kinds of painting to enforce the argument, and is by no means to be understood as belonging to one and the same method.

An interesting little work,‡ still in the form of a dialogue (Fabio and Lauro), appeared a year earlier; the author, Paolo Pino, was a Venetian painter. In speaking of the practical methods Fabio observes, as usual, that oil-painting is of all modes of imitation the most perfect, but his reasons for this opinion seem to have a reference to the Venetian

---

* "Della nobilissima Pittura e sua Arte," Venezia, 1549. Biondo is so ignorant as to attribute the Last Supper, by Leonardo da Vinci, to Mantegna.

† "Disegno del Doni," in Venezia, 1549.

‡ "Dialogo di Pittura," Venezia, 1548. Pino, in enumerating the celebrated contemporary artists, does not include Paul Veronese, for a very obvious reason, that painter being at the time only about 17 years of age. Sorte, who wrote thirty years later, mentions " l'eccellente Messer Paulino nostro," alone.

practice of going over the work repeatedly. Lauro asks whether it is not possible to paint in oil on the dry wall, as Sebastian del Piombo did. Fabio answers, " the work cannot last, for the solidity of the plaster is impenetrable, and the colours, whether in oil or distemper, cannot pass the surface." This might seem to warrant the inference that absorbent grounds were prepared for oil-painting, but there are proofs enough that resins as well as oil were used with the *gesso* to make the preparation compact. See Doni, Armenini, &c. This writer, again, does not speak of varnish. These appear to be the chief Venetian and Italian authorities* of the sixteenth and part of the following century; and although Boschini wrote latest, he appears to have had his information from good sources, and more than once distinctly quotes Palma Giovane.

In all these instances it will be seen that there is no allusion to the immixture of varnishes with the solid colours, except in painting on walls in oil, and that the processes of distemper and oil are always considered as separate arts.†

---

* The Dialogues of Lodovico Dolce, and various other works, are not referred to here, as they contain nothing on the subject in question. The latest authority at all connected with the traditions of Venetian practice, is a certain Giambatista Volpato, of Bassano : he died in 1706, and had been intimate with Ridolfi. The only circumstance he has transmitted relating to practical details is that Giacomo Bassan, in retouching on a dry surface, sometimes adopted a method commonly practised, he says, by Paul Veronese (and commonly practised still), namely, that of dipping his brush in spirits of turpentine ; at other times he oiled out the surface in the usual manner. Volpato left a MS. which was announced for publication in Vicenza in 1685, but it never appeared ; it, however, afterwards formed the ground-work of Verci's " Notizie intorno alla Vita e alle Opere de' Pittori di Bassano." Venezia, 1775. See also " Lettera di Giambatista Roberti sopra Giacomo da Ponte," Lugano, 1777. Another MS. by Natale Melchiori, of about the same date, is preserved at Treviso and Castel Franco : it abounds with historical mistakes ; the author says, for instance, that the Pietro Màrtyre was begun by Giorgione and finished by Titian. The recipes for varnishes and colours are very numerous, but they are mostly copied from earlier works.

† That distemper was not very highly esteemed by the Venetians may be inferred from the following observation of Pino :—" Il modo di colorir à guazzo è imperfetto et più fragile et à me non diletta onde lasciamolo all'

On the other hand, the prohibition of Boschini cannot be understood to be universal, for it is quite certain that the Venetians varnished their pictures when done.* After Titian had finished his whole-length portrait of Pope Paul III. it was placed in the sun to be varnished.† Again, in the archives of the church of S. Niccolo at Treviso a sum is noted (Sept. 21, 1521), "per far la vernise da invernisar la Pala dell' altar grando," and the same day a second entry appears of a payment to a painter, " per esser venuto a dar la vernise alla Pala," &c.‡ It is to be observed that in both these cases the pictures were varnished as soon as done;§ the varnish employed was perhaps the thin compound of naphtha (oglio di sasso) and melted turpentine (oglio d'abezzo), described by Borghini, and after him by Armenini : the last-named writer remarks that he had seen

oltremontani i quali sono privi della vera via." It is, however, certain that the Venetians sometimes painted in this style, and Volpato mentions several works of the kind by Bassan, but he never hints that he began his oil pictures in distemper.

* Boschini says, that the Venetians (he especially means Titian) rendered their pictures sparkling by finally touching on a dry surface (à secco). The absence of varnish in the solid colours, the retouching with spirit of turpentine, and even à secco, all suppose a dull surface, which would require varnish. The latter method, alluded to by Boschini, was an exception to the general practice, and not likely to be followed on account of its difficulty. Carlo Maratti, on the authority of Palomino, used to say, " He must be a skilful painter who can retouch without oiling out."

† See a letter by Francesco Bocchi, and another by Vasari, in the " Lettere Pittoriche" of Bottari. The circumstance is mentioned incidentally; the point chiefly dwelt on is, that some persons who passed were deceived, and bowed to the picture, supposing it to be the pope.

‡ Federici, " Memorie Trevigiane," Venezia, 1803. The altar-piece of S. Niccolo at Treviso is attributed, in the document alluded to, to Fra Marco Pensabene, a name unknown ; the painting is so excellent as to have been thought worthy of Sebastian del Piombo : for this opinion, however, there are no historical grounds. It was begun in 1520, but before it was quite finished the painter, whoever he was, absconded : it was therefore completed by another.

§ Titian's stay in Rome was short, and with respect to the Treviso altar-piece, a week or two only, at most, can have elapsed between the completion and the varnishing. Cennini, who recommends delaying a year at least before varnishing, speaks of pictures in distemper.

this varnish used by the best painters in Lombardy, and had heard that it was preferred by Correggio. The consequence of this immediate varnishing may have been that the warm resinous liquid, whatever it was, became united with the colours, and thus at a future time the pigment may have acquired a consistency capable of resisting the ordinary solvents. Not only was the surface of the picture required to be warm, but the varnish was applied soon after it was taken from the fire.*

Many of the treatises above quoted contain directions for making the colours dry :† some of these recipes, and many in addition, are to be found in Palomino, who, however defective as an historian,‡ has left very copious practical details, evidently of ancient date. His drying recipes are numerous, and although sugar of lead does not appear, cardenillo (verdigris), which is perhaps as objectionable, is admitted to be the best of all dryers. It may excite some surprise that the Spanish painters should have bestowed so much attention on this subject in a climate like theirs, but the rapidity of their execution must have often required such an assistance.§

One circumstance alluded to by Palomino, in his very minute practical directions, deserves to be mentioned. After

---

* See Borghini, Armenini, their Venetian copyist Bisagno, and Palomino. The last-named writer, though of another school and much more modern, was evidently well acquainted with the ancient methods : he says, "Se advierte que siempre que se huviere de barnizar alguna cosa conviene que la pintura y el barniz estèn calientes."—*El Museo Pictorico*, v. ii.

† Burnt alum, one of the ingredients recommended, might perhaps account for a shining fracture in the indurated pigment in some old pictures.

‡ Of the earlier Spanish writers Pacheco may be mentioned next to Palomino as containing most practical information. Carducho, De Butron, and others, seldom descend to such details. Palomino contains all the directions of Pacheco, and many in addition.

§ See Cean Bermudez, "Sobre la Escuela Sevillana," Cadiz, 1806. The same reasons induced the later Venetian machinists to paint on dark grounds, and to make use of (drying) oil in excess. See Zanetti, *Della Pittura Veneziana*, l. iv.

saying what colours should be preserved in their saucers under water, and what colours should be merely covered with oiled paper because the water injures them, he proceeds to communicate "a curious mode of preserving oil-colours," and of transporting them from place to place. The important secret is to tie them in bladders, the mode of doing which he enters into with great minuteness, as if the invention was recent. It is true, Christoforo Sorte, in describing his practice in water-colour drawing, says he was in the habit of preserving a certain vegetable green with gum-water in a bladder; but as the method was obviously new to Palomino, there seems sufficient reason to believe that oil-colours, when once ground, had, up to his time, been kept in saucers and preserved under water.* Among the items of expense in the Treviso document before alluded to, we find "a pan and saucers for the painters."† This is in accordance with Cennini's directions, and the same system appears to have been followed till after 1700.‡

The Flemish accounts of the early practice of oil-painting are all later than Vasari. Van Mander, in correcting the Italian historian in his dates, still follows his narrative in other respects verbatim. If Vasari's story is to be accepted as true, it might be inferred that the Flemish secret consisted in an oil varnish like copal.§ Vasari says, that Van

---

* Borghini, in describing the method of making a gold-size (the same as Cennini's), speaks of boiling the "buccie de' colori" in oil; this only means the skin or pellicle of the colour itself—in fact, he proceeds to say that they dissolve in boiling. Vasari, in describing the same process, uses the expression "colori seccaticci."

† "Maggio 4 (1520) Per un cadin (catino) per depentori. Per scudellini per li depentori."—*Mem. Trev.*, vol. i. p. 131. Pungileoni ("Memorie Istoriche di Antonio Allegri") quotes a note of expenses relating to two oil-pictures by Paolo Gianotti; among the items we find "colori, telari, et brocchette."—vol. ii. p. 75.

‡ Salmon, in his "Polygraphice" (1701), gives the following direction:— "Oyl colors, if not presently used, will have a skin grow over them, to prevent which put them into a glass, and put the glass three or four inches under water," &c.

§ This varnish appears to have been known some centuries before Van Eyck's time, but he may have been the first to mix it with the colours.

Eyck boiled the oils with other ingredients ; that the colours, when mixed with this kind of oil, had a very firm consistence ; that the surface of the pictures so executed had a lustre, so that they needed no varnish when done ; and that the colours were in no danger from water.*

Certain colours, as is well known, if mixed with oil alone, may be washed off after a considerable time. Leonardo da Vinci remarks, that verdigris may be thus removed. Carmine, Palomino observes, may be washed off after six years. It is on this account the Italian writers recommend the use of varnish with certain colours, and it appears the Venetians, and perhaps the Italians generally employed it solely in such cases. But it is somewhat extraordinary that Vasari should teach a mode of painting in oil so different in its results (inasmuch as the work thus required varnish at last) from the Flemish method which he so much extols—a method which he says the Italians long endeavoured to find out in vain. If they knew it, it is evident, assuming his account to be correct, that they did not practice it.

NOTE W.—Par. 608.

In the second volume Goethe gives the nomenclature of the Greeks and Romans at some length. The general notions of the ancients with regard to colours are thus described :—" The ancients derive all colours from white and black, from light and darkness. They say, all colours are between white and black, and are mixed out of these. We must not, however, suppose that they understand by this a mere atomic mixture, although they occasionally use the word μίξις ;† for in the remarkable passages, where they wish to express a kind of reciprocal (dynamic) action of the two contrasting principles, they employ the words κρᾶσις, union, σύγκρισις, combination ; thus, again, the mutual influence of light and darkness, and of colours among each

---

* See Vasari, Life of Antonello da Messina.
† See Note on Par. 177.

other, is described by the word κεράννυσθαι, an expression of similar import.

" The varieties of colours are differently enumerated; some mention seven, others twelve, but without giving the complete list. From a consideration of the terminology both of the Greeks and Romans, it appears that they sometimes employed general for specific terms, and *vice versâ*.

" Their denominations of colours are not permanently and precisely defined, but mutable and fluctuating, for they are employed even with regard to similar colours both on the *plus* and *minus* side. Their yellow, on the one hand, inclines to red, on the other to blue; the blue is sometimes green, sometimes red; the red is at one time yellow, at another blue. Pure red (purpur) fluctuates between warm red and blue, sometimes inclining to scarlet, sometimes to violet.

" Thus the ancients not only seem to have looked upon colour as a mutable and fleeting quality, but appear to have had a presentiment of the (physical and chemical) effects of augmentation and re-action. In speaking of colours they make use of expressions which indicate this knowledge; they make yellow redden, because its augmentation tends to red; they make red become yellow, for it often returns thus to its origin.

" The hues thus specified undergo new modifications. The colours arrested at a given point are attenuated by a stronger light darkened by a shadow, nay, deepened and condensed in themselves. For the gradations which thus arise the name of the species only is often given, but the more generic terms are also employed. Every colour, of whatever kind, can, according to the same view, be multiplied into itself, condensed, enriched, and will in consequence appear more or less dark. The ancients called colour in this state," &c. Then follow the designations of general states of colour and those of specific hues.

Another essay on the notions of the ancients respecting

the origin and nature of colour generally, shows how nearly Goethe himself has followed in the same track. The dilating effect of light objects, the action and reaction of the retina, the coloured after-image, the general law of contrast, the effect of semi-transparent mediums in producing warm or cold colours as they are interposed before a dark or light background—all this is either distinctly expressed or hinted at; "but," continues Goethe, "how a single element divides itself into two, remained a secret for them. They knew the nature of the magnet, in amber, only as attraction; polarity was not yet distinctly evident to them. And in very modern times have we not found that scientific men have still given their almost exclusive attention to attraction, and considered the immediately excited repulsion only as a mere after-action?"

An essay on the Painting of the Ancients* was contributed by Heinrich Meyer.

NOTE X.—Par. 670.

This agrees with the general recommendation so often given by high authorities in art, to avoid a tinted look in the colour of flesh. The great example of Rubens, whose practice was sometimes an exception to this, may however show that no rule of art is to be blindly or exclusively adhered to. Reynolds, nevertheless, in the midst of his admiration for this great painter, considered the example dangerous, and more than once expresses himself to this effect, observing on one occasion that Rubens, like Baroccio, is sometimes open to the criticism made on an ancient painter, namely, that his figures looked as if they fed on roses.

Lodovico Dolce, who is supposed to have given the *vivâ voce* precepts of Titian in his Dialogue,† makes Aretino

---

* Vol. ii. p. 69, first edition.

† "Dialogo della Pittura, intitolato l'Aretino." It was first published at Venice in 1557; about twenty years before Titian's death. In the dedication

say : " I would generally banish from my pictures those vermilion cheeks with coral lips; for faces thus treated look like masks. Propertius, reproving his Cynthia for using cosmetics, desires that her complexion might exhibit the simplicity and purity of colour which is seen in the works of Apelles."

Those who have written on the practice of painting have always recommended the use of few colours for flesh. Reynolds and others quote even ancient authorities as recorded by Pliny, and Boschini gives several descriptions of the method of the Venetians, and particularly of Titian, to the same effect. " They used," he says, " earths more than any other colour, and at the utmost only added a little vermilion, minium, and lake, abhorring as a pestilence *biadetti, gialli santi, smaltini, verdi-azzurri, giallolini*."* Elsewhere he says,† " Earths should be used rather than other colours :" after repeating the above prohibited list he adds, " I speak of the imitation of flesh, for in other things every colour is good ;" again, " Our great Titian used to say that he who wishes to be a painter should be acquainted with three colours, white, black, and red."‡ Assuming this

---

to the senator Loredano, Lodovico Dolce eulogises the work, which he would hardly have done if it had been entirely his own : again, the supposition that it may have been suggested by Aretino, would be equally conclusive, coupled with internal evidence, as to the original source.

* Introduction to the " Ricche Minere della Pittura Veneziana," Venezia, 1674. The Italian annotators on older works on painting are sometimes at a loss to find modern terms equivalent to the obsolete names of pigments. (See " Antologia dell'Arte Pittorica.") The colours now in use corresponding with Boschini's list, are probably yellow lakes, smalt, verditer, and Naples yellow. Boschini often censures the practice of other schools, and in this emphatic condemnation he seems to have had an eye to certain precepts in Lomazzo, and perhaps, even in Leonardo da Vinci, who, on one occasion, recommends Naples yellow, lake, and white for flesh. The Venetian writer often speaks, too, in no measured terms of certain Flemish pictures, probably because they appeared to him too tinted.

† " La Carta del Navegar Pitoresco," p. 338.

‡ Ib. p. 341. In describing Titian's actual practice (" Ricche Minere"), he, however, adds yellow (ochre). The red is also particularised, viz., the common terra rossa.

account to be a little exaggerated, it is still to be observed that the monotony to which the use of few colours would seem to tend, is prevented by the nature of the Venetian process, which was sufficiently conformable to Goethe's doctrine ; the gradations being multiplied, and the effect of the colours heightened by using them as semi-opaque mediums. Immediately after the passage last quoted we read, " He also gave this true precept, that to produce a lively colouring in flesh it is not possible to finish at once."* As these particulars may not be known to all, we add some further abridged extracts explaining the order and methods of these different operations.

" The Venetian painters," says this writer,† " after having drawn in their subject, got in the masses with very solid colour, without making use of nature or statues. Their great object in this stage of their work was to distinguish the advancing and retiring portions, that the figures might be relieved by means of chiaro-scuro—one of the most important departments of colour and form, and indeed of invention. Having decided on their scheme of effect, when this preparation was dry, they consulted nature and the antique ; not servilely, but with the aid of a few lines on paper (*quattro segni in carta*) they corrected their figures without any other model. Then returning to their brushes, they began to paint smartly on this preparation, producing the colour of flesh." The passage before quoted follows, stating that they used earths chiefly, that they carefully avoided certain colours, " and likewise varnishes and whatever produces a shining surface.‡ When this second painting was dry, they proceeded to scumble over this or that figure with a low tint to make the one next it come forward, giving another, at the same time, an additional light—for example,

---

* High examples here again prove that the opposite system may attain results quite as successful.

† Introduction to the " Ricche Minere."

‡ See Note to Par. 555. Here again, assuming the description to be correct, high authorities might be opposed to the Venetians.

on a head, a hand, or a foot, thus detaching them, so to speak, from the canvas." (Tintoret's *Prigionia di S. Rocco* is here quoted.) " By thus still multiplying these well-understood retouchings where required, on the dry surface, *(à secco)* they reduced the whole to harmony. In this operation they took care not to cover entire figures, but rather went on gemming them *(gioielandole)* with vigorous touches. In the shadows, too, they infused vigour frequently by glazing with asphaltum, always leaving great masses in middle-tint, with many darks, in addition to the partial glazings, and few lights."

The introduction to the subject of Venetian colouring, in the poem by the same author, is also worth transcribing, but as the style is quaint and very concise, a translation is necessarily a paraphrase.*

" The art of colouring has the imitation of qualities for its object ; not all qualities, but those secondary ones which are appreciable by the sense of sight. The eye especially sees colours, the imitation of nature in painting is therefore justly called colouring ; but the painter arrives at his end by indirect means. He gives the varieties of tone in masses ;†

---

* The following quatrain may serve as a specimen ; the author is speaking of the importance of the colour of flesh as conducive to picturesque effect :—

> " Importa el nudo ; e come ben l'importa !
> Un quadro senza nudo è come aponto
> Un disnar senza pan, se ben ghe zonto,
> Per più delicia, confetura e torta."—p. 346.

In his preface he anticipates, and thus answers the objections to his Venetian dialect—" Mi, che son Venetian in Venetia e che parlo de' Pitori Venetiani hò da andarme a stravestir ? Guarda el Cielo."

† The word *Macchia*, literally a blot, is generally used by Italian writers, by Vasari for instance, for the local colour. Boschini understands by it the relative depth of tones rather than the mere difference of hue. " By macchia," he says, " I understand that treatment by which the figures are distinguished from each other by different tones lighter or darker."— *La Carta del Navegar*, p. 328. Elsewhere, " Colouring (as practised by the Venetians) comprehends both the macchia and drawing ;" (p. 300) that is, comprehends the gradations of light and dark in objects, and the parts of objects, and consequently, their essential form. " The macchia," he adds, " is the effect of practice, and is dictated by the knowledge of what is requisite for effect."

he smartly impinges lights, he clothes his preparation with more delicate local hues, he unites, he glazes : thus everything depends on the method, on the process. For if we look at colour abstractedly, the most positive may be called the most beautiful, but if we keep the end of imitation in view, this shallow conclusion falls to the ground. The refined Venetian manner is very different from mere direct, sedulous imitation. Every one who has a good eye may arrive at such results, but to attain the manner of Paolo, of Bassan, of Palma, Tintoret, or Titian, is a very different undertaking."*

The effects of semi-transparent mediums in some natural productions seem alluded to in the following passage— " Nature sometimes accidentally imitates figures in stones and other substances, and although they are necessarily incomplete in form, yet the principle of effect (depth) resembles the Venetian practice." In a passage that follows there appears to be an allusion to the production of the atmospheric colours by semi-transparent mediums.†

NOTE Y.—Par. 672.

The author's conclusion here is unsatisfactory, for the colour of the black races may be considered at least quite as negative as that of Europeans. It would be safer to say that the white skin is more beautiful than the black, because it is more capable of indications of life, and indications of emotion. A degree of light which would fail to exhibit the finer varieties of form on a dark surface, would be sufficient to display them on a light one; and the delicate mantlings

---

* " Ma l'arivar a la maniera, al trato
  (Verbi gratia) de Paulo, del Bassan,
  Del Vechio, Tentoreto, e di Tician,
  Per Dio, l'è cosa da deventar mato."—p. 294, 297.

† The traces of the Aristotelian theory are quite as apparent in Boschini as in the other Italian writers on art; but as he wrote in the seventeenth century, his authority in this respect is only important as an indication of the earlier prevalence of the doctrine.

of colour, whether the result of action or emotion, are more perceptible for the same reason.

NOTE Z.—Par. 690.

The author appears to mean that a degree of brightness which the organ can bear at all, must of necessity be removed from dazzling, white light. The slightest tinge of colour to this brightness, implies that it is seen through a medium, and thus, in painting, the lightest, whitest surface should partake of the quality of depth. Goethe's view here again accords, it must be admitted, with the practice of the best colourists, and with the precepts of the highest authorities.—See Note C.

NOTE A A.—Par. 732.

Ample details respecting the opinions of Louis Bertrand Castel, a Jesuit, are given in the historical part. The coincidence of some of his views with those of Goethe is often apparent : he objects, for instance, to the arbitrary selection of the Newtonian spectrum; observing that the colours change with every change of distance between the prism and the recipient surface.—*Farbenl.* vol. ii. p. 527. Jeremias Friedrich Gülich was a dyer in the neighbourhood of Stutgardt : he published an elaborate work on the technical details of his own pursuit.—*Farbenl.* vol. ii. p. 630.

NOTE B B.—Par. 748.

Goethe, in his account of Castel, suppresses the learned Jesuit's attempt at colorific music (the claveçin oculaire), founded on the Newtonian doctrine. Castel was complimented, perhaps ironically, on having been the first to remark that there were but three principal colours. In asserting his claim to the discovery, he admits that there is nothing new. In fact, the notion of three colours is to be found in Aristotle ; for that philosopher enumerates no more in speaking of the rainbow,* and Seneca calls them by their right names.† Compare with Dante, Parad. c. 33. The relation between colours and sounds is in like manner adverted to by Aristotle; he says—" It is possible that colours may stand in relation to each other in the same manner as concords in music, for the colours which are (to each other) in proportions corresponding with the musical concords, are those which appear to be the most agreeable."‡ In the latter part of the 16th century, Arcimboldo, a Milanese painter, invented a colorific music; an account of his principles and method will be found in a treatise on painting which appeared about the same time. " Ammaestrato dal qual ordine Mauro Cremonese dalla viola, musico dell' Imperadore Ridolfo II. trovò sul gravicembalo tutte quelle consonanze che dall' Arcimboldo erano segnate coi colori sopra una carta."§

NOTE C C.—Par. 758.

The moral associations of colours have always been a more favourite subject with poets than with painters. This is to be traced to the materials and means of description as distinguished from those of representation. An image is more distinct for the mind when it is compared with something that resembles it. An object is more distinct for the eye when it is compared with something that differs from it. Association is the auxiliary in the one case, contrast in the

---

* " De Meteor.," lib. 3, c. ii. and iv. He observes that this is the only effect of colour which painters cannot imitate.

† " De Ignib. cœlest." The description of the prism by Seneca is another instance of the truth of Castel's admission. The Roman philosopher's words are—" Virgula solet fieri vitrea, stricta vel pluribus angulis in modo clavæ tortuosæ; hæc si ex transverso solem accipit colorem talem qualis in arcu videri solet, reddit," &c.

‡ " De Sensu et sensili."

§ " Il Figino, overo del Fine della Pittura," Mantova, 1591, p. 249. An account of the absurd invention of the same painter in composing figures of flowers and animals, and even painting portraits in this way, to the great delight of the emperor, will be found in the same work.

other. The poet, of necessity, succeeds best in conveying
the impression of external things by the aid of analogous
rather than of opposite qualities: so far from losing their
effect by this means, the images gain in distinctness. Comparisons that are utterly false and groundless never strike us
as such if the great end is accomplished of placing the
thing described more vividly before the imagination. In
the common language of laudatory description the colour of
flesh is like snow mixed with vermilion: these are the words
used by Aretino in one of his letters in speaking of a figure
of St. John, by Titian. Similar instances without end
might be quoted from poets: even a contrast can only be
strongly conveyed in description by another contrast that
resembles it.* On the other hand it would be easy to show
that whenever poets have attemped the painter's method of
direct contrast, the image has failed to be striking, for the
mind's eye cannot see the relation between two colours.

Under the same category of effect produced by association
may be classed the moral qualities in which poets have
judiciously taken refuge when describing visible forms and
colours, to avoid competition with the painters' elements,
or rather to attain their end more completely. But a
little examination would show that very pleasing moral
associations may be connected with colours which would
be far from agreeable to the eye. All light, positive colours, light-green, light-purple, white, are pleasing to the
mind's eye, and no degree of dazzling splendour is offensive.
The moment, however, we have to do with the actual sense
of vision, the susceptibility of the eye itself is to be considered, the law of comparison is reversed, colours become
striking by being opposed to what they are not, and their
moral associations are not owing to the colours themselves,

---

* Such as—
> " Her beauty hangs upon the cheek of night,
> Like a rich jewel in an Ethiop's ear."
> *Romeo and Juliet.*

but to the modifications such colours undergo in consequence of what surrounds them. This view, so naturally consequent on the principles the author has himself arrived at, appears to be overlooked in the chapter under consideration, the remarks in which, in other respects, are acute and ingenious.

NOTE D D.—Par. 849.

According to the usual acceptation of the term chiaroscuro in the artist world, it means not only the mutable effects produced by light and shade, but also the permanent differences in brightness and darkness which are owing to the varieties of local colour.

NOTE E E.—Par. 855.

The mannered treatment of light and shade here alluded to by the author is very seldom to be met with in the works of the colourists; the taste may have first arisen from the use of plaster-casts, and was most prevalent in France and Italy in the early part of the last century. Piazzetta represented it in Venice, Subleyras in Rome. In France "Restout taught his pupils that a globe ought to be represented as a polyhedron. Greuze most implicitly adopted the doctrine, and in practice showed that he considered the round cheeks of a young girl or an infant as bodies cut into facettes."*

NOTE F F.—Par. 859.

All this was no doubt suggested by Heinrich Meyer, whose chief occupation in Rome, at one time, was making

---

* See Taylor's translation of Merimée on oil-painting, p. 27. Barry, in a letter from Paris, speaks of Restout as the only painter who resembled the earlier French masters : the manner in question is undoubtedly sometimes very observable in Poussin. The English artist elsewhere speaks of the "broad, happy manner of Subleyras."—*Works*, London, 1809.

sepia drawings from sculpture (see Goethe's Italiänische Reise). It is hardly necessary to say that the observation respecting the treatment of the surface in the antique statues is very fanciful.

NOTE G G.—Par. 863.

This observation might have been suggested by the drawings of Claude, which, with the slightest means, exhibit an harmonious balance of warm and cold.

NOTE H H.—Par. 865.

The colouring of Paolo Uccello, according to Vasari's account of him, was occasionally so remarkable that he might perhaps have been fairly included among the instances of defective vision given by the author. His skill in perspective, indicating an eye for gradation, may be also reckoned among the points of resemblance (see Par. 105).

NOTE I I.—Par. 902.

The quotation before given from Boschini shows that the method described by the author, and which is true with regard to some of the Florentine painters, was not practised by the Venetians, for their first painting was very solid. It agrees, however, with the manner of Rubens, many of whose works sufficiently corroborate the account of his process given by Descamps. "In the early state of Rubens's pictures," says that writer,* "everything appeared like a thin wash; but although he often made use of the ground in producing his tones, the canvas was entirely covered more or less with colour." In this system of leaving the shadows transparent from the first, with the ground shining through them, it would have been obviously destructive of richness to use white mixed with the darks, the brightness, in fact, already existed underneath. Hence the

* " La Vie des Peintres Flamands," vol. i.

well-known precept of Rubens to avoid white in the shadows, a precept, like many others, belonging to a particular
practice, and involving all the conditions of that practice.*
Scarmiglione, whose Aristotelian treatise on colour was
published in Germany when Rubens was three-and-twenty,
observes, " Painters, with consummate art, lock up the
bright colours with dark ones, and, on the other hand,
employ white, the poison of a picture, very sparingly."
(Artificiosissimè pictores claros obscuris obsepiant et contra
candido picturarum veneno summè parcentes, &c.)

NOTE K K.—Par. 903.

The practice here alluded to is more frequently observable in slight works by Paul Veronese. His ground was
often pure white, and in some of his works it is left as such.
Titian's white ground was covered with a light warm colour,
probably at first, and appears to have been similar to that
to which Armenini gives the preference, namely, " quella
che tira al color di carne chiarissima con un non so che di
fiammeggiante."†

---

* The method he recommended for keeping the colours pure in the lights,
viz. to place the tints next each other unmixed, and then slightly to unite
them, may have degenerated to a methodical manner in the hands of his followers. Boschini, who speaks of Rubens himself with due reverence, and
is far from confounding him with his imitators, contrasts such a system
with that of the Venetians, and adds that Titian used to say, " Chi de imbra-
tar colori teme, imbrata e machia si medemi."—*Carta del Navegar*, p. 341.
The poem of Boschini is in many respects polemical. He wrote at a time
when the Flemish painters, having adopted and modified the Venetian principles, threatened to supersede the Italian masters in the opinion of the
world. Their excellence, too, had all the charm of novelty, for in the seventeenth century Venice produced no remarkable talent, and it was precisely
the age for her to boast of past glories. The contemptuous manner in which
Boschini speaks of the Flemish varnishes, of the fear of mixing tints, &c., is
thus always to be considered with reference to the time and circumstances.
So also his boasting that the Venetian masters painted without nature, which
may be an exaggeration, is pointed at the *Naturalisti*, Caravaggio and his
followers, who copied nature literally.

† " Veri Precetti della Pittura," p. 125.

NOTE L L.—Par. 919.

The notion which the author has here ventured to express may have been suggested by the remarkable passage in the last canto of Dante's " Paradiso"—

> " Nella profonda e chiara sussistenza,
> Dell' alto lume parvemi tre giri
> Di tre colori e d'una continenza," &c.

After the concluding paragraph the author inserts a letter from a landscape-painter, Philipp Otto Runge, which is intended to show that those who imitate nature may arrive at principles analogous to those of the " Farbenlehre."

THE END.